State Building and Development

Why does a huge income gap still exist between developed and developing countries? Plausible causes on the surface may be the difference in technology, the quality of human resources and economic institutions, but on the deeper level the gap reflects the success and failure of state building which is vital for economic development. This book provides cutting-edge knowledge on state building, economic development, and democratization based on case studies of Japan, ASEAN, South Asia, and selected countries in Sub-Saharan Africa.

The book examines the interaction between land policies and the state building in Sub-Saharan Africa. It also pays special attention to corruption, which affects the relationship between the state and the development, and decentralization, which exerts influences on the contentious politics. Finally, the book also sheds new light on the failure and success of industrial policies based on a literature review and a case study of the rapidly growing pharmaceutical industry in Bangladesh.

This book is one of the few studies which squarely addresses state building and economic development, and will be of use to those interested in this subject, development practitioners, and policymakers in developing countries.

Keijiro Otsuka is Professor of Development Economics at GRIPS. He has held positions at Tokyo Metropolitan University, the International Rice Research Institute, the International Food Policy Research Institute, and the World Bank. He has been conducting a large number of comparative case studies on industrial development and agricultural development in Asia and Sub-Saharan Africa.

Takashi Shiraishi currently serves as President, GRIPS (since 2011) and President of the Institute of Developing Economies-JETRO (since 2007). He served as Executive Member, Council for Science and Technology Policy (CSTP), Cabinet Office (2009–12). He has taught at the University of Tokyo (1979–87), Cornell University (1987–98), Kyoto University (1996–2005), and GRIPS (2005–09).

Routledge studies in the modern world economy

1 Interest Rates and Budget Deficits
A study of the advanced economies
Kanhaya L Gupta and Bakhtiar Moazzami

2 World Trade after the Uruguay Round
Prospects and policy options for the twenty-first century
Edited by Harald Sander and András Inotai

3 The Flow Analysis of Labour Markets
Edited by Ronald Schettkat

4 Inflation and Unemployment
Contributions to a new macroeconomic approach
Edited by Alvaro Cencini and Mauro Baranzini

5 Macroeconomic Dimensions of Public Finance
Essays in honour of Vito Tanzi
Edited by Mario I. Blejer and Teresa M. Ter-Minassian

6 Fiscal Policy and Economic Reforms
Essays in honour of Vito Tanzi
Edited by Mario I. Blejer and Teresa M. Ter-Minassian

7 Competition Policy in the Global Economy
Modalities for co-operation
Edited by Leonard Waverman, William S. Comanor and Akira Goto

8 Working in the Macro Economy
A study of the US labor market
Martin F. J. Prachowny

9 How Does Privatization Work?
Edited by Anthony Bennett

10 The Economics and Politics of International Trade
Freedom and trade: Volume II
Edited by Gary Cook

11 The Legal and Moral Aspects of International Trade
Freedom and trade: Volume III
Edited by Asif Qureshi, Hillel Steiner and Geraint Parry

12 Capital Markets and Corporate Governance in Japan, Germany and the United States
Organizational response to market inefficiencies
Helmut M. Dietl

13 Competition and Trade Policies
Coherence or conflict
Edited by Einar Hope

14 Rice
The primary commodity
A. J. H. Latham

15 Trade, Theory and Econometrics
Essays in honour of John S. Chipman
Edited by James C. Moore, Raymond Riezman and James R. Melvin

16 Who benefits from Privatisation?
Edited by Moazzem Hossain and Justin Malbon

17 Towards a Fair Global Labour Market
Avoiding the new slave trade
Ozay Mehmet, Errol Mendes and Robert Sinding

18 Models of Futures Markets
Edited by Barry Goss

19 Venture Capital Investment
An agency analysis of UK practice
Gavin C. Reid

20 Macroeconomic Forecasting
A sociological appraisal
Robert Evans

21 Multimedia and Regional Economic Restructuring
Edited by Hans-Joachim Braczyk, Gerhard Fuchs and Hans-Georg Wolf

22 The New Industrial Geography
Regions, regulation and institutions
Edited by Trevor J. Barnes and Meric S. Gertler

23 The Employment Impact of Innovation
Evidence and policy
Edited by Marco Vivarelli and Mario Pianta

24 International Health Care Reform
A legal, economic and political analysis
Colleen Flood

25 Competition Policy Analysis
Edited by Einar Hope

26 Culture and Enterprise
The development, representation and morality of business
Don Lavoie and Emily Chamlee-Wright

27 Global Financial Crises and Reforms
Cases and caveats
B.N. Ghosh

28 Geography of Production and Economic Integration
Miroslav N. Jovanović

29 Technology, Trade and Growth in OECD Countries
Does specialisation matter?
Valentina Meliciani

30 Post-Industrial Labour Markets
Profiles of North America and Scandinavia
Edited by Thomas P Boje and Bengt Furaker

31 Capital Flows without Crisis
Reconciling capital mobility and economic stability
Edited by Dipak Dasgupta, Marc Uzan and Dominic Wilson

32 International Trade and National Welfare
Murray C Kemp

33 Global Trading Systems at Crossroads
A post-Seattle perspective
Dilip K. Das

34 The Economics and Management of Technological Diversification
Edited by John Cantwell, Alfonso Gambardella and Ove Granstrand

35 **Before and Beyond EMU**
Historical lessons and future prospects
Edited by Patrick Crowley

36 **Fiscal Decentralization**
Ehtisham Ahmad and Vito Tanzi

37 **Regionalisation of Globalised Innovation**
Locations for advanced industrial development and disparities in participation
Edited by Ulrich Hilpert

38 **Gold and the Modern World Economy**
Edited by MoonJoong Tcha

39 **Global Economic Institutions**
Willem Molle

40 **Global Governance and Financial Crises**
Edited by Meghnad Desai and Yahia Said

41 **Linking Local and Global Economies**
The ties that bind
Edited by Carlo Pietrobelli and Arni Sverrisson

42 **Tax Systems and Tax Reforms in Europe**
Edited by Luigi Bernardi and Paola Profeta

43 **Trade Liberalization and APEC**
Edited by Jiro Okamoto

44 **Fiscal Deficits in the Pacific Region**
Edited by Akira Kohsaka

45 **Financial Globalization and the Emerging Market Economies**
Dilip K. Das

46 **International Labor Mobility**
Unemployment and increasing returns to scale
Bharati Basu

47 **Good Governance in the Era of Global Neoliberalism**
Conflict and depolitization in Latin America, Eastern Europe, Asia and Africa
Edited by Jolle Demmers, Alex E. Fernández Jilberto and Barbara Hogenboom

48 **The International Trade System**
Alice Landau

49 **International Perspectives on Temporary Work and Workers**
Edited by John Burgess and Julia Connell

50 **Working Time and Workers' Preferences in Industrialized Countries**
Finding the balance
Edited by Jon C. Messenger

51 **Tax Systems and Tax Reforms in New EU Members**
Edited by Luigi Bernardi, Mark Chandler and Luca Gandullia

52 **Globalization and the Nation State**
The impact of the IMF and the World Bank
Edited by Gustav Ranis, James Vreeland and Stephen Kosak

53 **Macroeconomic Policies and Poverty Reduction**
Edited by Ashoka Mody and Catherine Pattillo

54 **Regional Monetary Policy**
Carlos J. Rodríguez-Fuentez

55 Trade and Migration in the Modern World
Carl Mosk

56 Globalisation and the Labour Market
Trade, technology and less-skilled workers in Europe and the United States
Edited by Robert Anderton, Paul Brenton and John Whalley

57 Financial Crises
Socio-economic causes and institutional context
Brenda Spotton Visano

58 Globalization and Self Determination
Is the nation-state under siege?
Edited by David R. Cameron, Gustav Ranis and Annalisa Zinn

59 Developing Countries and the Doha Development Round of the WTO
Edited by Pitou van Dijck and Gerrit Faber

60 Immigrant Enterprise in Europe and the USA
Prodromos Panayiotopoulos

61 Solving the Riddle of Globalization and Development
Edited by Manuel Agosín, David Bloom, George Chapelier and Jagdish Saigal

62 Foreign Direct Investment and the World Economy
Ashoka Mody

63 The World Economy
A global analysis
Horst Siebert

64 Production Organizations in Japanese Economic Development
Edited by Tetsuji Okazaki

65 The Economics of Language
International analyses
Edited by Barry R. Chiswick and Paul W. Miller

66 Street Entrepreneurs
People, place and politics in local and global perspective
Edited by John Cross and Alfonso Morales

67 Global Challenges and Local Responses
The East Asian Experience
Edited by Jang-Sup Shin

68 Globalization and Regional Integration
The origins, development and impact of the Single European Aviation Market
Alan Dobson

69 Russia Moves into the Global Economy: Breaking Out
John M. Letiche

70 The European Economy in an American Mirror
Barry Eichengreen, Michael Landesmann and Dieter Stiefel

71 Working Time Around the World
Trends in working hours, laws, and policies in a global comparative perspective
Jon C. Messenger, Sangheon Lee and Deidre McCann

72 International Water Treaties
Negotiation and cooperation along transboundary rivers
Shlomi Dinar

73 Economic Integration in the Americas
Edited by Joseph A. McKinney and H. Stephen Gardner

74 Expanding Frontiers of Global Trade Rules
The political economy dynamics of the international trading system
Nitya Nanda

75 The Macroeconomics of Global Imbalances
European and Asian perspectives
Edited by Marc Uzan

76 China and Asia
Economic and financial interactions
Edited by Yin-Wong Cheung and Kar-Yiu Wong

77 Regional Inequality in China
Trends, explanations and policy responses
Edited by Shenggen Fan, Ravi Kanbur and Xiaobo Zhang

78 Governing Rapid Growth in China
Equity and institutions
Edited by Ravi Kanbur and Xiaobo Zhang

79 The Indonesian Labour Market
Shafiq Dhanani, Iyanatul Islam and Anis Chowdhury

80 Cost-Benefit Analysis in Multi-level Government in Europe and the USA
The case of EU Cohesion Policy and of US Federal Investment policies
Alessandro Ferrara

81 The Economic Geography of Air Transportation
Space, time, and the freedom of the sky
John Bowen

82 Cartelization, Antitrust and Globalization in the US and Europe
Mark LeClair

83 The Political Economy of Integration
Jeffrey Cason

84 Critical Issues in Air Transport Economics and Business
Rosario Macario and Eddy Van de Voorde

85 Financial Liberalisation and Economic Performance
Luiz Fernando de Paula

86 A General Theory of Institutional Change
Shiping Tang

87 The Dynamics of Asian Financial Integration
Edited by Michael Devereux, Philip Lane, Park Cyn-young and Wei Shang-jin

88 Innovative Fiscal Policy and Economic Development in Transition Economies
Aleksandr Gevorkyan

89 Foreign Direct Investments in Asia
Edited by Chalongphob Sussangkarn, Yung Chul Park and Sung Jin Kang

90 Time Zones, Communications Networks, and International Trade
Toru Kikuchi

91 Miraculous Growth and Stagnation in Post-War Japan
Edited by Koichi Hamada, Keijiro Otsuka, Gustav Ranis, and Ken Togo

92 Multilateralism and Regionalism in Global Economic Governance: Trade, Investment and Finance
Edited by Junji Nakagawa

93 **Economic Growth and Income Inequality in China, India and Singapore: Trends and Policy Implications**
Pundarik Mukhopadhaya, G. Shantakumar and Bhanoji Rao

94 **Foreign Direct Investment in China: Spillover Effects on Domestic Enterprises**
Deng Ziliang

95 **Enterprise Forms and Economic Efficiency: Capitalist, Cooperative and Government Firms**
Kazuhiko Mikami

96 **Diversity and Transformations of Asian Capitalism**
Edited by Boyer, Uemura and Isogai

97 **Knowledge Transfer in the Automobile Industry: Global-Local Production Networks**
Dessy Irawati

98 **Exchange Rates and Foreign Direct Investment in Emerging Asia: Selected Issues and Policy Options**
Ramkishen S. Rajan

99 **Singapore, the Energy Economy: From the First Refinery to the End of Cheap Oil, 1960 – 2010**
Ng Weng Hoong

100 **China-India Economics: Challenges, Competition & Collaboration**
Amitendu Palit

101 **Case Studies on Chinese Enterprises**
Edited by Donglin Xia

102 **Argentina's Economic Growth and Recovery**
Michael Cohen

103 **The Korean Labour Market After the 1997 Economic Crisis**
Edited by Joonmo Cho, Richard B. Freeman, Jaeho Keum and Sunwoong Kim

104 **China and India: the Quest for Energy Resources in the 21st Century**
Zhao Hong

105 **Beyond the Global Crisis: Structural Adjustments and Regional Integration in Europe and Latin America**
Edited by Lionello Punzo, Carmen Aparecida Feio and Martin Putchet Anyui

106 **The Global Economic Crisis in Latin America: Impacts and Responses**
Edited by Michael Cohen

107 **The Processes and Practices of Fair Trade: Trust, Ethics and Governance**
Edited by Brigitte Granville and Janet Dine

108 **Regional Development through Ecological Business: Unique Cases in Japanese Rural Regions**
Makoto Hirano

109 **Aging and Economic Growth Potentials in the Pacific Region**
Edited by Akira Kohsaka

110 **Crises of Global Economies and the Future of Capitalism: Reviving Marxian Crisis Theory**
Edited by Kiichiro Yagi, Nobuharu Yokokawa, Shinjiro Hagiwara and Gary A. Dymski

111 The Financial History of the Bank for International Settlements
Kazuhiko Yago

112 Freight Transport and the Modern Economy
Michel Savy and June Burnham

113 Thoughts on Economic Development in China
Edited by Ma Ying and Hans-Michael Trautwein

114 China's Ethnic Minorities: Social and Economic Indicators
Rongxing Guo

115 Globalization, Outsourcing and Labour Development in ASEAN
Shandre Thangavelu and Aekapol Chongvilaivan

116 The Role of Informal Economies in the Post-Soviet World
The End of Transition?
Colin C Williams, John Round and Peter Rodgers

117 Demystifying the Chinese Miracle: The Rise and Future of Relational Capitalism
Yongqin Wang

118 Globalism and Regional Economy
Edited by Susumu Egashira

119 Russia's Changing Economic and Political Regimes
The Putin years and afterwards
Andrey Makarychev and André Mommen

120 Innovation and Regional Development in China
Edited by Ingo Liefner and Yehua Dennis Wei

121 International Trade Negotiations and Domestic Politics
The intermestic politics of trade liberalization
Edited by Oluf Langhelle

122 Emerging Knowledge Economies in Asia: Current Trends in ASEAN 5
Edited by Dessy Irawati and Roel Rutten

123 The Internationalization of the Renminbi
International Monetary Institute, Renmin University of China

124 Financial Globalization and Regionalism in East Asia
Edited by Takuji Kinkyo, Yoichi Matsubayashi and Shigeyuki Hamori

125 Successful Business Dealings and Management with China Oil, Gas and Chemical Giants
EurIng. Henry K. H. Wang

126 State Building and Development
Edited by Keijiro Otsuka and Takashi Shiraishi

State Building and Development

Edited by Keijiro Otsuka and Takashi Shiraishi

Routledge
Taylor & Francis Group
LONDON AND NEW YORK

First published 2014
by Routledge
2 Park Square, Milton Park, Abingdon, Oxfordshire OX14 4RN

and published in the USA and Canada
by Routledge
711 Third Avenue, New York, NY 10017

First issued in paperback 2016

Routledge is an imprint of the Taylor & Francis Group, an informa business

British Library Cataloguing in Publication Data
A catalogue record for this book is available from the British Library

Library of Congress Cataloging in Publication Data
State building and development / edited by Keijiro Otsuka and Takashi Shiraishi.
pages cm. — (Routledge studies in the modern world economy ; 126)
Includes bibliographical references and index.
1. Economic development—Political aspects. 2. Nation-building—Economic aspects. 3. Political development—Economic aspects.
I. Otsuka, Keijiro. II. Shiraishi, Takashi, 1950–
HD75.S747 2014
338.9—dc23

2013027363

ISBN 13: 978-1-138-91812-2 (pbk)
ISBN 13: 978-0-415-70975-0 (hbk)

Typeset in Times New Roman
by RefineCatch Limited, Bungay, Suffolk

Contents

Tables

Figures

Contributors

Md. Nurul Amin is Deputy Commissioner of Taxes in the National Board of Revenue at the Ministry of Finance in Bangladesh. He graduated from the Department of Economics, University of Dhaka in 2004 and completed his Ph.D. in development economics at the National Graduate Institute for Policy Studies (GRIPS) in 2013.

Kaliappa Kalirajan is a Professor in the Crawford School of Public Policy at the Australian National University in Canberra, Australia, and an adjunct professor at the Madras School of Economics, Chennai, India. He was also a professor of development economics at GRIPS from 2001 to 2009.

Keijiro Otsuka is a Professor of Development Economics at GRIPS. He has held positions at Tokyo Metropolitan University, the International Rice Research Institute, the International Food Policy Research Institute, and the World Bank. He has been conducting a large number of comparative case studies on industrial development and agricultural development in Asia and sub-Saharan Africa.

Osamu Saito is a Professor Emeritus at Hitotsubashi University. He has served on the Executive Committee of the International Association of Economic History and is a past President of the Socio-Economic History Society of Japan. He has written on wide-ranging issues in economic history, mostly in a comparative perspective.

Takashi Shiraishi currently serves as President of GRIPS (since 2011) and President of the Institute of Developing Economies-JETRO (since 2007). He served as Executive Member of the Council for Science and Technology Policy (CSTP), Cabinet Office (2009–12). He has taught at the University of Tokyo (1979–87), Cornell University (1987–98), Kyoto University (1996–2005), and GRIPS (2005–09).

Tetsushi Sonobe is a Professor of Development Economics at GRIPS. He is an executive adviser to the President of the university and Director of the State Building and Economic Development Program. He is also an adviser to JICA's KAIZEN management programs in Ethiopia and Tanzania.

Shinichi Takeuchi is a director at the African Studies Group, Area Studies Center, Institute of Developing Economies Japan External Trade Organization (IDE-JETRO). Specializing in international relations and African studies, he has carried out field researches especially in the Central African countries.

Yuki Tanaka is a consultant at the Embassy of Japan in Uganda for the Grand Assistant for Grassroots Human Security Project. After obtaining a Ph.D. from GRIPS, she continued her research at GRIPS and worked part-time as a research assistant at the Japan International Cooperation Agency (JICA) Research Institute.

Keiichi Tsunekawa is currently Vice President of GRIPS, Senior Research Adviser of the Japan International Cooperation Agency Research Institute, and Professor Emeritus of the University of Tokyo. He served as Vice President of JICA and Director of JICA Research Institute between October 2008 and March 2011.

Takashi Yamano is Senior Scientist (Agricultural Economics) at the International Rice Research Institute (IRRI). He conducts social science research on technology adoption and impact evaluation among rice farmers in South Asia. He taught at GRIPS from 2002 to 2011, before joining IRRI.

Preface

Economic development is a challenging analytical issue, in part because it is multi-dimensional and highly complex and because the key variables and parameters are all endogenous, making it extremely difficult to establish causation. Economics is a leading social science in this area because development is fueled by investments in human capital, physical capital, social capital, scientific knowledge, and infrastructure, which are guided by their costs and benefits and shaped by economic policies and institutions. On the other hand, the nature and the process of state building not only determine the cost and return estimates of investments through long-term political and economic stability but also shape economic policies and institutions directly, thereby indirectly affecting the pace of economic development. The success and failure of economic development, in turn, affect state building. Obviously this is the field in which development economists and political scientists must collaborate to gain a deep understanding of the interactive processes between state building and economic development.

Yet, development economists and political scientists have tended to address the issue of state building and development independently, without much collaboration. As a result, economists have focused mainly on the effects of development policies on economic development, whereas political scientists concentrate on the effects of state building on political contentions and democratization. Such piecemeal approaches do not make much sense, because state building, development policies, economic development, and political contentions are all interdependent. The main thrust of this volume is to illuminate and analyze the interactive processes among them.

This volume is the outcome of the collaborative research project on "The Transferability of East Asian Development Strategies and State Building" undertaken by development economists and political scientists at the National Graduate Institute for Policy Studies (GRIPS), in collaboration with the institute's Ph.D. students, former staff, and affiliated scientists in the last five years. GRIPS is a graduate school newly established in 1997 by the Japanese government with a view to fostering inter-disciplinary social science studies. In fact, its goals are to "contribute to the betterment and advancement of democratic governance around the world" and to "promote interdisciplinary policy studies." In other words, GRIPS is committed to implementing inter-disciplinary social science research concerned with worldwide issues. *State Building and Development* is an appropriate topic for GRIPS' faculty of economists and political scientists. The project has been generously funded by the Global Center of Excellence (GCOE) Program of the Ministry of Education and Science of the Japanese government.

GCOE members regularly organized seminars and workshops, which culminated in a mid-term conference in Hakone in December 2009, and in a final symposium in Tokyo in September 2012. At the inception of the project, the members decided to re-examine carefully the economic and political history of Japan since the Meiji Restoration in 1968, because the reality of Japanese economic development and state building has been largely misunderstood by the literature on that period. This is unfortunate, because the modern history of Japan's development is widely considered as a successful model of state building and development. While proper understanding of the Japanese experience is the main pillar of the entire study, critically interrogating the applicability of Japanese and other East Asian experiences to other regions of the world is the common thread running through other case studies. Although we admit that we cannot cover all the facets of state building and development, we are confident that we have shed new light on some of the key aspects of this fundamentally important but analytically elusive issue.

In the preparation of this volume, we have been indebted to many researchers for their useful and constructive comments. In particular, we would like to thank James Robinson of Harvard University, John Page of the Brookings Institution, Finn Tarp of UN-WIDER, and Takehiko Nakao of the Asian Development Bank. We would also like to express our gratitude to participants in the symposium held in GRIPS in September 2012: Nobuhiro Aizawa, of the Institute of Developing Economies and JETRO, Kenta Goto of Kansai University, Keiichiro Oizumi of the Japan Research Institute, and Khoo Boo Teik of the Institute of Developing Economies and JETRO. Our colleagues in GRIPS, Jonna P. Estudillo, Yonosuke Hara, Motoko Kawano, Tomoya Matsumoto, Alistair Munro, Takeshi Onimaru, and Chikako Yamauchi made valuable contributions. Finally, we thank Paul Kandasamy, Kazuko Yamamura, and Maki Nakajima for their editorial assistance.

1 Introduction: towards a new paradigm on state building and development

*Keijiro Otsuka and Takashi Shiraishi**

1 Introduction

Why does a huge income gap still exist between developed and developing countries? How did Japan become the first advanced country outside the western world? Why has the economic performance of the Philippines and Indonesia been better compared with their higher-income neighbors, Malaysia and Thailand, in recent years? Why have South Asian countries, including India and Bangladesh, begun growing fast? On the surface, the income gap and different growth performance reflect the differences in technology, quality of human resources, and economic policies, but at the deeper level they reflect, in large measure, the success and failure of state building conducive to economic development. It is the contention of this volume that the issues raised above can be interpreted in a consistent manner within a broader analytical framework that subsumes the interactive processes between state building, contentious politics, and economic development.

A critical question is how a state conducive to development can be built. In this context, it is noteworthy that the case of Japan since the Meiji Restoration in 1868 is widely regarded as an example of successful state building and development (see for example Johnson 1982). Thus, it is certainly worth exploring the extent to which successful state building led to sustainable development, and asking the question "Which was more important during this interactive process?": the evolution of an acceptable form of government (i.e. democratization), the ability of the state to implement effective and sustainable development policy, or the ability to reduce distributional conflicts that successful economic development may have generated between social groups, for Japan from a historical perspective. What becomes clear from the analyses in Chapters 2 and 3 in this volume is not only the importance of state building per se in promoting economic development but also the critical roles played by interactive processes among state building, economic development, and contentious politics in shaping the development paths that eventually – after the disastrous empire-building in the 1930s and first half of the 1940s – led to full democratization under occupational forces after World War II.

As with the case of Japan, a new state emerges out of internal conflicts, political reforms, or independence, and the first task that it must accomplish is to build new institutions. At this stage, the state is in many cases non-democratic, dominated by the elites, particularly landed elites and urban bourgeoisie representing the interests of the rich economic class. Without exception, new institutions lead to conflicts of interest of various sorts. Ethnic or class conflicts may, for example, arise when new institutions favor certain ethnic groups or certain economic classes at the expense of the majority of the people. Under such situations, economic development, if successful, is likely to lead to distributional inequity, which, in turn, may lead to contentious politics, social unrest, and repression. Such social and political instability, in turn, will depress incentives to make long-term investments, which are vital for long-term economic development.

In order to contain such conflicts, the dominant political group or the elites may decide to choose democracy, which is pro-majority, or even pro-poor, compared with non-democracy which is pro-elites. Or the state may adopt more equitable institutions and sustainable development strategies. Indeed, the term "developmental state," which aims at economic development as a major purpose of politics, is commonly applied to relatively equitable development-oriented states in Asia, beginning with Japan, followed by the Newly Industrialized Countries of Singapore, Taiwan, Hong Kong, and Korea, and later by ASEAN countries such as Malaysia, Thailand, and Indonesia. Furthermore, in low-income countries, labor-intensive industries are often the only viable industries, and technology change may involve using more labor. Such development may be able to confer benefits to the majority of the population and thereby lessen the pressure on the state to democratize. On the other hand, economic dynamism increases the returns to human capital (Schultz 1975) and stimulates human capital accumulation (Otsuka *et al.* 2009). As a result, the importance of land as a factor of production decreases and landed elites tend to lose political influence. Instead, the educated middle-income class emerges as a new political force that may expedite democratization in favor of them or deter it as the social conflict between the rich and poor is defused. If democracy is created and consolidated, social and economic stability is likely to be established, thereby leading to sustainable economic development. Economic development, however, does not guarantee the endurance of democracy, as in the case of pre-war Japan (see Chapter 3).[1] Thus, how state building, economic development, and contentious politics as well as democratization interact is a fundamental issue in development economics and political science.

Despite the close inter-dependence between state building, contentious politics, and economic development, there have been relatively few studies which squarely address the relationship between them.[2] An exception is *Why Nations Fail* by Daron Acemoglu and James Robinson (2012). While their book primarily focuses on why there are so many extractive states, our volume explores the processes by which extractive states can be transformed into inclusive states, to use their terminology. Another book by the same authors (2006), *Economic Origins of Dictatorship and Democracy*, is very useful to understand the causes and processes of democratization, but the analysis of economic development and development policies is lacking. Other closely related books are *Contention and Democracy in Europe, 1650–2000* and *Democracy* by Charles Tilly (2004, 2007), which analyze how contentious politics associated with state building lead to different degrees of democratization in different countries. Although we basically agree with both Acemoglu and Robinson's and Tilly's argument that democracy is born of contentious politics, we would like to point out that their books focus mainly on state building rather than the interactions between state building and economic development.

This volume attempts to synthesize diverse views on state building and economic development by critically reviewing the historical experience in Japan, exploring contemporary issues of state building and development in ASEAN and sub-Saharan Africa (SSA), and charting the success and failure of state policies for economic development in South Asia as well as SSA. By providing cutting-edge knowledge on state building and economic development based on a number of case studies, we hope to shed new light on this exceedingly difficult but important subject in the study of economic development.

The organization of this chapter is as follows. Section 2 presents the common analytical framework of this study, while Section 3 discusses how state building affects economic development by facilitating the long-term stability of the economy, and Section 4 explores the role of economic policies in economic development and state building. Section 5 provides an overview of the organization of the book.

2 Analytical framework

Following OECD (2008), state building may be defined as "an endogenous process to enhance capacity, institutions, and legitimacy of the state driven by state-society relations." In our view, the state-society relations can be specified by the degree to which contentions among social forces or between the elites and social groups are contained or managed. "Institutions" refers to the political and economic institutions, including market and non-market institutions, property rights institutions, centralized and decentralized political institutions, and democratic and nondemocratic institutions, among others. Legitimacy is regarded as the acceptance of political authority by a population, whereas capacity pertains to administrative capacity in surveillance, maintenance of peace and order, taxation, allocation of budgets, and implementation of appropriate economic policies. Successful state building ensures political stability that leads to an economic environment conducive to long-term investments.

As shown in Figure 1.1,[3] state building affects economic development because it is the state that provides public goods such as security and safety of people and property and implements industrial and agricultural development policies and macroeconomic policies. But state building is also shaped by development because development improves the legitimacy of the state and expands the tax base.

The two-way causal relationship between state building and economic development may also have negative results. Corruption, for example, adversely

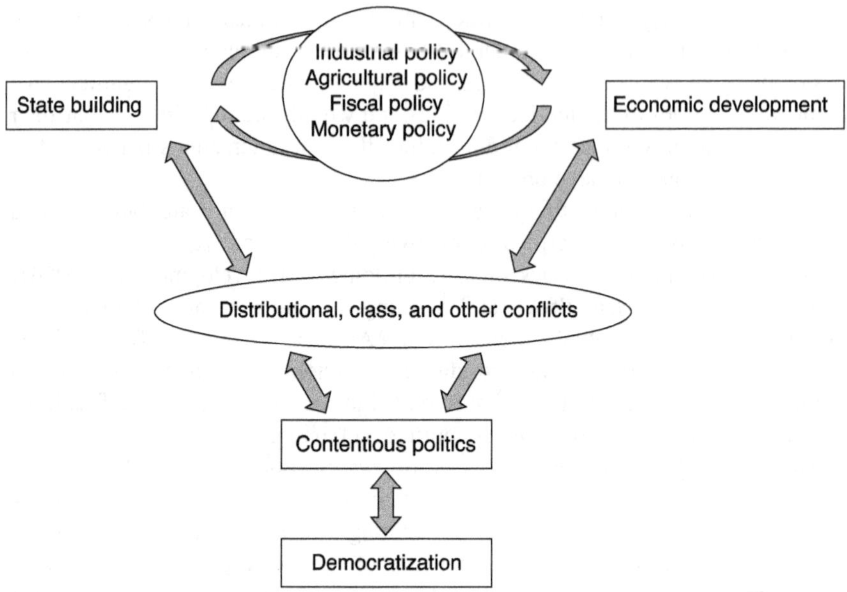

Figure 1.1 Analytical framework on the relationships among state building, economic development, and contentious politics

affects economic development and the legitimacy of the state in many cases as it reduces private returns to investment and distributes private benefits for policymakers (Shleifer and Vishny 1993). With or without corruption, however, both state building and economic development lead to changes in the distribution of economic benefits among ethnic groups, income classes, and the rural and urban population, changes that may trigger contentious politics and influence the course of democratization. In what follows, we sketch how state building, economic development, and contentious politics interact.

State building

State building in the developing countries is frequently affected by the land issue because land is a major asset in such countries and the majority of the population is engaged in farming. When land is abundant relative to labor, land does not command scarcity value and, hence, nobody has strong interest in the private ownership of land. However, because some cultivable land areas are uncultivated, such land is often claimed to be government land and later distributed to the politically influential class. Historically, this practice became one of the major sources of the inequitable ownership distribution of land and social injustice in poor countries (Lipton 2009). Historically, colonial governments consolidated large tracts of land and established large estates and haciendas. The landed elites thereby created often dominate not only in farming but also in commerce, industry, and politics, and oppose democratization that may lead to redistributive politics.

This is unfortunate not only politically but also economically because there are no scale advantages in farming in low-income countries where labor-intensive cultivation practices are adopted and monitoring hired workers in spatially dispersed and ecologically diverse conditions is costly (Hayami and Otsuka 1993). As a result, an inverse correlation is often observed between farm size and productivity, suggesting that small farms relying on family labor are more efficient than large farms relying on hired labor in both Asia and SSA (e.g. Holden *et al.* 2009, 2013; Larson *et al.* 2013; Lipton 2009).

As discussed above, almost without exception, large farms have been created by the colonial and post-colonial governments, not by free market forces. There are also countries in which governments claim ultimate ownership of the entire land area. The basic cause of contentious politics in many countries in SSA, including Rwanda and Kenya, to be discussed in Chapters 5 and 6 respectively, is land conflict arising from the reallocation of farmland by the government to particular ethnic groups.

In contrast to the unequal land distribution, decentralization of political institutions affects the path of state building in a positive way because a decentralized political institution can be a critical device to reduce inter-ethnic conflicts by guaranteeing minority ethnic groups fair shares of the political and economic resources. As minority groups tend to be concentrated in certain geographical areas, they can be the majority groups in local jurisdictions, so that their preference can be incorporated into local politics in decentralized political systems. The decentralized political system stimulates competition among local governments in the provision of basic economic services, such as health care and education as well as infrastructure (Shleifer and Vishny 1993). If policies to allocate the budget of the central government to lower-level governments are in place, decentralization can be an effective means to reduce inter-regional inequity and conflicts. These arguments illustrate the importance of decentralized political institutions for equitable and sustainable economic development.

Effective state building enhances the capacity of the state to design and implement effective development policies and macroeconomic policies for stabilizing the economy. Such capacity is critical to the new state or the state undergoing political reforms. Economists have long ignored the development of effective industrial and agricultural development policies. But we now have enough evidence to show that the state plays a critical role in economic development, particularly the development of the manufacturing sector in accordance with the comparative advantage of the economy (see Chapters 9 and 10). The capacity of the state, particularly the bureaucrats, to design and implement development policies is a key factor in determining the fate of development-oriented states.

One of the obstacles in implementing an effective development policy is corruption. Corruption may result in policies that accrue benefits to policymakers and private rent seekers but not necessarily to the general public and the national economy. Unnecessary road construction with bribes to politicians is a classic example. Bribes also discourage investments by firms not only because they are like an "investment tax" for firms but also because the secrecy and uncertain amount of bribes increases the transaction costs and uncertainty in investment returns (Shleifer and Vishny 1993). At present, land grabbing or the sale of government land that is already occupied by people to foreign companies in SSA has become an important source of conflicts between people and the state as charges of corruption accompany such sales (Deininger and Byerlee 2012).

Needless to say, corruption, if discovered, reduces the legitimacy of the state, leads to political instability, and undermines sustainable economic development. Economic stagnation in turn hampers state building. Insofar as the purpose of the state is to achieve sustainable economic development, its legitimacy rests principally on the success of economic development. An undemocratic Singapore has seldom experienced social conflicts or political unrest because the economy has grown rapidly and equitably, thereby securing the legitimacy of the state (Acemoglu and Robinson 2006).

Economic development and conflicts

Economic development is usually accompanied by the uneven development of economic sectors, regions, and firms of different sizes, thereby creating distributional inequity and conflicts, even though the mobility of labor mitigates such inequity. The agricultural sector lags behind in the course of economic development, leading to serious rural-urban income gaps (Hayami and Godo 2005). The Japanese economy during the inter-war years grew rapidly due mainly to the development of capital-intensive heavy industries and the adoption of labor-saving technologies. There was a dramatic rise in income inequality between rural and urban societies as well as between workers and the bourgeoisie (see Chapter 2). If the unskilled labor-intensive manufacturing industry develops, the income of uneducated urban workers improves relative to property-owning classes, educated workers, and farmers. In contrast, if the computer-related service industries develop, educated workers tend to gain relative to uneducated workers. Furthermore, many of the manufacturing sectors form industrial clusters in selected areas to take advantage of the agglomeration economies, viz., information spillovers, low transaction costs of parts and intermediate inputs among firms, and the formation of skilled labor markets, and, hence, industrial development tends to create regional inequalities (Sonobe and Otsuka 2006, 2011; World Bank 2008).

All these changes generate distributional conflicts, resulting in strikes, demonstrations, riots, and internal wars, or severe party competition. It is well known that agricultural protection is a response to rural dissatisfaction with widening income gaps between farmers and urban workers (Anderson 2009; Anderson and Hayami 1986). In China, widening income gaps between rapidly growing coastal areas and less developed inland areas, and between rural and urban areas are a major policy issue (Rozelle and Huang 2012).

Contentious politics and democracy

As mentioned above, distributional conflicts affect contentious politics and may eventually trigger the move towards democratization. Acemoglu and Robinson (2006) argue that inequitable income and wealth distribution are often the main causes of social conflict, which, in turn, is an important cause of democratization in many societies. The relationship, however, is non-linear. While equitable distribution can be compatible with non-democratic systems, as in the case of Singapore, extremely inequitable distribution may also deter democratization because the elites would lose substantially from redistributive policies under democracy and because they might have the wealth and political power to repress the opposition. In other words, there may exist an "optimum" degree of inequality in facilitating democracy.

The benefit and loss of democratization for the elites and masses are bound to change with changes in technology and the composition of wealth (land, human capital, and physical capital). Technological change in agriculture that uses more labor and fertilizer relative to land will reduce the relative income position of the landed elites and contributes to poverty reduction. The development of unskilled labor-using industries and technologies will reduce poverty and improve income distribution. Consequently, risks which upper classes anticipate from democracy and resultant redistribution will be lowered. Similarly, active investment in human capital will contribute to the formation of an educated middle-income class and the prospect of democracy.

Given our current knowledge of the democratization process, identifying the conditions under which democracy is created is a formidable task. The rapid economic development in Asia provides a rare opportunity to deepen our understanding of this issue (see particularly Chapter 4).

3 State building for development

Since the issue of state building and economic development is highly complex, and involves complex interactions among institutions, the legitimacy and capacity of the state, a variety of conflicts, contentious politics, development policies, and development outcomes, this volume does not presume to cover all the issues of state building relevant for economic development. Instead, we focus on the issue of what the developmental state is and on two of the key institutions relevant for economic development: a decentralized political regime and land rights institutions. In this section we examine these issues, while reviewing the development paths of all the countries covered by this study in terms of changes in the purchasing power parity (PPP)-adjusted per capita gross domestic product (GDP) over time and its differences across countries.

Developmental state

According to Chalmers Johnson's *MITI and the Japanese Miracle* (1982), any state whose *raison d'être* is the attainment of economic development and whose intervention in a market economy is administered via a governmental planning agency may be called a developmental state. Such a planning agency is supposed to aim at promoting industrial development by industrial policies based on a partnership with the private sector. Saito (Chapter 2) argues, however, that the Japanese government during the Meiji era (1868–1912) was far less developmental than generally thought. In fact, it was not industrialization from above but rather private initiative from below that led to the development of modern industries, for example, the cotton spinning industry (Otsuka *et al.* 1988). It is also important to note that much of the economic growth during the Meiji era was achieved by the modernization of traditional rural industries, for example, local weaving clusters or districts (e.g. Hashino and Otsuka 2013), rather than the development of the modern industries which the Meiji government initially intended to establish (Hashino and Saito 2004).

Consistent with the arguments in Chapter 2, the growth rate of the PPP-adjusted per capita GDP in Japan before World War II was comparable to the West, which may be represented by the US, as shown in Figure 1.2, where the logarithm is taken for per capita GDP so that the slope of the curve shows the growth rate.[4] Considering that the existence of a huge income gap means huge potential for the less developed country to learn advanced technology and know-how from more developed countries, the performance of the Japanese economy from 1890 to 1930 was not particularly commendable. Nor was her performance in other policy areas impressive: successive governments were reluctant to invest in health and welfare and did nothing to curb the rising trends in distributional inequality. Over the period in question, moreover, sustainable economic growth was never put before military build-up as the nation's goal. It was after World War II that the Japanese economy successfully caught up with the US, when the contentious politics after Japan's defeat and the democratization and dismantling of the landed elite under US occupation gave rise to a democratic and stable political regime (see Chapter 3).

That Japan was not uniquely successful in economic development is clear from Figure 1.2, which shows that Taiwan and Korea recorded equally rapid growth with a time lag. Similar to post-war Japan, Taiwan and Korea may be regarded as successful "developmental states."[5] Yet it is interesting to observe that as the growth rate of the Japanese economy slowed down gradually decade by decade and has become stagnant since the 1990s, so did the growth rates of Taiwan and Korea, with a time lag of one to two decades. Although developmental states may develop their economies fast in the process of catch-up, such development is often not sustainable, once the catch-up is largely completed.[6] It is also interesting to observe the exceptionally enduring and rapid growth of the Chinese economy. This is not surprising, however, if the pace of catch-up depends on the technology gap, which can be measured roughly by the income gap, as China was much poorer than other East Asian economies in the 1960s and 1970s before the economic reform began.

Malaysia under the leadership of Prime Minister Mahathir Mohamad (1981–2003), Thailand under the dominance of military and bureaucratic elites

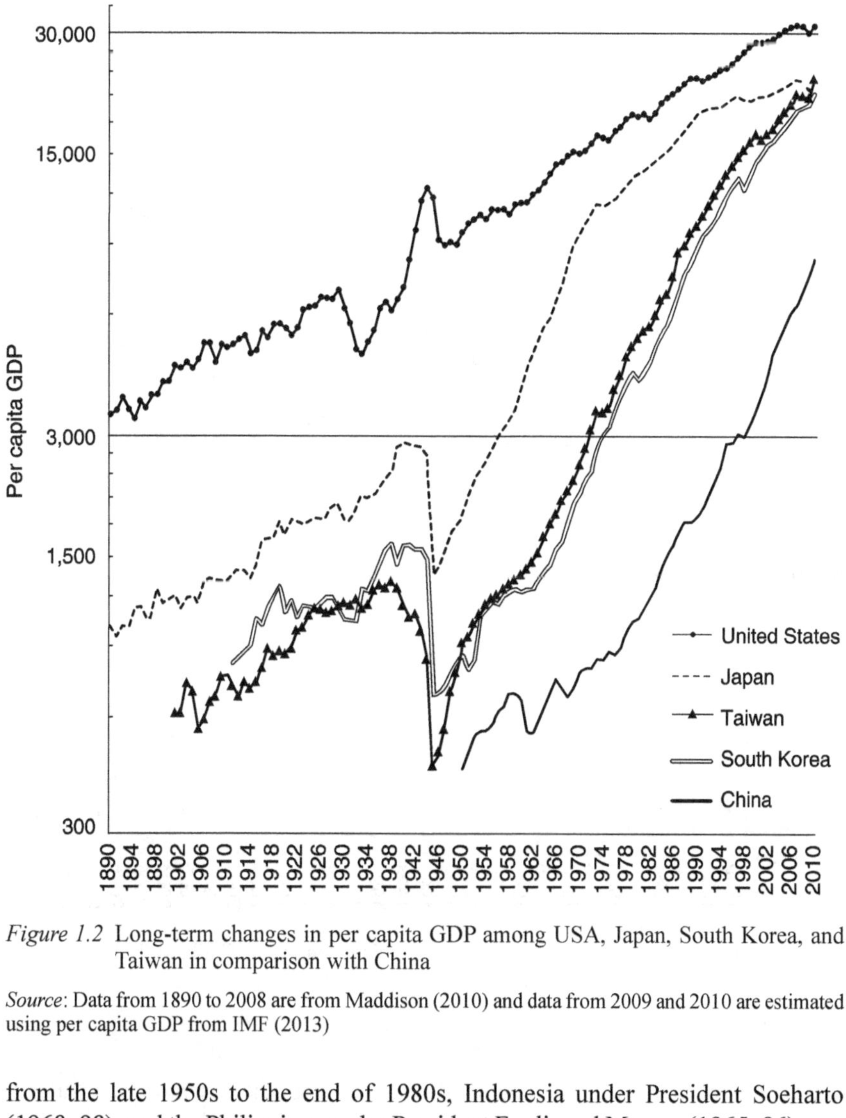

Figure 1.2 Long-term changes in per capita GDP among USA, Japan, South Korea, and Taiwan in comparison with China

Source: Data from 1890 to 2008 are from Maddison (2010) and data from 2009 and 2010 are estimated using per capita GDP from IMF (2013)

from the late 1950s to the end of 1980s, Indonesia under President Soeharto (1968–98), and the Philippines under President Ferdinand Marcos (1965–86), can arguably be examined in light of the developmental state paradigm (see Chapter 4). According to Figure 1.3, which shows changes in the PPP-adjusted per capita GDP in these ASEAN countries in comparison with China from 1980 to 2010, these countries, except for the Philippines, experienced rapid growth from the 1980s to 1997, when the Asian financial crisis broke out. Such trends indicate that the developmental state can be conducive to economic development, containing contentious politics and achieving political stability. Foreign direct investment (FDI) was equally important, and stimulated the development of domestic industries in Southeast Asia. In contrast, contentious politics intensified in

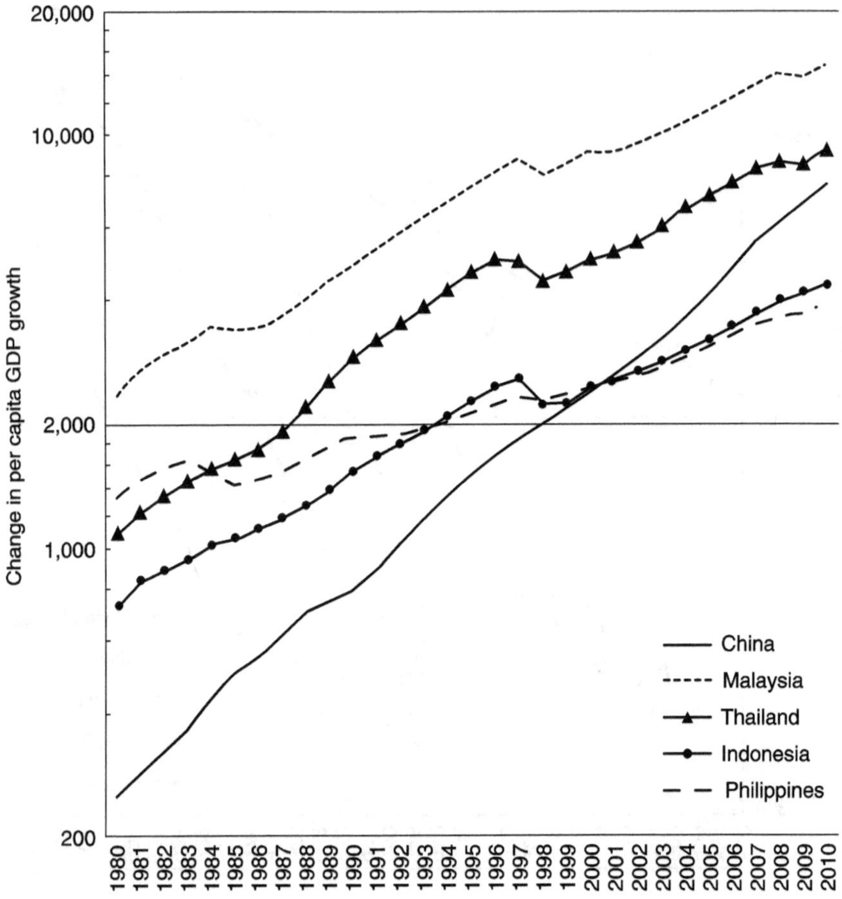

Figure 1.3 Changes in per capita GDP among China, Malaysia, Thailand, Indonesia, and the Philippines, 1980–2010

Source: IMF (2013)

Malaysia and Thailand in the course of recovery from the Asian crisis, resulting in less rapid growth in these countries, as will be discussed in more detail in Chapter 4. Formerly lower-performing countries in Southeast Asia, Indonesia and the Philippines recorded high growth in the first decade of this century, at least, in part, because of the establishment of a stable and relatively "clean" democracy and their success in containing contentious politics.[7]

Decentralization

While Japan's state building process involved shifting from a decentralized to a centralized system rather than the other way round, in many developing countries which have heterogeneous ethnic groups and are vulnerable to ethnic conflicts, decentralization can be a policy option to render the interactive process of state building and development smooth and stable. This volume covers Indonesia (Chapter 4), India (Chapter 7), and Kenya (Chapter 6), as examples of such states. Minority groups in the state tend to reside in concentrated areas, so that they may be majority groups in particular jurisdictions. Thus, constructing decentralized political institutions can be an effective component of state building, leading to lessened ethnic conflicts and a stable relationship between the state and constituencies, if such efforts do not collaterally strengthen secessionist pressures (Okamoto 2011). Chapter 4 discusses the favorable effect of transformation from developmental authoritarianism to the decentralized democratic system in Indonesia, notably under President Susilo Bambang Yudhoyono (2004–14). The unexpectedly steady growth in per capita GDP in this country after the downturn due to the Asian financial crisis can be partly attributed to such decentralization.

India is an interesting country from the viewpoint of state building, as it introduced market-oriented institutional reforms in 1991 and a series of constitutional reforms in 1993 to empower local administrative institutions at the third tiers of local governance (district, sub-district, and village levels), beyond the two tiers of central and state governments. Decentralization reforms were designed to achieve equitable development. According to Figure 1.4, the growth rate in per capita GDP in India accelerated from the early 1990s when market-oriented reforms were introduced.[8] A critically important observation is that human development indictors, such as life expectancy, infant mortality rates, and literacy rates, and infrastructure development indicators, such as telecommunication density and electricity consumption per capita, tend to be equalized across states in India (see Chapter 7).

Kenya is an ethnically diverse country and was relatively wealthy among developing countries. Indeed, its per capita GDP was somewhat higher than India's until the mid-1990s and was equaled by Bangladesh only in 2010. As will be discussed in Chapter 6, ethnic relations were politicized by the reallocation of land from white settlers to politically strong ethnic groups, rather than to ethnic groups that originally owned the land occupied by white settlers. Ethnic conflict heightened as a result of the "unfair" land allocation. The failure to establish fair and secure land ownership rights is a clear case of a failure in state building. Although a concrete and peaceful solution is hard to contemplate, ethnic-cum-land conflicts are location specific and as such the decentralization of the political system in Kenya, which is highly centralized now, seems to be a prerequisite for the ultimate solution.

Land rights institutions

De Soto (1989) argues that although entrepreneurship is potentially abundant in urban areas in developing countries, its potential has not been mobilized because of the lack of secure land ownership rights, which can be used as collateral for formal-sector credit. It is not, however, the lack of credit but the lack of

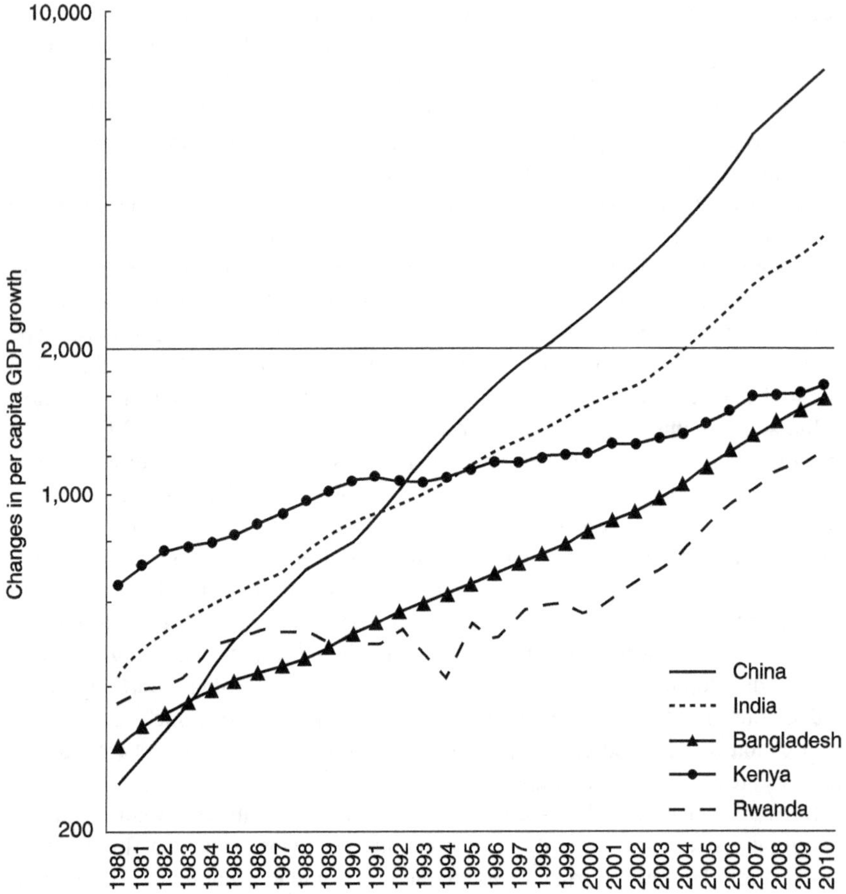

Figure 1.4 Changes in per capita GDP among India, Bangladesh, Kenya, and Rwanda in comparison with China, 1980–2010

Source: IMF (2013)

entrepreneurship that deters the development of micro and small enterprises (MSEs) in developing countries (Bloom and Van Reenen 2007, 2010; Bloom *et al.* 2010, 2011; Sonobe and Otsuka 2006, 2011). In other words, the lack of secure land rights does not seem to be a serious constraint on the development of MSEs in the urban sector of developing economies.

Land tenure security is more important for rural development. In an economy where agriculture accounts for more or less 30 than percent of GDP and 60 to 70 percent of employment, which is common in SSA, the establishment of private land ownership rights has been a central element of the political agenda in recent years when farmland has become scarce due to a population explosion (see Chapter 5). When land is abundant, slash-and-burn or shifting cultivation is the "optimum" farming system, in which crops are grown in one or two seasons followed by 20 to 30 years of fallow to restore soil fertility (Boserup 1965). Since life expectancy is short and land is abundant, there is little incentive for the cultivator to claim individual ownership of cultivated land. Thus, land is owned by clan, lineage, or extended family and allocated to its members by the chief with equity considerations (Otsuka and Place 2001). As population increases and land becomes scarce, it becomes important to invest in land improvement, for example, planting trees and tree crops, terracing, and irrigating for sedentary farming (Hayami and Ruttan 1985). In order to do so, the security of land ownership rights must be guaranteed to provide appropriate incentives for investors (Besley 1995). According to Otsuka and Place (2001), the individualization of land rights has been taking place spontaneously in native societies in SSA. Such land, however, cannot be used as collateral for credit from formal financial sectors, as the transfer rights (e.g., the right to sell to outsiders) are not clearly given. In such a situation, land titling or the provision of formal land transfer rights by providing land certificates makes sense, particularly in areas where new technology is being introduced and so the demand for credit is high (Holden *et al.* 2013).

In order to achieve sustainable agricultural development, not only must new profitable technologies be developed but land rights institutions must also be in place to ensure the sustainable management of soil fertility. Yamano *et al.* (2011) and Otsuka and Larson (2013) conclude that the establishment of land tenure security is a fundamental issue of agricultural development in SSA.

4 State building and development policies

The capacity of the state to implement development policies and macroeconomic policies governs the pace of economic development, whereas successful economic development offers an expanded tax base for the state, which, in turn, can be used to mitigate various conflicts and, hence, contain contentious politics. Although this book does not deal with macroeconomic policies, it is widely known from cross-country regression analyses that macroeconomic stability is positively associated with economic growth (Bleaney 1996; Fischer 1993; Sirimaneethan and Temple 2013). This section focuses on industrial polices.

At the outset, it must be pointed out that there are no universally accepted, effective development policies, not to mention policies to support the development of service sectors. Economists have failed to develop such polices. As a result, the World Bank's *World Development Report*, which is supposed to summarize the up-to-date theoretical and empirical knowledge of development economics, is surprisingly silent about strategies to develop industries (World Bank 2008, 2012).[9] We are still in the process of searching for effective development policies.

Industrial policy

Bangladesh was one of the poorest countries in the world in the early 1980s, much poorer than Kenya and Rwanda (see Figure 1.4), and its population density has been one of the highest. Beginning with such adverse conditions, the country has grown steadily over the last three decades, owing primarily to the development of the garment industry (Mottaleb and Sonobe 2011). In our view nothing is more instructive than the development experience of the garment industry in Bangladesh in designing effective industrial policies. Let us review its development process in this subsection.

When Daewoo Corporation of the Republic of Korea teamed up with Desh Ltd to initiate export-oriented garment production in Bangladesh in 1979, there was no modern garment sector in this country. Yet, since then, the number of garment factories has increased dramatically, and direct manufacturing employment has expanded rapidly (see Figure 1.5). In the 2000s, the industry accounted for as much as 75 percent of the country's exports. As of 2010–11, out of 3.6 million workers, female workers accounted for 80 percent.

The story began when Desh sent 130 newly recruited educated employees to Daewoo's garment factory in the Republic of Korea in 1979, where they participated in an eight-month intensive training course covering diverse topics from sewing skills to factory management, quality control, and international procurement and marketing. Within a few years, however, almost all the trainees had left Desh to start their own garment businesses. There is consensus among

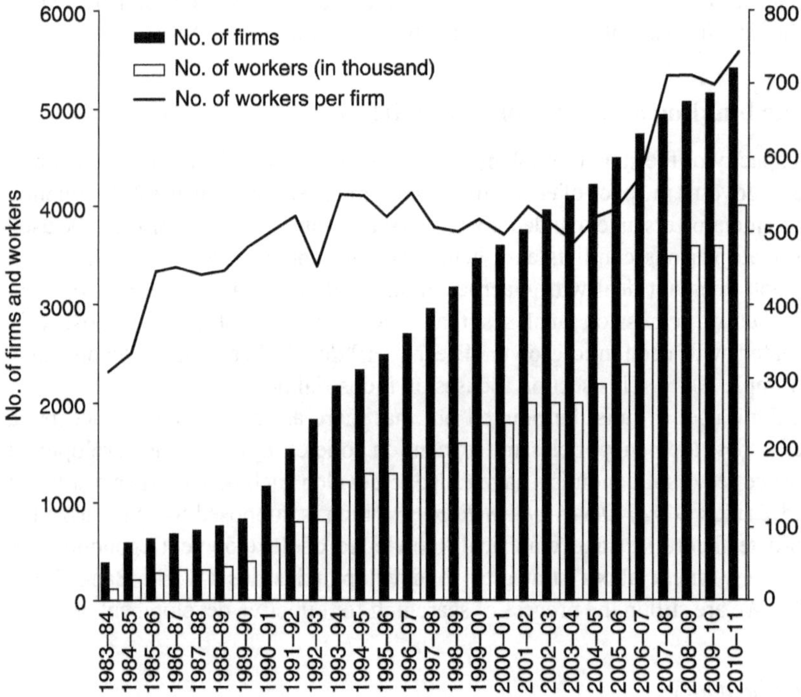

Figure 1.5 Growth of the garment industry in Bangladesh

Source: Bangladesh Knitwear Manufacturers and Exporters Association (2011)

observers of this industry that the Desh-Daewoo training kick-started the garment industry in Bangladesh.

Some of the ex-Desh workers joined new garment factories established by affluent businessmen, while others founded trading houses, which have contributed to the proliferation of garment manufacturers by providing a variety of valuable services including international procurement and marketing, making samples, and design re-engineering to new manufacturers. Observing Desh's profitable start in exporting followed by the success of ex-Desh workers, highly educated people entered the market in large numbers and wealthy families actively invested in this industry. As a result, the size of garment firms has been quite large since the beginning; the average employment size was 300 workers in 1983–84 and 700 workers in 2010–11. As of 2005, the owners of garment firms went to school for 15 years on average and about 60 percent of them completed college or university education.

Learning from abroad continued. Some entrepreneurs participated in training programs in Singapore, Japan, and Europe. Garment enterprises in newly industrialized countries in East Asia followed Daewoo in the operation in Bangladesh and the provision of training for Bangladeshi workers and managers. Thus, many Bangladeshi traders and manufacturers had work experience in garment trading and production, including the experience of working at joint ventures, before starting their current businesses. According to Mottaleb and Sonobe (2011), prior formal training and marketing and production experience, as well as the schooling of entrepreneurs, are critical determinants of successful enterprise performance in this industry.

The development experience of the garment industry in Bangladesh provides prima facie evidence that entrepreneurship can be fostered by learning advanced management practices and technologies through training and work experience. However, the initial Daewoo-Desh experience shows that it does not fully pay for private enterprises to invest in training for the acquisition of new knowledge because the useful knowledge spills over to other enterprises. The Daewoo-Desh decision to send new employees to the garment factory in Korea for training was a mistake from the private point of view, even though it was socially beneficial. In fact, the same or a similar employee training strategy has never been adopted by other private companies. Here, the role of prudent industrial policy proved to be critical in nurturing entrepreneurship and facilitating the transfer of useful technological and managerial knowledge from abroad.

Chapter 10 provides another instructive case study of the pharmaceutical industry in Bangladesh, which proves once again the importance of the education of entrepreneurs (e.g., through the establishment of the Department of Pharmacy) and learning from advanced countries (e.g., through attractive FDI policies) for successful industrial development. These results suggest that an effective industrial policy must promote investment in both general and specific human capital and the acquisition of useful knowledge from abroad.

Although in this volume we do not explicitly discuss polices to develop service sectors, particularly fast-growing computer-based modern service sectors, the principles are the same as those for industrial development policy: to invest in human capital and to facilitate learning from advanced countries (Jensen 2011). India and the Philippines are good examples. The modern service sectors, however, are human capital-intensive, so that investment in human capital by the state holds the key to success in the development of the modern service sector (Goswami *et al.* 2012).

5 Organization of the book

Aside from this chapter, which sets the stage for the analyses in subsequent chapters, there are two parts; Part I on "State building for development" and Part II on "State failures and successes." The central theme of the volume is to inquire into the dynamic processes by which states with weak institutions, legitimacy, and capacity are transformed into states with the institutional capacity to guarantee political stability, provide basic public goods, and implement effective development policies.

The first two chapters in Part I (Chapters 2 and 3) carefully re-examine how the state has interacted with economic development in modern Japanese history since the Meiji era. Chapter 4 looks into the process of political and economic transformation from non-democratic or even authoritarian states to more democratic states and the effects of the class, ethnic, and distributional conflicts associated with such transformations on contentious politics and state building among the ASEAN-4 during recent decades. The analysis clearly indicates that contentious politics, if mired in political stalemate, hinders economic development. At the same time, decisions taken by policymakers and state officials may have unexpected results in charting the economies of these ASEAN-4 countries even under conditions of political stalemate.

In SSA, agriculture is still the dominant economic sector and, hence, economic development as well as job creation hinges on agricultural development (World Bank 2012). The role of land policies and institutions in the state building in SSA are reviewed with a special reference to Rwanda in Chapter 5, which has experienced devastating internal conflicts followed by swift economic recovery in recent years. This chapter clearly demonstrates *latent* but eruptive political contention due to the implementation of overly swift and sweeping land reform.

Part II examines how state building interacts with economic policies. Chapter 6 demonstrates how unfair land distribution policy in favor of politically strong ethnic groups implemented by the non-democratic, post-colonial state in the past led to land tenure insecurity and the recent post-election violence in Kenya. Holden *et al.* (2013) suggest that facilitating land transfer through markets from land-abundant to labor-abundant farm households by means of a progressive land tax and loans from land banks may effectively mitigate such land-related conflict.

Chapter 7 attempts to assess the extent to which fiscal decentralization contributed to equity across states and between urban and rural areas in the Indian economy. The rapid growth in the Indian economy since the early 1990s might not have been sustainable if market-based development had resulted in inequitable distribution of income between the educated and uneducated, prosperous and stagnant states, and urban and rural areas. This is likely to be serious because so far the engine of growth in the Indian economy has been computer-based or related to modern service sectors, which offer lucrative employment opportunities primarily to the educated middle- to high-income classes but not to the urban uneducated class and the agricultural labor force (Ghani 2010). The fiscal decentralization will contribute to at least a partial alleviation of such unequalizing trends.

Chapter 8 explores how corruption norms, which are proxies for the quality of state or state building, are related to economic development. It is found that the corruption norm is negatively correlated with per capita income, which suggests that economic development contributes to the legitimacy of the state by reducing corruption. It is also found that corruption norms vary from person to person, indicating that the corrupt behaviors of policymakers are so variable that they create uncertainties in business environments, particularly in low-income economies.

Finally, the last two chapters attempt to shed new light on the conditions for the failure and success of industrial policies, based on the results of a large number of case studies conducted by the authors themselves (Chapter 9), and a case study of the spectacularly growing pharmaceutical industry in Bangladesh, where the government is known to be corrupt (Chapter 10). Two keys to successful industrial development are identified: human capital and learning from abroad. Since new knowledge acquired by educated entrepreneurs from training, work experience at foreign firms, and their own efforts tends to be imitated by competing firms, private return to the acquisition of new knowledge falls short of social return. This spillover effect provides the basis for government support for education, training, and foreign direct investment. A critically important observation is that industrial development led by educated entrepreneurs and based on the transfer of technological and managerial knowledge from more advanced countries and multinational companies is common in East Asia (Sonobe and Otsuka 2006, 2011). In other words, the pattern of development in Bangladesh shows that regional development since the 1960s in East Asia is no longer limited to "East Asia" per se, as other countries experience similar robust economic growth. An interesting implication is that government support for education, training, and foreign direct investment is far more important than a strong state, which was assumed to be the precondition for a "developmental state" for economic development in this globalizing world, as people, capital, technology, and knowledge circulate across borders and allow people and countries to seize opportunities, maximize their niches, and improve their living standards.

Notes

* The authors are grateful to Osamu Saito, Keiichi Tsunekawa, and Tetsushi Sonobe for their useful comments on the earlier version of this chapter.

1 The reversion to a non-democratic regime, however, does not take place once an economy exceeds the middle income level (Przeworski *et al.* 2000).

2 For further review of the relevant literature on economic development and democratization, see Section 2 in Chapter 3.
3 We are indebted to K. Tsunekawa for the development of Figure 1.1, which is a modified version of Figure 3.1 in Chapter 3.
4 Data of per capita GDP between 1890 and 2008 are taken from Maddison (2010), which uses 1990 international dollars. For the estimation of per capita GDP in 2009 and 2010, the growth rates from the previous year are calculated by using per capita GDP data between 2008 and 2010 from IMF (2013), and then the calculated growth rates are used to compute per capita GDP in 2009 and 2010.
5 As in the case of post-war Japan, how effectively the state led the industrial development by industrial policy in Korea and Taiwan is debated among economists (Amsden 1989; Komiya *et al.* 1988; Kuznets 1988; Wade 1990;).
6 Hamada *et al.* (2011) argue that as of now, Japanese economic institutions are still geared to the imitation of foreign technologies and not to the creation of frontier knowledge.
7 In the case of the Philippines, per capita income is much higher than per capita GDP because of the remittances from a large number of overseas workers.
8 Although per capita GDP in India is much lower than in China, the gap is likely to be overestimated because the informal sectors, which are not well covered by official statistics, account for a large share of the whole economy in India. Such underestimation, however, is not a major problem in China.
9 Similarly, no clear-cut development strategy to develop agriculture is prescribed in the *World Development Report* on agriculture (World Bank 2007).

References

Acemoglu, D. and Robinson, J.A. (2006) *Economic Origins of Dictatorship and Democracy*, Cambridge: Cambridge University Press.

Acemoglu, D. and Robinson, J.A. (2012) *Why Nations Fail: The Origins of Power, Prosperity, and Poverty*, New York: Crown Business.

Amsden, A. (1989) *Asia's Next Giant: South Korea and Late Industrialization*, New York: Oxford University Press.

Anderson, K. (ed.) (2009) *Distortions to Agricultural Incentives: A Global Perspective, 1955–2000*, Washington, DC: World Bank.

Anderson, K. and Hayami, Y. (eds.) (1986) *The Political Economy of Agricultural Protection*, Sydney: Allen & Unwin.

Bangladesh Knitwear Manufacturers and Exporters Association (2011) *History of Development of Knitwear of Bangladesh*, Bangladesh: BKMEA.

Besley, T. (1995) "Property rights and investment incentives," *Journal of Political Economy*, 103 (5): 913–37.

Bleaney, M. (1996) "Macroeconomic stability, investment and growth in developing countries," *Journal of Development Economics*, 48 (2): 461–77.

Bloom, N., and Van Reenen, J. (2007) "Measuring and explaining management practices across firms and countries," *Quarterly Journal of Economics* 122 (4): 1351–409.

Bloom, N., Mahajan, A., McKenzie, D., and Roberts, J. (2010) "Why do firms in developing countries have low productivity?" *American Economic Review*, 100 (2): 619–23.

Bloom, N., Eifert, B., Mahajan, A., McKenzie, D., and Roberts, J. (2011) "Does management matter? Evidence from India," Policy Research Working Paper No. 5573, World Bank.

Boserup, E. (1965) *The Conditions of Agricultural Growth*, Chicago: Aldine.

Deininger, K. and Byerlee, D. (2012) "The rise of large farms in land-abundant countries: Do they have a future?" *World Development*, 40 (4): 701–14.

de Soto, H. (1989) *The Other Path: The Invisible Revolution in the Third World*, New York: Harper & Row.

Fischer, S. (1993) "The role of macroeconomic factors in growth," *Journal of Monetary Economics*, 32 (3): 485–512.

Ghani, E. (2010) *The Service Revolution in South Asia*, New York: Oxford University Press.

Goswami, A.G., Matoo, A., and Saez, S. (2012) *Exporting Services: A Developing Country Perspective*, Washington, DC: World Bank.

Hamada, K., Otsuka, K., Ranis, G., and Togo, K. (eds.) (2011) *Miraculous Growth and Stagnation: Lessons from the Experience of Postwar Japanese Economic Development*. London: Routledge.

Hashino, T. and Otsuka, K. (2013) "Hand looms, power looms, and changing production organizations: the case of the Kiryū weaving district in early twentieth-century Japan," *Economic History Review*, 66 (3): 785–804.

Hashino, T. and Saito, O. (2004) "Tradition and interaction: research trends in modern Japanese industrial history," *Australian Economic History Review*, 44 (3): 241–58.

Hayami, Y. and Godo, Y. (2005) *Development Economics: From the Poverty to the Wealth of Nations*, Oxford: Oxford University Press.

Hayami, Y. and Otsuka, K. (1993) *The Economics of Contract Choice: An Agrarian Perspective*, Oxford: Clarendon Press.

Hayami, Y. and Ruttan, V.W. (1985) *Agricultural Development: An International Perspective*, Baltimore, MD: Johns Hopkins University Press.

Holden, S., Otsuka, K., and Place, F. (eds.) (2009) *The Emergence of Land Markets in Africa: Assessing the Impacts on Poverty, Equity, and Efficiency*, Baltimore, MD: Resources for the Future.

Holden, S., Otsuka, K., and Deininger, K. (eds.) (2013) *Land Tenure Reforms in Asia and Africa: Assessing Impacts on Poverty and Natural Resource Management*, Basingstoke: Palgrave Macmillan.

IMF (International Monetary Fund) (2013) *World Economic Outlook Database April 2013*, Washington, DC: IMF.

Jensen, J.B. (2011) *Global Trade in Services*, Washington, DC: Peter G. Peterson Institute for International Economics.

Johnson, C. (1982) *MITI and the Japanese Miracle: The Growth of Industrial Policy, 1925–1975*, Stanford, CA: Stanford University Press.

Komiya, R., Okuno, M., and Suzumura, K. (eds.) (1988) *Industrial Policy of Japan*, New York: Academic Press.

Kuznets, P.W. (1988) "An East Asian model of economic development: Japan, Taiwan, and South Korea," *Economic Development and Cultural Change*, 36 (3): S11–43.

Larson, D., Matsumoto, T., Kilic, T., and Otsuka, K. (2013) "Should African rural development strategies depend on smallholder farms? An exploration of the inverse productivity hypothesis," *Agricultural Economics*, forthcoming.

Lipton, M. (2009) *Land Reform in Developing Countries: Property Rights and Property Wrongs*, Oxfordshire: Routledge.

Maddison, A. (2010) Data on population and GDP, https://sites.google.com/site/econgeodata/maddison-data-on-population-gdp.

Mottaleb, K.A. and Sonobe, T. (2011) "An inquiry into the rapid grwoth of the garment industry in Bangladesh," *Economic Develoment and Cultural Change*, 60 (1): 67–89.

OECD (2008) (Organization for Economic Cooperation and Development) "State building in situations of fragility," initial findings, Paris: OECD.

Okamoto, M. (2011) "Minshuka shita taminzoku kokka Indonesia ni okeru antei no politics" ["Politics of stability in democratized, multi-ethnic Indonesia"], Ph.D. dissertation, Kyoto University.

Otsuka, K., Estudillo, J.P., and Sawada, Y. (2009) *Rural Poverty and Income Dynamics in Asia and Africa*, London: Routledge.

Otsuka, K. and Larson, D. (eds.) (2013) *An African Green Revolution: Finding Ways to Boost Productivity on Small Farms*, Dordrecht: Springer.

Otsuka, K. and Place, F. (eds.) (2001) *Land Tenure and Natural Resource Management: A Comparative Study of Agrarian Communities in Asia and Africa*, Baltimore, MD: Johns Hopkins University Press.

Otsuka, K., Ranis, G., and Saxonhouse, G. (1988). *Comparative Technology Choice in Development: The Indian and Japanese Cotton Textile Industries*. London: Macmillan.

Przeworski, A., Alvarez, M.R., Cheibub, J.A., and Limongi, F. (2000) *Democracy and Development: Political Institutions and Well-being in the World, 1950–1990*, Cambridge: Cambridge University Press.

Rozelle, S. and Huang, J. (2012) "China's labor transition and the future of China's rural wages and employment," Background paper for *World Development Report 2013: Jobs*. Washington, DC: World Bank.

Schultz, T.W. (1975) "The value of ability to deal with disequilibria," *Journal of Economic Literature*, 13 (3): 827–46.

Shleifer, A. and Vishny, R.W. (1993) "Corruption," *Quarterly Journal of Economics*, 108 (3): 599–617.

Sirimaneetham, V. and Temple, J.R.W. (2013) "Macroeconomic stability and the distribution of growth rates," *World Bank Economic Review*, 23 (3): 443–79.

Sonobe, T. and Otsuka, K. (2006) *Cluster-Based Industrial Development: An East Asian Model*. Basingstoke: Palgrave Macmillan.

Sonobe, T. and Otsuka, K. (2011) *Cluster-Based Industrial Development: A Comparative Study of Asia and Africa*, Basingstoke: Palgrave Macmillan.

Tilly, C. (2004) *Contention and Democracy in Europe, 1650–2000*, Cambridge: Cambridge University Press.

Tilly, C. (2007) *Democracy,* Cambridge: Cambridge University Press.

Wade, R. (1990) *Governing the Market: Economic Theory and the Role of Government in East Asian Industrialization*, Princeton, NJ: Princeton University Press.

World Bank (2007) *World Development Report 2008: Agriculture for Development*, Washington, DC: World Bank.

World Bank (2008) *World Development Report 2009: Reshaping Economic Geography*, Washington, DC: World Bank.

World Bank (2012) *World Development Report 2013: Jobs*, Washington, DC: World Bank.

Yamano, T., Otsuka, K., and Place, F. (eds.) (2011) *Emerging Development of Agriculture in East Africa: Markets, Soil, and Innovations*, Amsterdam: Springer.

Part I

State building for development

2 Was modern Japan a developmental state?

*Osamu Saito**

1 The problem

Meiji Japan has long been regarded as a strong, developmental state. The early Meiji government's key figure, Ōkubo Toshimichi,[1] noted in his 1874 policy document that:

> The strength of a country depends on the prosperity of its people which, in turn, is based on the level of output. To increase output, industrialization is essential. However, no country has ever initiated the process of industrialization without official guidance and promotion.
>
> (Quoted in Ohno 1998: 7)

This passage reflects what he learnt when he visited Victorian Britain, the Workshop of the World, as a vice-ambassador of a mission sent by the new government to America and Europe from 1871 to 1873. Conceived originally as an attempt to revise the 'unequal treaties' with the West, the delegation led by Prince Iwakura turned out to be one of the most significant learning missions that modern Japan undertook. Its one-and-a-half-year tour exposed Ōkubo and other able leaders in the government to the wealth of western industrial nations. They were dazzled by the affluence that the people of the West enjoyed and realized in how many aspects Japan lagged behind the western countries. The British representative in Japan, Sir Harry Parkes, who accompanied the mission on their tour of Lancashire, Britain's industrial heartland, told the visitors that 'as far as Japan's future traffic with the world and the promotion of new enterprise is concerned, this is the single most significant tour of inspection you are likely to have' (quoted in Nish 1998: 44). From London, Ōkubo wrote to a friend in Tokyo, saying that 'Now I know why Britain is so rich and strong' (quoted in Banno and Ohno 2010: 18). It was 'iron and coal' that transformed British industry: both were turned 'into manufactured goods, which they export again to other countries for sale' (Kume 2002: 419). In another letter from London, Ōkubo remarked that Britain was 50 years ahead of Japan (*Ōkubo Toshimichi Monjo* 1927–29: IV, 467–70). Kume Kunitake, the mission's official chronicler, shared Ōkubo's view: 'It is since 1800 that Europe has attained its present wealth; and it is only in the last forty years that it has achieved the truly remarkable level of prosperity we now see' (Kume 2002: 57). Undoubtedly, there was a sense of economic backwardness among the Meiji leaders. They believed, as Gerschenkron argued, that the frontrunners were not unreachable if advanced technology and systems were made available to the latecomers. Thus, as predicted by Gerschenkron, the tour led Ōkubo and other leaders to the conviction that the state should play an active role in Japan's industrialisation (Gerschenkron 1962: Ch. 1 and postscript).

Indeed, the government set a series of goals for the economy since the Meiji Restoration of 1868, summed up in the slogan 'rich nation, strong military' (*fukoku kyōhei*). According to Chalmers Johnson's book on *MITI and the Japanese Miracle*, any state whose *raison d'être* is the attainment of economic development, and whose intervention in a market economy is administered via a governmental planning agency (such as post-World War II Japan's Ministry of International Trade and Industry, MITI), may be called a developmental state. Under this regime, ideas for economic planning come first from the state, conjoining private-sector efforts with state guidance. Economic growth thus generated may be called 'plan rational' but not 'market rational' (i.e. pro-market). Also it should be distinguished from the Soviet-type 'plan irrational' command economy since much of actual production decision-making is left to the private sector. Government intervention is justified from a long-term economic perspective and is in many cases intertwined with nationalist politics (Johnson 1982; Murakami 1996: Ch. 5; Woo-Cumings 1999). While Johnson's analysis focused on Japan's industrial policy in the 1925–75 period, contemporary development specialists believe that Meiji Japan's 'success' in this regard served as a 'prototype' for the emergence of developmental states in East Asia in the post-World War II period (Watanabe 1998).

However, it now seems that the role of Meiji statism in the country's economic development has been grossly overestimated. First, as political historian Junji Banno has made clear, leaders of the Restoration period were never unified in pursuing the revolutionary goals, nor were leaders in the newly-formed government. There were four separate goals held by separate groups in the government. While two of the four were political and constitutional, the other two were directly related to the issue of economic development: industrialisation (which most of the *fukoku* group actually meant) and military build-up (*kyōhei*). There was competition between these multiple goals, with setbacks, coalitions, and phase shifts over the nation-building process that lasted from 1868 to the early 1880s (Banno 2001; Banno and Ohno 2010). The picture which emerges from such interpretations is certainly different from the image of the Meiji government as an authoritarian developmental state.

Second, this early-Meiji trial of industry promotion was short-lived. There is evidence that from 1885 to c. 1930 much was left to private initiatives and market forces. Tetsuji Okazaki and Juro Teranishi, to name only two, have found that in this period the level of state intervention was lower, money and employment markets more flexible, and corporate governance provided more by shareholders than in the post-World War II period (Okazaki and Okuno-Fujiwara 1999;

Teranishi 2005). Teranishi believes that what he calls the Meiji-Taisho[2] system 'emerged in the 1890s, . . . peaking more or less with the 1919–20 boom, stumbling badly after 1927, and finally collapsing in the mid-1930s' (Teranishi 2005: 42), although we can push back the beginning a little earlier, i.e. to 1885 since the first surge in firms' activity, one of Teranishi's own criteria, occurred in the late 1880s, and since the year 1881 is considered a turning point in the political history of macroeconomic management as we will see below. Whichever the dates, however, it is interesting to note here that in Johnson's 1982 book the original time frame he chose was from 1925 to 1975. He suggested that from 1914 to 1925 was a period in which 'an approximation of laissez faire was in vogue' (Johnson 1982: 33); and he still believes that the chosen period is 'a distinct unity' (Johnson 1999: 55). As the laissez faire period is likely to have begun much earlier than Johnson initially thought, we should now question the established image of Meiji or even modern Japan, because much of pre-World War II Japan was market rational, rather than plan rational. However, Johnson did say in passing that 'modern Japan began in 1868 to be plan rational and developmental' and that even after about a decade of experimentation with state entrepreneurship, when it shifted to collaboration with the private sector, 'Japan was and remained plan rational' (Johnson 1982: 23) – phrases which fit nicely with the stereotyped image of the Meiji government as a promoter of industrialisation from above.

Third, there is now consensus among economic historians that the Meiji government's economic policy was far from consistent during this nation-building period. As we will see later, after an initial, unsuccessful, measure of note issues to meet all the administrative as well as more enterprising expenses, a new central government had to make a selective attempt at 'industrialisation from above' with state entrepreneurship and other hands-on measures. However, this policy was reformulated by the Ōkubo administration in the mid-1870s, and was eventually scrapped by Finance Minister Count Matsukata in 1881, suggesting that none of those policies resulted in a positive result. Thus the country's first surge in firms' activity in the 1885–89 period – which is often called Meiji Japan's 'industrial revolution' since a number of modern, western-style firms were set up in cotton spinning and some other manufacturing industries – cannot be attributed to any action the government made in the 1870s and 1880s, questioning the growth process as industrialisation from above.

Finally, taking a little longer view, economic development in the period before World War I should no longer be viewed as a period of spectacular growth. Take for example Angus Maddison's historical statistics. According to his real gross domestic product (GDP) per capita estimates (Maddison 2003: Tables 1c, 2c, 5c), Japan's average annual growth rate between two benchmark years of 1870 and 1913 was 1.5 per cent, lower than that of the USA (1.8 per cent) and marginally higher than that of western Europe (1.3 per cent). And in 1913 when Japan's per capita GDP reached $1,387, that of the west European countries stood at $3,458 (both in 1990 international dollars), indicating that catch-up with the West did not take place during the Meiji period. Comparatively better performance was achieved later, especially in the late 1910s and in the period immediately after the Great Depression. Despite its dramatic impact Japan's record of growth (1.0 per cent per annum) for the 1930–35 period compared favourably with that of western countries: that of the USA stood as low as 0.1 per cent while western Europe's was 0.4 per cent. This may be taken to suggest that catch-up began in the inter-war period, but it should be realised that average growth rates declined in this period across the major industrial nations including Japan. Even an average annual growth rate of 2 per cent, according to Robert Allen's calculation, was 'not fast enough' for a latecomer like Japan to catch up with the west (Allen 2011: 126). Also, inter-war Japan experienced a dramatic rise in income inequality between social classes as well as between rural and urban societies. As a result, growth in this period became much less stable than that of the period before 1913. Takafusa Nakamura once noted that the period from World War I to the Pacific War was an era of 'unbalanced growth'; in other words, economic growth before 1913 was much less dynamic but 'balanced', suggesting that there occurred moderate growth of both traditional and modern economies (Hashino and Saito 2004; Nakamura 1983). The fact that there was no head start of the modern, capitalist sector under Meiji rule also questions the supposed linkage between state guidance and rapid economic growth in the pre-World War I period.

It is important therefore to examine critically whether the early Meiji state was actually plan rational and developmental, and to explore what accounted for changes in the government's attitude towards development policy in relation to other national objectives, both political and military, over the period from 1885 to the 1930s.

Governments can influence the process of economic development by, for example, building tariff barriers in order to protect strategically important domestic industries, by giving subsidies to those industries, by setting up state enterprises or investment banks, by providing macroeconomic planning and administrative guidance to the private sector, or by combining any of these options. Which options are actually chosen by a government is dependent on circumstances in a given period as well as its past circumstances, both economic and political. For Japan, the second half of the nineteenth century was not just a period of economic transformation, but also of a regime change: a civil war and the resultant change of government paved the way for the building of a nation state. Thus, the next section will take a brief look at the political economy at both shogunal and daimyo levels on the eve of the change from the Tokugawa 'feudal' polity to Meiji Japan's centralized nation state. Then, Section 3 examines two experiments of industry promotion, policies actually implemented in the early Meiji period. Section 4 turns to the situation after 1885, and government spending in several areas will be examined in relation to the early Meiji national objectives of rich nation and strong military. Emphasis will be on the fact that much was left to the private sector in that period. The final section therefore discusses the question of why the state withdrew so suddenly after 1885. A few hypotheses will be put forward in relation to Japan's position in international relations of the long nineteenth century as well as the domestic situation she had reached by the end of Tokugawa rule.

2 Late-Tokugawa political economy[3]

Tokugawa Japan, a closed economy, consisted of the shogunal and 280 daimyo territories and each daimyo government kept fiscal as well as macroeconomic autonomy in its own territory (called 'domain'). During the last decades of Tokugawa rule, Japan's so-called 'seclusion' policy was under strong pressure from abroad: western powers knocked on the doors, demanding the opening of trade and diplomatic relations with the West. The Japanese took the demand as a military threat. The shogunal government set out various plans for coastal defence, ordering local daimyo to share the artillery and financial burdens. Eventually this led to a freer than ever discussion on defence and foreign policies among the daimyo and samurai officials, which in turn developed into a growing schism between the shogunal government and several daimyo powers (for an overview of the process towards the opening of the country in 1859, see Mitani 2006).

Among the latter group of samurai officials and intellectuals, there also emerged a view that Tokugawa Japan's decentralised 'feudal' structure should be replaced by a unified state system. The open confrontation led to a civil war and then to the collapse of the Tokugawa regime in 1868. In this sense, the Meiji Restoration can be regarded as a step towards the creation of a nation state. In fact, only three years later this programme for political unification took shape with the abolishment of the 280 daimyo domains. However, it is interesting to note that before the civil war a kind of consensus had already been reached by key figures for the establishment of a 'feudal assembly'. In 1864, for example, one from an anti-Tokugawa domain and another from the shogunal government met and came to an agreement that the best way to cope with the western impact was to create an assembly of four or five daimyo 'of clear wisdom'. Similar proposals were made by others. And it is this that 'provided the theoretical background that later legitimized the political policy orientation of the Meiji government' (Banno and Ohno 2010: 13). Indeed, Article 1 of the Charter Oath promulgated soon after the Restoration promised a government by public deliberation under Meiji rule, which undoubtedly reflected the political half of the late Tokugawa consensus.

The consensus included an economic element as well, which reflected the experience and skills of samurai bureaucrats accumulated in various daimyo domains. The pre-1858 discussion of defence and diplomatic issues led samurai officials in the domains to the realisation that military build-up and wealth creation should go hand in hand to cope with the national crisis. This domain-level understanding is the prototype that was transformed later into Meiji Japan's slogan 'rich nation, strong military'. One important component of this economic policy package was money supply, which today is rarely considered a development policy tool. The money supply under the Tokugawa system had been controlled by both central and local authorities. Gold and silver coins were under direct control of the shogunate, while each daimyo's domainal government was allowed to issue its own notes for circulation within the domain. By the end of the Tokugawa period, it is likely that the number of domainal governments issuing paper money had gradually grown (Shimbo and Saito 1999: 352). Not all of them were successful, but it should be stressed that many domainal governments were able to sustain their note prices at reasonable levels, and that some of the governments which had experienced monetary crises did recover and rehabilitate their money supplies. Know-how concerning the management of a 'paper-money economy' was indeed one of the important legacies of the Tokugawa period. The other important element was export promotion by setting up a trade bureau in the domainal government. Local merchants were involved in the trade bureau scheme to buy up a product for 'export' to metropolitan and, after 1859, overseas markets via treaty ports, and profits thus acquired went to cover the payments for arms the daimyo government wanted to buy from the West. The number of daimyo domains introducing a similar plan increased more noticeably than in the case of paper money (Nishikawa and Amano 1999).

Well-known are reform plans of the 1840s in the four south-western domains that later led the anti-shogunate campaign, and the number of such reforms kept increasing in the decade immediately after the opening of the treaty ports. This fact is significant, for many of the leaders of the reforms proposed ideas and measures quite similar to those of the Meiji policymakers. In other words, '*fukoku*' became the domains' goal, emphasising the importance of trade as a source of the 'benefit of the domain' (*kokueki*). According to a recent survey of early modern economic thought literature, such late-Tokugawa '*kokueki* policies in the domainal states were institutional innovations that tended to persist through conjunctional phases of budgetary expansion and retrenchment' (Metzler 2010: 240). Many domainal governments thus encouraged the production of cash crops and manufactured goods by monopsonising and 'exporting' them to Osaka and other commercial centres. In so doing the domains often issued paper money which, it was hoped, would serve as the supply of capital to the producers of their 'export' goods. Better known, perhaps, is the case of Fukui domain. In 1858, Mitsuoka Hachiro (renamed to Yuri Kimimasa later) took the initiative to issue notes to buy up raw silk and other products in the domain, which were then sent to Nagasaki. Yuri called the notes *kōsan shihei* (paper money for industry promotion), and the domainal government profited as much as 50,000 ryō from this operation. Although details are not available, leading village entrepreneurs and wealthy merchants from the castle town were involved in the scheme. It seems that the supply of money in the form of domainal notes through the town merchant-financiers to the silk-producing villages had a positive effect (this success in Fukui helped Yuri to gain charge of finance in the new-born Meiji government; but, as we will see later, his national-level paper money scheme failed). It is likely therefore that the policy package of note issue and export promotion, a kind of tested knowledge as far as the domainal economy was concerned, formed part of a late-Tokugawa legacy passed on to the new Meiji central government (Nishikawa and Amano 1999).

3 Two models of industry promotion

Having had a cursory look at the pre-Meiji political economy, it should be noted that there was another model of development policy ready for the Meiji government

Table 2.1 Chronology, 1859–1938

1859	Yokohama and other ports opened for foreign trade under the so-called 'unequal treaties' with the West
1868	Meiji Restoration (the Meiji era begins)
	Charter Oath promulgated
1870	Ministry of Public Works established
1871	Iwakura mission departs
1872	National banking system introduced
1873	Ōkubo Toshimichi returns from Europe
	Land tax reform announced (with uniformly set tax rate of 3 per cent of the cash value of land)
	'Conquer Korea' argument defeated in government
	Ōkuma Shigenobu appointed Minister of Finance
	Ministry of Home Affairs established. Ōkubo takes office as first Home Minister
1874	Petition for the 'Opening of a popularly elected national assembly' submitted
1876	National Bank Regulations revised
1877	Land tax rate lowered to 2.5 per cent
	Satsuma rebellion
1878	Ōkubo assassinated
1880	Government enterprises sold to private interests
1881	Ministry of Agriculture and Commerce established
	Finance Minister Ōkuma dismissed. Matsukata Masayoshi takes over
1882	National banking system scrapped. Bank of Japan established
1885	Cabinet system established
	Ministry of Public Works abolished
1885–9	First surge in firms' industrial activity
1889	Promulgation of the Meiji Constitution
1890	First general election
1894	Declaration of war on Qing China
1895	Taiwan annexed to Japan
1897	Gold standard adopted
1902	Anglo-Japanese Alliance signed
1904	Declaration of war on Russia
1910	Korea annexed to Japan
1911	'Unequal treaties' revised
1912	Taisho era begins
1914–18	World War I. Japan taken off the gold standard in 1917
1926	Showa era begins
1929	Stock market crash in New York. The Great Depression begins
1930	Lifting of the gold embargo

(Continued)

Table 2.1 (Continued)

1931	Manchurian Incident. Abandons the gold standard permanently
1936	Failed coup d'etat (February 26 Incident)
1937	Marco Polo Bridge Incident, starting the second Sino-Japanese War
1938	National General Mobilisation Law promulgated. Wartime economy begins

to adopt. The new government, although they had bitterly criticised the shogunal government's conciliatory policy towards the western powers, pursued a programme of westernisation from the start. While the traditional model of export promotion was undoubtedly one option, it was the transplantation of an 'iron and coal' production system that the Meiji government wanted to try first. In 1870, the Ministry of Public Works[4] was established, under which a substantial amount of money was sunk into government-run enterprises. A half of its total investments went to railways, 30 per cent to mining and 13 per cent to the construction of telegraphs. Outside the Public Works Ministry, model factory projects were launched under the auspices of the Ministry of Home Affairs, which was set up in 1873. The silk-reeling factories at Maebashi and Tomioka, the cotton mills in Aichi and Hiroshima, and the Senju woollen mill are such examples; also, the government bought spinning machinery with 2,000 spindles from England in 1879. But the Home Ministry's expenditures on those projects were considerably smaller in comparison with those of the Public Works Ministry.

However, the Meiji government was under serious financial constraints. First, the new government's budgetary position was extremely fragile. The tax base the government inherited from the Tokugawa shogunate did not cover the vast territorial areas for 280 daimyo governments. In both shogunate and daimyo territories, the major source of revenue had been the land tax: there had been no excise, no market tax, and no customs duty. According to the so-called unequal treaties, which may in fact be interpreted as a manifestation of British-led 'free trade' imperialism of the long nineteenth century (Gallagher and Robinson 1953), import duties were fixed at the low rate of 5 per cent *ad valorem* for most commodities coming into Japan. Under this treaty port system, therefore, the Meiji government was 'robbed' of a means to increase revenue and, more importantly, to take control of its macro economy. It was the land tax reform of 1873 that enabled the treasury to stabilise the taxation structure, maintaining roughly the same level of revenue in aggregate terms as in Tokugawa days. However, the reform led to several peasant revolts against the government, which helped fuel a nationwide movement for people's rights led by a former government councillor Itagaki Taisuke that started almost simultaneously. The government was thus forced to lower the land tax rate from 3 to 2.5 per cent in 1877. The Ministry of Finance, therefore, tried to broaden the tax base by introducing a number of new taxes, but most of them failed: it was a long way to go for them to establish a firmer tax base outside the land sector.

Second, the government was increasingly worried about the adverse balance of foreign trade. According to trade statistics for the period 1860–1900 (Sugiyama 1988: 46–47), the balance of payments was in favour for a brief period after the opening of the treaty ports as raw silk and, to a lesser extent, silkworm eggs, found unexpectedly huge markets abroad. In 1867, however, imports exceeded exports considerably with the imbalance reaching 20 million yen in current prices. Between 1871 and 1874 its level remained within the range of 4–9 million yen annually but in 1875 it rose again to 13 million yen. The extraordinary burden of these deficits stands out clearly against the statistics of government revenue and expenditure in the same period: the total of yearly ordinary revenue was 283 million yen, with capital investment in state-run enterprises alone amounting to 19 million yen, for seven and a half years from December 1867 to June 1875 (Smith 1955: 71). This balance of payments problem was an inevitable consequence of the policy the government adopted: while Japanese raw silk exports kept increasing, imports also increased substantially, i.e. imports of cotton goods as well as more expensive items such as merchant vessels, warships, munitions and machinery, all needed to carry out the westernisation programme.

With these two constraints, the government made a significant change in development policy in the early 1870s. It was indeed the outcome of a power struggle within the government. By the year 1873, there had emerged a serious disagreement over policy towards Korea. Most vociferous was a pro-military group of councillors who had proposed an ambitious foreign expedition. Having returned from the Iwakura mission, Ōkubo successfully objected to their 'Conquer Korea' argument. In his famous October 1873 critique of the war proposal, he stated:

> Today government expenditures are tremendous, which our incomes cannot cover. Thus if we open fire and send several tens of thousands of men abroad we will incur enormous expenses. This will require heavy taxes or foreign loans or the issuance of paper money, which will lead to higher prices, social unrest and uprisings . . . Our government has started to stimulate industries, but it will be several years before we get results . . . If we now begin an unnecessary war, spend a huge amount of money, shed blood, and worsen the daily life of people, all these government works will break like a bubble and lose several decades of time . . . Regarding the foreign trade situation, each year there is one million yen deficit . . . and our specie reserve decreases. Thus our international credit worsens, leading to inflation and our people's livelihood becoming hard. Also the export of our products faces difficulties.
>
> (quoted in Lu 1997: 325)

He underestimated the level of trade deficits while he was undoubtedly too optimistic to say that their industry promotion policy would bear results in several years' time. But his stance was clear: while rejecting the proposed 'unnecessary' war for the reason of the twin deficit problem, he placed an unmistakable priority on 'stimulating industries'. In other words, he effectively declared that 'rich nation' and 'strong military' were separable as policy objectives. Under his rule, therefore, 'rich nation' was the nation's primary goal with 'strong military' put aside.

With the pro-warfare campaign quashed, Ōkubo seized power within the government. In 1874 he spelt out an outline of the government's industrial and trade policy. As quoted earlier, he saw both governmental 'guidance' and 'encouragement' as the key to the successful development of a latecomer like Meiji Japan. However, he stopped short of making specific proposals in the 1874 document. In fact, the actual industrial and trade policies adopted by the Ōkubo administration subsequently were different from what one might expect from those 'industrialisation from above' lines. His May 1875 policy document made it clear that the nation's industrial objective rested on 'increasing exports and restraining imports', while the expenditure on railway construction was cut back in 1875, lavishly-paid foreign advisers and engineers were sacked, and finally state-owned factories and mines were sold 'on easy terms' to private enterprises from 1884 onwards. It is evident that export promotion and the encouragement of traditional industry became the government's new development policy (*Ōkubo Toshimichi Monjo* 1927–9: IV, 363–66).

As in the late Tokugawa domainal economies, the Meiji government's export promotion was backed by the printing of paper money. This time, however, it was the private sector that was expected to supply notes. The national banks, authorised by the 1872 Regulations, were the first western-style, private-sector banking institutions. Having faced the chaotic financial situation caused by the opening of the treaty ports and the collapse of the old domainal system, the Meiji government sent one councillor to the USA, who brought back a model of national banking with him. This decentralised American system had been implemented to supersede the even more decentralised 'state banks' in the USA but was still in sharp contrast to the central banking system. Although government ministers knew that it was the centralised system that had been adopted by European countries, a proposal which favoured it was rejected by a majority of the ministers. According to the 1872 Regulations, the banks were required to issue their own notes with the backing of specie reserves. In August 1876, however, the National Bank Regulations were amended by the Ōkubo administration's Finance Minister Ōkuma Shigenobu, a pragmatic Restoration leader. In an 1875 policy document, he too had mentioned the twin deficit problem as the most serious difficulty that the government had been facing. The underlying causes for such difficulties, said Ōkuma, were inadequate transport systems and the tightness in financial markets, especially in local markets. It was noted that the 300 or so domainal governments of the past had themselves effectively been 'running banking and other businesses for the people'; hence, it was argued, their abolition by the new government meant the disappearance of such functions, which were indispensable for the local economy (*Ōkuma Monjo* 1958–63: III, 127). It is along this line of understanding that Ōkuma's monetary policy was framed. His amendment of the 1872 Regulations allowed the banks to issue their own notes if convertible to government currency. Since the government notes were not convertible to specie, this amendment actually meant that they were now able to issue non-convertible bank notes. In the following years, a number of banks were set up under this scheme, not only in the metropolitan and treaty port cities but in many provincial towns as well. The increase in the number of national banks began in 1877 and continued until it exceeded the government-set limit of 150. So did national bank notes issued; and the rate of increase in the bank notes in circulation remained high until 1879. The popularity of Ōkuma's amendment among financiers in the countryside suggests that the increase in money supply was welcomed by local merchants and producers, many of whom must have been export-oriented. In other words, Ōkubo and Ōkuma favoured the old system in modern guise.

However, the paper money economy of the early Meiji period has not been regarded as a success story. The orthodox interpretation is that the decentralised system of national banks ended with inflation and financial crises. In order to examine the impact of the 1875 amendment, the graphs of annual gross national product (GNP) and wholesale price series are set out in Figure 2.1. A close look at the graphs, as well as additional information about exports and currency in circulation (available from Teranishi 1983), reveals that there was a 20-fold increase in national bank notes issued for the first three years, which meant a 1.5-fold increase in total currency in circulation. Inevitably a high price rise took place from 1878 onwards. Moreover, in 1877 an uprising of ex-samurai from Satsuma took place. The rebellion was led by Saigo Takamori, one of the 'Conquer Korea' proponents; thus, their surrender meant that the pro-military group reduced political influence considerably. But it also meant an unexpected expenditure for the government, the costs of which were met by an increase in notes issued. As a result of all this, the year-on-year rate of inflation became two-digit from 1879 to 1881. However, output in current prices also grew strongly from 1879 on with a similarly strong increase in exports: in fact, growth in output and exports was stronger than the price rise as far as 1879 and 1880 are concerned. To put it differently, the economy grew and exports expanded in real terms as a result of the 1876 amendment of the National Bank Regulations. The rate of increase in the latter was a little over 13 per cent, while that in the former went down to 7 per cent. Since it was only exports that were still growing at a pace faster than the price rise, people's incomes and consumption must have declined noticeably in 1881. In other words, it is not unlikely that money supply had exerted some positive effect until 1880, but as Ōkuma himself admitted, the supply of paper money had gone excessive. Inflation became uncontrollable. In 1880 Ōkuma started working out a plan to redeem bank notes. In October 1881, however, Ōkuma was ousted from the government. Matsukata Masayoshi took over his financial portfolio. Next year, note issue was centralised. An austerity budget was introduced with a drastic redemption plan for bank notes, and a deflation spiral began.

The Meiji leaders firmly believed that the nation should be guided by the state to achieve the proclaimed objectives of 'rich nation' and/or 'strong military'.

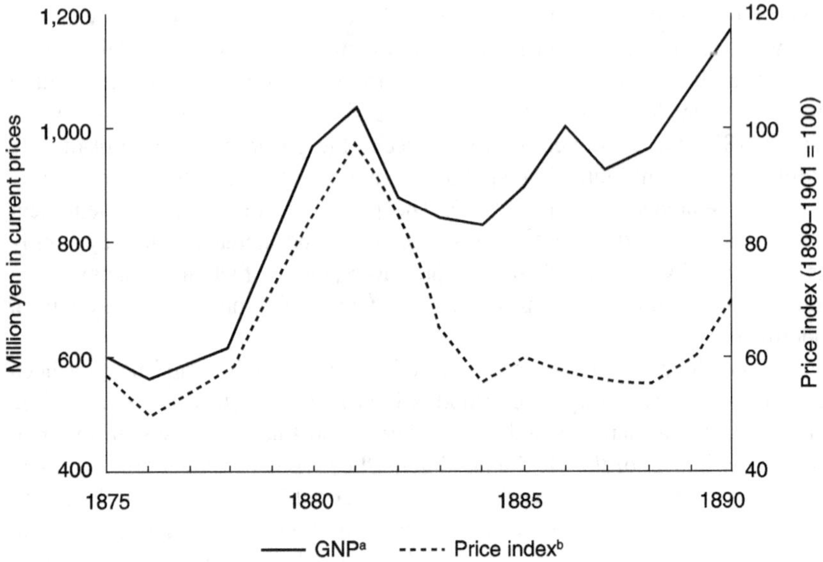

Figure 2.1 Yearly changes in GNP and the Tokyo wholesale price index, 1875–90

Source: Saito (forthcoming), Table 2.1

Notes: [a] The GNP series is Teranishi's estimates and does not cover investment in non-primary industrial construction and inventory, for which data are unavailable before 1880. Estimates are made in current prices. No attempt has been made to estimate a GNP deflator series for the period before 1885.

[b] The price index is Arita and Nakamura's estimates for wholesale prices in Tokyo. The baseyears are converted from 1934–36 to 1899–1901.

Nevertheless, after the brief period of experiments with hands-on policies, the government realised that both hands-on development policy and pro-military objectives should be shelved – for the time being, at least. As the Ōkubo-Ōkuma regime kept the 'rich nation' target alive, they inevitably had to resort to the traditional model of export promotion with the increased supply of paper money in the hope of stimulating the export-oriented rural sector. By 1881, however, both models went bankrupt.

4 The laissez faire period, 1885–1937

It is widely agreed that the Matsukata deflation period of 1881–84 was a turning point in the economic history of Meiji Japan. The decentralised age of a paper money economy for industry promotion was over. The national banking system was taken over by a new financial regime based on a central banking system. With the Bank of Japan (BOJ) established in 1882 and the government-issued paper money and national bank notes brought to par, all bank note issue was centralised.

Thus, in the late 1880s the country saw its economy entering a new phase. From 1888 a number of new firms were set up in spinning and railways. Most of the firms were large in size and employed modern technology. This first surge in the private sector's business activity, therefore, witnessed the take-off of a modern sector. However, such growth of the modern sector was not at the expense of traditional industries. The traditional sector also grew. Export-oriented silk reeling continued to grow while cotton weaving and other rural industries found a growing domestic market during the rest of the Meiji period. It was, therefore, a parallel growth of the modern and traditional sectors. Much of Meiji economic growth was still achieved within a pre-modern, rural setting, with some interactions with the emerging modern sector (Hashino and Saito 2004; Nakamura 1983).

After the Matsukata recession the economy returned to the growth track. The late 1880s saw firms' industrial output and, hence, the nation's total product start to increasing (see Figure 2.1). The subsequent growth had differential effects on the two major constraints that the new Meiji government had faced. While it failed to exert much influence on the balance of payments before World War I, the government's tax revenue increased gradually. Since the Restoration of 1868, the Meiji government had tried to broaden its tax base. Following a period of trials and errors in the areas of miscellaneous indirect taxes and excises, the government succeeded in sorting out the mess with respect to the direct and indirect demarcations, as well as to the central and local governmental divisions, by the turn of the century. As the land tax decreased its share gradually since the reduction of its tax rate to 2.5 per cent, indirect duties such as the tax on alcoholic beverages emerged as one of the major sources of public revenue, together with the newly introduced income and corporate taxes (the former was introduced in 1887 and the latter in 1900). As Table 2.2 reveals, people's tax burden increased by 90 per cent from 1880 to 1913 and nearly doubled from 1913 to 1935, a reflection of the state's ability to collect taxes increasing over time. Also shown in the table is that the government's total revenue increased at a higher pace, which implies that its ability to borrow also increased over time.

In politics too, the period saw a structural change, i.e. the introduction of a parliamentary cabinet system in 1885, the promulgation of the Meiji Constitution in 1889, and the first general election in 1890 with an electorate of nearly half a million, about 5 per cent of the total male population aged 25 and over. A sort of 'government by public deliberation', promised by the Charter Oath of 1868, came into being at last. This made the formation and re-formation of political alliances, which had already been common in the Restoration period, more open. It also paved the way to tax rate increases, which the government had long craved for, in exchange for public expenditure growth, which could now be spent on local projects to win the vote for the political parties' favour (Banno and Ohno 2010; Nakabayashi 2012).

With the government's capacity to raise tax revenue enhanced noticeably, the once pigeonholed national objectives of 'rich nation' and 'strong military' returned

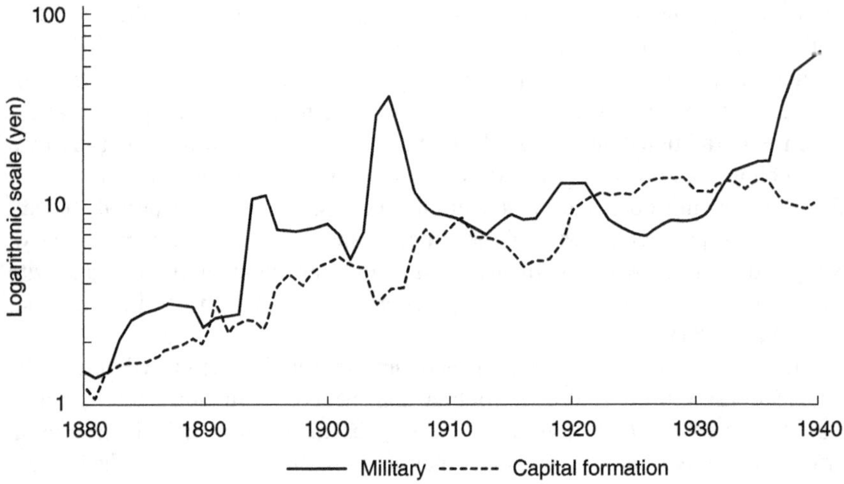

Figure 2.2 Changes in government military and capital expenditures, 1880–1940 (annual per capita series in 1934–36 prices)

Source: Saito (forthcoming)

as policy agendas. In 1886, as shown in Table 2.2, the share of the government in national income was low: the share of the government's total expenditure in gross national expenditure (GNE) stood as low as 11 per cent, a level comparable to most of the west European countries in the pre-World War I period. This suggests that after the two models of development policy collapsed, the state remained cautious with respect to government spending. The share increased to 15 per cent in 1913, then to 21 per cent in 1935. This upward trend in the early twentieth century is found in most industrialised countries of the day; however, it should be noted that while in Britain and other western countries the growth in government expenditure was accounted for by the expansion of welfare spending, the Japanese pattern does not fit this explanation. Japan was one of the few nations who 'resisted' the long rise of social spending (Lindert 2004: 15). As Table 2.2 indicates, spending on welfare services was meagre and could not keep pace with revenue growth – in fact, its level declined noticeably from 0.19 yen to 0.02 yen in 1913, so that even in 1935 its share in GNE did not return to the 1886 level of 0.2 per cent, all controlling for population increase. On the other hand, both military and current capital expenditure areas (the latter excluding military investments) expanded at a speed considerably greater than the other areas throughout the entire period in question. Overall expenditure in the two areas increased more than five times: in 1880 the per capita burden of military expenditure was 0.9 yen and that of capital expenditure 0.8 yen; the figure increased to 7.6 yen and 6.7 yen respectively in 1913, then to 16 yen and 13 yen in 1935. It seems, therefore, that most of the finance ministers from the turn of the century onwards gave in to the demands from both the pro-military and industrialisation camps.

As far as the industrialisation-from-above programme is concerned, however, there was no sign of its return to the political arena until the late 1920s. With protectionist measures unadoptable, the early Meiji government opted for loans and subsidies to industries. This situation did not change until 1911 when the revision of the so-called 'unequal treaties' entered into full effect. Even after tariff autonomy was achieved, however, customs and import quotas were not major policy tools. It is true that tariffs were eventually raised in order to protect some industries with strong import-substitution potentials, but the government's industrial policy during the late Meiji period remained concentrated on the granting of small amounts of subsidies to industries, as in the case of shipping and shipbuilding under the Navigation Subsidy Act and the Shipbuilding Encouragement Act (both of 1896), and to agriculture in the inter-war period. Another policy measure was the allocation of industry-specific funds through 'special' banks such as the Yokohama Specie Bank and the Industrial Bank of Japan, as well as through various trade associations in local industrial districts. These schemes may be regarded as precursors of the post-World War II Ministry of International Trade and Industry (MITI)'s industrial policy.

However, these schemes involved substantially smaller amounts of government money. Indeed, the successive governments after 1885 were not particularly generous fiscally. According to the penultimate row of Table 2.2, the per capita burden of all current government subsidies (including those to agriculture)

Table 2.2 Changing levels of government revenue and expenditure estimated for the years of 1880, 1886, 1913 and 1935[a]

	Government revenue and expenditure (per capita in 1934–36 prices)				*% of GNE*[b]		
	1880	1886	1913	1935	1886	1913	1935
Total revenue	10.9	14.4	25.5	54.4	13.3	16.1	20.7
Tax	11.1	12.4	21.0	39.6	11.4	13.3	15.1
Total expenditure	—	12.0	23.5	53.9	11.1	14.9	20.5
Military[c]	1.4	3.0	7.6	16.3	2.7	4.8	6.2
Capital formation	1.2	1.7	6.7	12.6	1.6	4.2	4.8
Subsidies	0.11	0.33	0.42	0.03	0.3	0.3	0.01
Social welfare[d]	0.19	0.17	0.02	0.26	0.2	0.01	0.1

Source: Ohkawa and Shinohara (1979), Tables A1, A44-46, A50, A53; Ohkawa *et al.* (1967), Table 1, and Emi and Shionoya (1966), Table 13

Notes: [a] The price index used is the GNE deflator series (in 1934–36 prices), which is extended to the 1879–81 period by using an aggregate series of consumers' and investment goods prices derived from Ohkawa *et al.* (1967). All the figures are three-year averages centred on the year indicated.

[b] Percentages of GNE are calculated on a current-price basis.

[c] Military investments are not included in capital formation.

[d] Social welfare spending does not include annuities and pensions for public-sector employees (civil servants and military officers), but includes assistance payments to soldiers and their families.

remained generally low. The figure increased from 0.1 yen in 1880 to 0.3 yen in 1886, stayed on roughly the same level to 1913, and then dropped suddenly to 0.03 yen in 1935, suggesting that industrial policy in the 1885–1929 period utilised subsidies more often than in years before and after that period. However, it should be noticed that the levels of subsidies even in that period were low: they represented only 0.3 per cent of GNE in both 1886 and 1913 (the proportion declined from 2.7 per cent to 1.8 per cent if calculated in relation to the government's total expenditure). This share in GNE was definitely lower compared with levels in Japan's post-war period of 1955–73, the 'high growth' period in which Chalmers Johnson thought MITI's industrial policy was most relevant. The percentage was at the same 0.3 per cent level in 1955, which increased thereafter and reached the 1 per cent mark in 1968 (all three-year averages calculated from Ohkawa and Shinohara 1979: Tables A1, A2, A44). In conclusion, therefore, the government's subsidies to industry should not be overestimated. As early as 1937, George Allen found that 'Before 1929 the State exercised far less control over economic life than is usually supposed'; however, he went on to note that 'by the beginning of 1937 an important part of Japan's economy has passed under State regulation' (Allen 1940: 783, 784). The crucial change took place between 1929 and 1937.

Much of the government's spending on capital formation went to the construction of infrastructure. The new Meiji government announced that the state would take primary responsibility for 'public utilities', and investments in rail and road networks followed. The post-1885 period saw railways, roads, harbours, waterworks and schools all attracting the attention of party politicians. When the first general election was held, the Jiyūtō (liberal party) was the major opposition to the non-parliamentarian conservatives in government. The origin of the party can be traced back to a petition for the 'opening of a popularly elected national assembly' submitted in 1874 by Itagaki and several other Restoration leaders who had left the government. One of them had just returned from Britain, bringing in new democratic ideas. One of the principles they declared was that 'The people, who have the duty to pay taxes to the government, concurrently possess the rights to be informed of the state affairs and to approve or reject such matters' (Itagaki 1957–8: I, 90). Those who signed the 1874 petition were all ex-samurai, but this statement was taken to imply that the 'people's rights' notion could be extended to the commoners, allowing them to 'voice' by themselves. Since then, therefore, the people's rights movement was enthusiastically supported by local gentlemen, most of whom were landowners engaged also in industry and trade in the countryside. It was no surprise, therefore, that when they fought the first general election, one of the party slogans was a demand for the 'reduction of the people's burden' (*minryoku kyūyō*), i.e. a demand for tax reduction. Having already won the reduction in the land tax rate from 3 per cent to 2.5 per cent of the cash value of land in 1877, they also resisted the trend of tax increase in areas outside the land sector. In other words, Meiji Japan's liberal party politicians wanted to say 'no' to the government's spending policy. There occurred a major shift, however. After their defeat in the 1894 election, they abandoned the people's burden slogan, which enabled the government to increase military expenditure when war on China was declared (Banno 2001: 82). But there was another impact: the budgets for public works also started to increase gradually. This became clearer when the Seiyūkai, an illegitimate successor to the old liberal party, was formed in 1900 and their 'pork barrel' politics began to influence the rural electorate. The country gentlemen began to accept tax increases in exchange for the tangible fruits local candidates would bring in, i.e. railways, stations, highways, and also subsidies to regional economies. This may be called a new approach to industry promotion under different circumstances. That said, however, it should be emphasised that they never endorsed the state interventionist approach to economic development. Government spending was welcomed when and only when it benefited their constituencies (Teranishi 2005: 85–86).

In Table 2.2 above, the calculations were all made for peacetime budgets. However, in order to examine the relationships between these two areas of government spending, the entire period ought to be covered. Figure 2.2 thus compares the annual series of real per capita burden of military and current non-military capital expenditures over the period from 1880 to 1940 (note that the vertical axis is logged, so that the slope of the curve can be interpreted as the rate of change). It is indicated that the long-run increase in government non-military capital expenditure was gradual but steady until World War I, while changes in military expenditure were extremely volatile. Because of waging the two Northeast Asian wars, the trend line of its growth process in the period before 1913 was generally stronger than that of capital formation, but the military group in the government suffered a setback from 1914 to 1929, the period when 'laissez faire was in vogue'. Moreover, it seems that there was an opposite correlation between the military and capital expenditure curves in Figure 2.2, suggesting that the strong rivalry seems to have remained between the two camps. The battle line was still between the warfare (*kyōhei*) and industry promotion (*fukoku*) groups, not between the latter and the pro-market camp as far as the period before 1929 is concerned. Even after the Great Depression, the Seiyūkai cabinet's Finance Minister Takahashi Korekiyo tried to resist the demands for a substantial expansion of military budgets from the Army and Navy. However, the political balance of power changed in the inter-war years: the increase in domestic infrastructural spending slowed down. Then in the 1930s it stopped altogether, whereas military expenditure skyrocketed. Overall, therefore, military spending grew more rapidly in this 60-year period than Table 2.2 implies, and the rivalry with the new industry promotion group let the government to go more for spending policy (Okazaki 2004).

5 Discussion

The foregoing exploration of the political economy of pre-World War II Japan suggests that the concept of 'developmental state' is not particularly helpful in making sense of policy design and economic development during her state building period. Meiji Restoration leaders were neither consistent in implementing schemes and policy measures, nor persistent in pursuing long-term development policy. This may sound puzzling since the Meiji leaders believed that strong governmental guidance was necessary for the nation to achieve the twin goal of 'rich nation' and 'strong military', which were supposed in turn to enable Japan to build a nation state to be ranked with the western powers in the long run. One may argue that the Meiji government was not quite competent to pursue such active roles. While that is certainly true, it should be realised that the level of government competence has always been dependent on historical circumstances. Had Japan opened her trading ports after World War II, the political-economic regime would probably have looked more developmental. Not just because the policymakers could have better access to socialist, Keynesian or social engineering theories, but also because international environments could have been different. The use of tariffs and subsidies may well have been in different shape, and the role of foreign direct investment could have been greater. In other words, the fact that Japan had to start under the regime of free trade imperialism, not under the American umbrella in the Cold War era, should not be underestimated.[5]

After the initial attempts at the two competing models of industry promotion had failed, there was a rather sudden turn to a laissez faire regime with successive governments adopting more or less pro-market policies in much of the post-1885 period. One may wonder if this was of choice. Given government leaders' deep-rooted belief in statism, however, probably not. Indeed, there was not much choice left after 1885. The only channel through which government ministers could exert influence was via party politicians. Much infrastructural investment in the countryside was made through this channel. Also, subsidies to local trade and agricultural associations were transmitted through much the same route. Benefits, though not particularly large, were thus siphoned off, as we saw in Table 2.2, and went into the hands of landowners and merchants who agreed to increases in the tax burden in exchange. According to Juro Teranishi's words, a 'consensus' was reached between the government and the private sector. The former was 'entrusted' to 'pursue state objectives', while the latter was 'allowed to engage in economic activities, more or less free from government interventions' (Teranishi 2005: 78).

What made the government's pursuit of state objectives compatible with the prevalence of the pro-market approaches to the economic questions in this period? One possible factor is the persistent impact of free-trade imperialism. The long nineteenth century was under pax Britannica. Unlike mercantilist approaches to economic supremacy, 'the most common political technique of British expansion' was to enforce treaties of free trade with countries in her 'informal empires' (Gallagher and Robinson 1953). Although most Japanese were unhappy about extraterritoriality and the lack of tariff autonomy that featured in the commercial treaties with Britain as well as other western nations, the Anglo-Japanese alliance, signed in 1902, can be considered both an invitation to the system of European states 'as a kind of guest member' and a diplomatic expression of the Japanese government's acceptance of the free trade imperialist regime (Metzler 2006: 258).

Another important decision made by the Meiji government in the post-1885 period was the adoption of the gold standard in 1897. Together with the introduction of a central bank, it had been part of the prescription Matsukata gave when he took office as Finance Minister. Having acquired a large amount of indemnity (worth £38 million) after the first Sino-Japanese War, the government decided to use it for the switch from silver to gold: the move was regarded as an occasion for Japan to take rank with the world powers. It was also expected to make the issuing of government and corporate bonds easier in international capital markets such as London and New York, thus raising the nation's ability to borrow internationally. The establishment of the Industrial Bank of Japan, a public-sector banking corporation, was designed specifically to provide long-term industrial financing by importing western capital. Moreover, since the silver-gold exchange ratio had long been declining in the international markets, the switch to gold meant that Japan opted for imports of cheaper battleships and other related goods, rather than exports of competitive products of the domestic traditional industrial sector. This decision can therefore be considered a manifestation of the Meiji government's will to build a militarily strong state and, for that purpose, to complete the industrialisation process geared towards import-substituting, 'heavy' industries, rather than export-oriented, 'light' industries (Teranishi 1982, 228).

Despite all these expectations, the immediate effect of the adoption of the gold standard was stagnation. Deficits emerged in the balance of payments, which resulted in a recession at the turn of the century. Then came heavy borrowing for the war on Russia. As a result, 'passive economic policies were adopted from 1910 to 1913, producing stagnation in the domestic economy' (Nakamura 1983: 34). In a sense, this outcome seems to have been consistent with the argument that nations who went onto the classical gold standard adopted financially 'orthodox' policies (Bordo and Rockoff 1996). Successive Japanese governments also tended to refrain from running a heavy budget deficit and the Bank of Japan from increasing money supply. As Mark Metzler puts it, while Japan's adoption of the gold standard paved the way to her empire building in Asia, it was 'fully compatible with the workings of the liberal international financial order' (Mezler 2006: 259). As late as 1930, a decision was made by Finance Minister Inoue Junnosuke, an ex-Bank of Japan Governor; and this can be cited as indicating how widely this orthodox view of the liberal international financial order was shared. The gold standard, suspended during World War I, was restored in Britain and other countries in the 1920s. Inoue argued that Japan too should follow suit. His plan was to lift the gold embargo at the pre-war parity, not at a post-October 1929 parity, and with an unpopular austerity budget, but successfully persuaded his colleagues in the government. The timing was disastrously bad. The recession deepened. Eleven months later Japan left the gold standard permanently. In February 1932 Inoue was assassinated. Financial liberalism was 'discredited and abandoned' (Metzler 2006: 247). That said, however, the above finding concerning the relationship between the gold standard and growth outcome suggests that there was some other dimension specific to Meiji Japan. Given the fact that Meiji growth was largely export-led with traditional manufacturing being the major export industry, the government's decision made in 1897 meant that building a military-industrial state should be given priority over export gains and, hence, a richer nation. But what we know is that this decision led eventually to a phase of unbalanced growth – unbalanced between the rich and poor, between the urban and rural sectors, and also between the 'rich nation' and 'strong military' objectives.

More than half a century ago, Arthur Lewis, the 1979 Nobel laureate in economics, noted in his textbook on economic growth that:

> The behaviour of governments plays as important a role in stimulating or discouraging economic activity . . . It is, however, harder to get into perspective because of political prejudice. On the one side are those who distrust individual initiative, and are anxious to magnify the role of government. On the other side are those who distrust governments, and are anxious to magnify the role of individual initiative.
>
> (Lewis 1955: 376)

The same remark may be made about the Meiji government. As I have suggested in this chapter, Meiji Japan was not a developmental state. But this concluding statement should not be taken to imply that the Restoration leaders had the courage to leave economic decision-making to 'individual initiative' and market mechanisms. On the contrary: their conviction that the state should lead the country up to the rank of world powers never waned. Such conviction alone, however, would lead nowhere. During a half-century from 1885, 'the role of individual initiative' is likely to account for much of reasonable if not strong growth. However, the statesmen's deep-rooted conviction remained intact, so that statism could return as soon as circumstances changed. It is therefore likely that the 1879 move from silver to gold was a manifestation of their collective conviction. Also likely is that this conviction had some bearing on the sudden turn from pro-market to collectivist thinking that took place as soon as the ill-timed readoption of gold in 1930 collapsed, the critical turn which led to a plan-irrational experiment under the wartime regime.

There are also path-dependent factors. One is the question of democracy in Meiji politics. Soon after imperial rule was restored, as we have seen, the Charter Oath declared that the new government would establish a government by public deliberation, which was a reflection of the consensus that had already been reached on both pro- and anti-Tokugawa sides before the Restoration. The issue of how and when had not been settled, however. Thus a serious division among the Restoration leaders emerged and a group led by Itagaki, who had strongly demanded an immediate establishment of parliament and left the government, launched an anti-government action that is now called the 'people's rights movement'. Thus a 'popularly elected assembly' did not come into being until 1890, but the fact that different goals, alliances and leaders existed and evolved without solidifying into a simple hard structure in Meiji Japan carries weight (Banno and Ohno 2010). This political structure, though far from a democratic ideal, must have played a part in preventing an autocratic developmental state of the late twentieth-century East Asian type from emerging. Another factor is the nationalist obsession with a 'strong military' objective. It had also been an important element in the Restoration leaders' political agenda and, with the exception of the Ōkubo-Ōkuma period, remained virtually unchanged over the entire period in question. There was rivalry between the new industry promotion advocates and the military, but sustainable economic development was never put before military build-up as the nation's objective. Furthermore, the state was reluctant to invest in health and welfare and did virtually nothing to curb the rising trend in income inequality. I therefore cannot stop arguing, as Yasukichi Yasuba did in his article on the relationship between militarism and resource shortage in pre-World War II Japan (Yasuba 1996), that had Japan abandoned military ambition earlier, or had she not joined the gold standard in 1897, then the pre-World War II economy could have benefited more from exports; hence, growth would have been less volatile and more sustainable, and the quality of people's living higher.

Notes

* The author is grateful to Yonosuke Hara for his helpful comments and suggestions on earlier versions of this chapter.

1 The Meiji period dates from 1868 to 1912 (Table 2.1). Historical Japanese names in the text, as well as names of the authors of Japanese-language publications in the list of references, are printed in Japanese order with the surname first.

2 Like Meiji, Taisho is an era name, dating from 1912 to 1926 (Table 2.1).

3 This and the next section draw largely on Saito (forthcoming).

4 *Kōbushō* in Japanese, which could also be translated as Ministry of Industry. For the chronology of political, diplomatic and economic events in this period, consult Table 2.1.

5 However, this does not necessarily imply that the thesis put forward by Chalmers Johnson (1982) or Yasusuke Murakami (1996) is useful and tenable if it is for the post-World War II period of high growth. It is a separate question, both conceptually and empirically. In fact, there are many economists who believe that the role of MITI and other government agencies has been grossly exaggerated. For example, Ryutaro Komiya has found 'a considerable gap' between the policies actually implemented and the bureaucrats' guiding principles or catchphrases publicised in that period; he also points out that many competitive industries grew 'without any dependence on industrial protection and promotion policies', while leverage excised by the government in the period of post-war reconstruction became marginalised over the period of the 1960s and 70s (Komiya 1988: 7–9).

References

Allen, G.C. (1940) 'Economic policy: public enterprise, tariffs and subsidies' and 'Economic policy: state intervention in industrial organization', in E.B. Schumpeter (ed.) *The Industrialization of Japan and Manchukuo, 1930–40*, part II, London: Macmillan.

Allen, R.C. (2011) *Global Economic History: A Very Short Introduction*, Oxford: Oxford University Press.

Banno, J. (2001) *Democracy in Pre-war Japan. Concepts of Government, 1871–1937: Collected Essays*, London: Routledge.

Banno, J. and Ohno, K. (2010) 'The flexible structure of politics in Meiji Japan', Developmental Leaders, Elites and Coalition Programme Research Papers, No.7, University of York.

Bordo, M.D. and Rockoff, H. (1996) 'The gold standard as a good housekeeping seal of approval', *Journal of Economic History*, 56 (2): 389–428.

Emi, K. and Shionoya, Y. (1966) *Government Expenditure. Long-term Economic Statistics of Japan*, Vol.7, Tokyo: Toyo Keizai Shimposha.

Gallagher, J. and Robinson, R. (1953) 'The imperialism of free trade', *Economic History Review*, second ser., 6 (1): 1–15.

Gerschenkron, A. (1962) *Economic Backwardness in Historical Perspective: A Book of Essays*, Cambridge, MA: Belknap Press of Harvard.

Hashino, T. and Saito, O. (2004) 'Tradition and interaction: research trends in modern Japanese industrial history', *Australian Economic History Review*, 44 (3): 241–58.

Itagaki, T. (ed.) (1957–8) *Jiyūtō-shi* [*History of the Jiyūtō*], reprinted edn, 3 vols, Tokyo: Iwanami Shoten.

Johnson, C. (1982) *MITI and the Japanese Miracle: The Growth of Industrial Policy, 1925–1975*, Stanford, CA: Stanford University Press.

Johnson, C. (1999) 'The developmental state: odyssey of a concept', in M. Woo-Cumings (ed.) *The Developmental State*, Ithaca, NY: Cornell University Press.

Komiya, R. (1988) 'Introduction', in R. Komiya, M. Okuno and K. Suzumura (eds) *Industrial Policy of Japan*, New York: Academic Press.

Kume, K. (2002) *The Iwakura Embassy 1871–73, Vol. II: Britain*, trans G. Healey, Richmond: Curzon Press.

Lewis, W.A. (1955) *The Theory of Economic Growth*, London: Allen & Unwin.

Lindert, P.H. (2004) *Growing Public: Social Spending and Economic Growth since the Eighteenth Century*, Vol.1, Cambridge: Cambridge University Press.

Lu, D.J. (ed.) (1997) *Japan: A Documentary History*, Vol. II, New York: M.E. Sharpe.

Maddison, A. (2003) *The World Economy: Historical Statistics*, Paris: OECD.

Metzler, M. (2006) *Lever of Empire: The International Gold Standard and the Crisis of Liberalism in Prewar Japan*. Berkeley, CA: University of California Press.

Metzler, M. (2010) 'Policy space, polarities, and regimes,' in B. Gramlich-Oka and G. Smits (eds) *Economic Thought in Early Modern Japan*, Leiden: Brill.

Mitani, H. (2006) *Escape from Impasse: The Decision to Open Japan*, Tokyo: LTCB International Library for the International House of Japan.

Murakami, Y. (1996) *An Anticlassical Political-Economic Analysis: A Vision for the Next Century*, Stanford, CA: Stanford University Press.

Nakabayashi, M. (2012) 'Rise of the Japanese fiscal state', in B. Yun-Casalilla and P.K. O'Brien (eds) *The Rise of Fiscal States: A Global History, 1500–1914*, Cambridge: Cambridge University Press.

Nakamura, T. (1983) *Economic Growth in Prewar Japan*, New Haven, CT: Yale University Press.

Nish, I. (ed.) (1998) *The Iwakura Mission in America and Europe: A New Assessment*, London: Curzon Press.

Nishikawa, S. and Amano, M. (1999) 'Domains and their economic policies,' in A. Hayami, O. Saito and R.P. Toby (eds) *Emergence of Economic Society in Japan, 1600–1859*, Oxford: Oxford University Press.

Ohkawa, K. and Shinohara, M. (eds.) (1979) *Patterns of Japanese Economic Development: A Quantitative Appraisal*, New Haven, CT: Yale University Press.

Ohkawa, K. *et al.* (1967) *Prices. Long-term Economic Statistics of Japan*, Vol. 8, Tokyo: Toyo Keizai Shimposha.

Ohno, K. (1998) 'Overview: creating the market economy,' in K. Ohno and I. Ohno (eds) *Japanese Views on Economic Development: Diverse Paths to the Market*, London: Routledge.

Okazaki, T. (2004) 'Seiji Sisutemu to Zaisei Pafōmansu: Nihon no Rekishiteki Keiken' [Political system and fiscal performance: Japan's historical experience], in M. Aoki and K. Tsuru (eds) *Nihon no Zaisei Kaikaku* [*Fiscal Reforms in Japan*], Tokyo: Toyo Keizai Shimposha.

Okazaki, T. and Okuno-Fujiwara, M. (1999) 'Japan's present-day economic system and its historical origins', in T. Okazaki and M. Okuno-Fujiwara (eds) *The Japanese Economic System and its Historical Origins*, Oxford: Oxford University Press.

Ōkubo Toshimichi Monjo [*Ōkubo Toshimichi Papers*] (1927–29) 10 Vols, Tokyo: Nihon Shiseki Kyōkai.

Ōkuma Monjo [*Ōkuma Papers*] (1958–63) 6 Vols, Tokyo: Waseda Daigaku Shakai Kagaku Kenkūyjo.

Saito, O. (forthcoming) 'The economic history of the Restoration period, 1853–1885', manuscript for Volume 2 of Oxford University Press's Japanese Economic History series, http://hermes-ir.lib.hit-u.ac.jp/rs/bitstream/10086/18886/1/gd10-163.pdf.

Shimbo, H. and Saito, O. (1999) 'The economy on the eve of industrialization', in A. Hayami, O. Saito, and R.P. Toby (eds) *Emergence of Economic Society in Japan 1600–1859*, Oxford: Oxford University Press.

Smith, T.C. (1955) *Political Change and Industrial Development in Japan: Government Enterprise, 1868–1880*, Stanford, CA: Stanford University Press.

Sugiyama, S. (1988) *Japan's Industrialization in the World Economy 1859–99: Export Trade and Overseas Competition*, London: The Athlone Press.

Teranishi, J. (1982) *Nihon no Keizai Hatten to Kinyū* [*Japan's Economic Development and Finance*], Tokyo: Iwanami Shoten.

Teranishi, J. (1983) 'Matsukata Defure no Makuro-Keizaigakuteki Bunseki' [A macroeconomic analysis of the Matsukata deflation period], in M. Umemura, and T. Nakamura (eds) *Matsukata Zaisei to Shokusan Kōgyou Seisaku* [*The Matsukata Financial Regime and Industry Promotion Policy*], Tokyo: Tokyo Daigaku Shuppankai.

Teranishi, J. (2005) *Evolution of the Economic System in Japan*, Cheltenham: Edward Elgar.

Watanabe, T. (1998) 'Designing Asia for the next century', in K. Ohno and I. Ohno (eds) *Japanese Views on Economic Development: Diverse Paths to the Market*, London: Routledge.

Woo-Cumings, M. (1999) 'Introduction: Chalmers Johnson and the politics of nationalism and development', in M. Woo-Cumings (ed.) *The Developmental State*, Ithaca, NY: Cornell University Press.

Yasuba, Y. (1996) 'Did Japan ever suffer from a shortage of natural resources before World War II?', *Journal of Economic History*, 56 (3): 543–60.

3 State building, economic development, and democracy in modern Japan 1868–1968

Keiichi Tsunekawa

1 Introduction

Japan experienced democratization twice: during the pre-World War II period and in the postwar period. Both were associated with the process of state building (in the case of the postwar period, state-rebuilding) and economic development. Prewar democracy took a long time to develop, and when it was established as the "Taisho Democracy," it was short-lived. Postwar democracy was established under foreign occupation but has endured since. The primary purpose of this chapter is to analyze how state-building and democratization developed in Japan over two different periods and to explain why the nature and the longevity of the two democracies differ. This chapter will also examine how the economic development of modern Japan interacted with state building and democratization in complex ways. The effort to build a modern state inadvertently created pressures for democratization while the establishment of a stable state helped foster economic development during the Meiji period. The resultant semi-democracy and economic development in turn created pressures for further democratization. However, the breakdown of prewar democracy demonstrates that economic development did not guarantee the endurance of democracy because state building during the Meiji period had left political and ideational legacies that were ultimately detrimental to democracy. The success of postwar democracy is largely due to the fundamental transformation of these legacies.

The first section of the chapter will review the basic literature on democratization (transition and/or consolidation) and present my own framework of analysis. The following three sections will be dedicated to historical analysis of three consecutive periods: (1) the building of the Meiji state and limited democratization; (2) Taisho Democracy and its demise, and (3) postwar reforms and enduring democracy. The chapter concludes with the argument that both prewar and postwar democracies in Japan were largely shaped by conflict and compromise between the forces fighting over state building and/or economic distribution and that the nature of the compromise determined the different longevities of the two democracies. Finally, this chapter will explore the policy implications for people in search of the appropriate means of state building and economic development in the contemporary developing world.

2 Theories of democratization

Theories of democratization are broadly categorized into objective and subjective approaches. The objective approach identifies concrete conditions such as levels of economic development and/or specific social-class relations and explores how these factors precipitate or retard democratization. For instance, the early modernization theory literature represented by Lipset (1959, 1960) and Scott (1959) argues that economic development brings about social diversification and the growth of the middle class, which in turn facilitate moderation and pluralism. More recently, Przeworski and his associates offered quantitative analysis showing that higher per capita income is significantly correlated with the endurance of democracy, although it does not explain the transition from authoritarian to democratic regimes. According to their study, democratic countries with gross domestic product (GDP) per capita of above $6,055 (1985 purchasing power parity – PPP) have never experienced a regime breakdown (Przeworski *et al.* 2000: 94, 98).

Authors such as Moore (1966), Rueschemeyer *et al.* (1992), and Mahoney (2001) highlight another set of objective conditions for democratization. They argue that certain configurations of social-class relations precipitate or impede democratization. Moore looks at the relations among the crown, landed elites, urban bourgeoisie, and the peasantry while Rueschemeyer and his associates focus on landed elites, bourgeoisie, middle sectors, and the proletariat. Mahoney analyzes the trajectory of Central American countries, focusing on the relationship among the export-agriculture sector, liberals, state elites, and the peasantry. Moore, for instance, argues that the combination of a weak crown, bourgeoisified landed elites, strong urban bourgeoisie, and a shrunken peasantry facilitated the early emergence of parliamentary democracy in England while a strong king supported by influential landed elites, weak bourgeoisie, and a large, repressed peasantry laid the groundwork for an authoritarian form of modernization in Prussia.

In contrast with the objective approach, the subjective approach rejects the existence of common objective conditions for democratization. Instead, it emphasizes the process in which stakeholders interact with one another. Choices and strategies of the contending forces are the most important factors for this approach. The arguments of Linz and Stepan (1978) and O'Donnell and Schmitter (1986) are among the most typical in this field. Interestingly, both deal with transition (not consolidation): democracy to authoritarianism in the former and authoritarianism to democracy in the latter. Both emphasize the importance of specific choices made by relevant actors. According to O'Donnell and Schmitter, the period of transition is so full of uncertainties that no predetermined factor can condition the path of transition. Choices and strategies taken by democratic leaders vis-à-vis hard-liners and soft-liners in the authoritarian regime are, therefore, crucial.

Alexander (2002), in contrast, regards the choices of the rightwing elites as crucial. Comparing the experiences of Spain and some other European countries, he concludes that democratization, including its long-term endurance, develops only when rightwing elites finally judge with confidence that their basic preferences such as property right and physical safety are no longer threatened by leftwing forces.

While Alexander's view reflects the influence of the rational choice approach, Tilly (2004, 2007) presents a more nuanced historical approach. For him, it is state formation and inter-state rivalry that ignite the contentious politics, which in turn affect the path toward democracy or non-democracy. State builders, in order to effectively extract physical and human resources from society, need to integrate parochial power centers and trust networks into the domain of national public politics and standardize local units and networks so that categorical inequalities do not jeopardize the public domain. Since the state builders' efforts usually violate existing values and practices in local societies, they frequently face violent resistance against which they choose either repression or compromise. Compromise can take the form of establishing mechanisms for consultation with the affected people. This means the enhancement of freedom and participation. However, reversal (de-democratization) can occur when the state builders opt for autocratic measures against autonomy-seeking local forces or groups. Consequently, the strengthening of the central authority and the process of democratization take a zigzag course in any country. Tilly negates the existence of common objective conditions for democratization and limits his discussion to describing how the zigzag occurred historically in various countries.

Acemoglu and Robinson (2006) attempt to integrate objective and subjective approaches to democratization. They take into account both strategic interactions (subjective factors) and structural constraints/incentives (objective factors) in their explanation of democratization. They share with Tilly the view that contentious politics is the basic source of democratization. However, for Acemoglu and Robinson, the contention most relevant to democratization is not the one between state builders and resistant forces but the distributional conflict between the elites (usually rich) and the masses (usually poor). Just like Alexander, Acemoglu and Robinson regard the cost calculation by elites as crucial to their choice of repression, distributional compromise, or institutional compromise. This last alternative most likely leads to an enduring democracy.

Besides posing policy choices for the elites, Acemoglu and Robinson offer many objective conditions which arguably facilitate or constrain democratization. These conditions include the strength of civil society, sources of income and composition of wealth, the nature of initially adopted political institutions, inter-group inequality, the strength of the middle class, and globalization.

In explaining democratization in modern Japan, this chapter adopts Acemogulu and Robinson's eclectic approach by taking into account both objective and subjective factors. In line with Tilly and Acemoglu and Robinson, it places contentious politics in the center of the analysis. This chapter, however, offers an analysis of contentious politics from a broader perspective than the distributional conflicts between the rich and the poor. State builders are not necessarily rich people. As can be seen below, state builders in Japan taxed propertied classes to extract resources necessary for their endeavor, an act that proved highly contentious. The chapter also considers ideational conflicts along with material conflicts since contenders fight not only for distribution of costs and benefits of state building or economic development but also for the extent and scope of participation and for promotion and realization of cultural or religious values.

In terms of structural conditions for democratization, the chapter focuses on factors affecting the cost calculation of the contending forces, since democratization advances only when the cost of exclusion exceeds the cost of inclusion in contenders' calculation. Such cost calculation is most probably realized when the powers of the contending forces are more or less equal. Repressive policy under such a state of power balance is bound to provoke fierce and stubborn resistance from the opponents and deeply hurt not only the opponents but also the ruling elites.

However, because the cost calculation is based on subjective judgment, there is no guarantee that fierce resistance will lead ruling elites to assess the cost of exclusion as prohibitively high. But since contention under such circumstances is expected to be prolonged, contenders will most probably learn the cost of exclusion through their own repeated experiences. It is more difficult to expect the same degree of learning about the cost of inclusion, since inclusion has been less frequently experienced in countries that are not yet democratic. In the final analysis, power distribution cannot be a determinate factor for explaining the path toward democracy. There remains a sizeable room for judgment and choice by the stakeholders.

This chapter also considers another structural factor, namely, the constraints and opportunities stemming from external relations. As discussed by Tilly, state formation does not occur in a vacuum, but rather, in an environment in which many state builders compete with one another. Therefore, the external structure in which a state builder is enmeshed does affect the process of both state formation and democratization.

Although explanation of economic development is not the main purpose of this chapter, frequent references to economic development will be made in recognition of the fact that state building and democratization are deeply intertwined with the process of economic development, even though we should not assume that there are causal relations among them.

The relationship between state building and economic development is highly complicated. On the one hand, state builders need to extract resources from society to finance their costly endeavors: the establishment, training, and maintenance of administrative and security organizations and the building of physical and cultural infrastructure for communication, transportation, education, and health necessary for the consolidation of a centralized nation-state. If the economy is already developed, it will ease state builders' efforts at raising money. An underdeveloped economy, in contrast, poses great financial difficulties for state builders. Even in a relatively wealthy society, however, efforts at state building may obstruct economic development by crowding out private initiatives or by using national resources inefficiently. On the positive side, state building can help economic development in many ways. For one thing, the consolidation of a centralized authority will help enlarge and standardize the market. A centralized state can also nurture entrepreneurial activities more directly by securing disciplined labor, easing company finance, and assisting technology transfers.

The resultant economic development, however, does not guarantee democratization. Modernization theorists once expected economic development to generate enough wealth to moderate inter-class animosities and contribute to democratization. This expectation, however, has been frequently betrayed by de-democratization or the long-term survival of autocrats in many high-growth developing countries. As mentioned above, the quantitative analysis by Przeworsky and his associates negates any correlation between economic development and the transition to democracy. Economic development inevitably diversifies the social structure. New social forces emerge and jeopardize the existing mode of distribution and domination and give birth to new conflicts for redistribution and participation. Frequently, these conflicts lead to stalemate or authoritarian backlash (Huntington 1968; O'Donnell 1973).

Figure 3.1 shows the analytical framework to be used in this chapter, which takes into account the complex relations among state building, economic development and democratization. Both state building and economic development are characterized by – and themselves create – contentious politics over the distribution of material costs and benefits as well as various ideational issues. These conflicts affect democratization in both positive and negative directions. Democratization most probably advances when contentious politics unfolding under certain (domestic and external) structural constraints/incentives make stakeholders' cost calculation tilt toward compromise. If they continue to exclude one another, democracy never comes.

In Figure 3.1, "Democratization or de-democratization" is posited as the final destination of contentious politics. In practice, causal relations can be bidirectional. As happened during the turn of the century (from the nineteenth to the twentieth) in Japan, partial democratization of an autocratic regime can broaden the space for freer political actions, which in turn can affect the process of state building

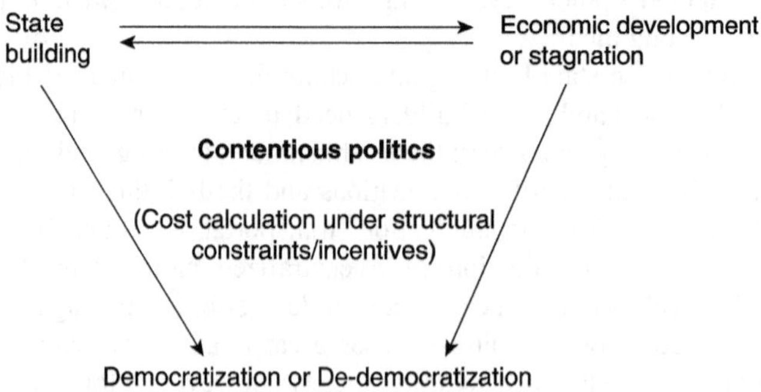

Figure 3.1 Analytical framework of state building, economic development, and democratization

and/or economic development. To avoid excessive complications, however, Figure 3.1 treats "Democratization or de-democratization" as the final destination since it is the main dependent variable of this chapter. The historical analysis that follows will be made in accordance with this framework.

3 Building the Meiji state and limited democratization

In line with Tilly's framework of state building and democratization, the first signs of democratization in Japan emerged toward the end of the nineteenth century as a result of political contention between state builders, on the one hand, and the forces affected by the state building attempts, on the other hand. The processes of state building and partial democratization, however, were deeply affected by Japan's position in the world at the time.

For one thing, the movement for establishing a centralized state was initially sparked by a series of treaties that the Tokugawa government was forced to sign with the western powers between 1854–58. By 1858, Japan had been stripped of the autonomy to decide the level of import tariffs. Moreover, foreigners living in the settlements were placed outside the jurisdiction of Japanese courts. Japan became virtually a semi-independent country.

The feudal rule of the Tokugawa Shogunate was finally overthrown in 1868 by rebel forces in the name of the Emperor. At that time, the political and economic situation in Japan was extremely fragile. In many of the fiefs ruled by feudal lords, especially in western Japan, the traditional hierarchical order was crumbling. An anti-Tokugawa movement led mostly by lower-class samurai emerged. Amidst the general loosening of discipline that had long kept order in the country, numerous uprisings by peasants and urban masses broke out. In the meantime, the Tokugawa Shogunate, feudal lords, and the anti-Tokugawa forces accumulated huge debts to finance their efforts for modernization and military operations. The general social disorder, violent clashes between Tokugawa and anti-Tokugawa forces, and financial difficulties of the central and local governments all jeopardized productive and commercial activities, debilitating the economy. Under such a fragile situation, the government newly established in 1868 faced multiple difficulties as it attempted to build a modern centralized state and to regain complete independence from foreign powers through successful renegotiation of the unequal treaties.

First, the Meiji government had to establish a national army and a centralized administrative system in a country still ruled by approximately 270 feudal lords. For the purpose of centralizing the military forces and administrative structures, the government implemented a series of administrative reforms during its first six years (1868–73). Functionally diverse ministries (such as Finance, Foreign Affairs, Military, Justice, Education, Industry, and Home Affairs) were established;[1] fiefs were abolished and integrated into a smaller number of prefectures; and centralized military forces composed of former samurai were established to defend the capital as well as the country's four regions.[2] Government leaders believed, however, that a broadly based army would be necessary to face external threats and therefore decided to introduce a universal conscription system in 1873, notwithstanding the threat that this measure posed against the privileged position of the former samurai class (Danno 2007: 90–104; Gordon 2003: 66).[3]

All these tasks of centralization aggravated the fiscal burdens of the central government. The state had to take over the feudal lords' job of paying salaries to the former samurai subjects. The former samurai class numbered 1.8 million, or 5.5 percent of the total population of 33 million, in 1872. As much as a quarter of the entire expenditure of the new government was used to feed them between December 1867 and June 1875 (Ando 1975: Table 1.51, Table 1.61). The state also needed money to build a modern army and to set up a transportation and communication network and a national education system. The first railroad in Japan was constructed in 1872 to connect Tokyo and Yokohama. In the early 1880s, railroad construction was entrusted to the private sector but, in 1890, public railroads counted for as much as 886km or 40 percent of the total length of 2,250km constructed (Ando 1975: Table 13). The Meiji government also announced its intention to build a national education system with the Ordinance of Education of 1872. It was replaced by a new ordinance in 1879 and revised several times thereafter. One of the major purposes of these ordinances was to make primary education compulsory in every corner of the country.

The Meiji government even played an entrepreneurial role in the first 15 years. During the Tokugawa era, rich merchants and farmers had accumulated a large amount of capital but hesitated to invest it under the highly uncertain conditions of the early Meiji period. Part of the uncertainties stemmed from the government decision of refusing to repay 80 percent of the debts it had taken over from feudal lords (Nakamura 1985: 21). The government, regarding economic development as crucial to strengthen the military capability for domestic and external security, built a series of western-style manufacturing factories in the textile, cement, glass, ship-building, and machinery sectors. Most of these enterprises proved unprofitable and had to be privatized after the early 1880s. Thereafter, economic development was led by private investors.

This, however, does not mean that economic development in prewar Japan was mostly market-based. The state played indispensable roles as guarantor and supporter of private investment, if not as direct producer. In the early Meiji years, it introduced modern technologies from the West and trained technicians who installed and ran modern facilities. The state also helped lay the foundation of the banking sector by allowing the bankers to use national bonds for initial capitalization, chartering the banks to issue banknotes, depositing public money, and granting credit to these banks (Teranishi 2005: 73–74). It was also the state that built the economic, legal and social infrastructure to enhance the standardized domestic market. The state took the initiative to expand the railroad and telegraph/postal networks and build public schools and agricultural experimental stations. The Commercial Law and Civil Code were enacted in 1890 and 1896, respectively, although their full implementation came only in the late 1890s.

Equally important was the consolidation of long-term political stability through successful state building. A politically volatile and violent environment

Table 3.1 Share of tax revenues (%)

Tax on	*1875*	*1890*	*1905*	*1920*	*1935*
Agricultural land	85.0	60.7	32.0	10.1	6.3
Personal income		1.7	6.2	8.5	14.4
Corporate income			3.1	17.5	10.1
Business activity			7.5	8.5	5.9
Alcoholic beverages	4.4	21.0	23.5	22.4	22.6
Sugar			4.5	5.5	9.2
Imports	2.9	6.7	14.6	9.5	16.3

Source: Ando (1975), Table 26

deters owners of production factors from long-term commitment of their resources. Without such commitment, it is difficult to expect economic development. Long-term stability is not endogenous to economic development. It usually comes after a painful process of contentious politics associated with state building.

In Meiji Japan, contentious politics were most typically observed in the struggle over the distribution of the burdens of state building. In 1873, the government centralized and standardized the tax on agricultural lands to strengthen its fiscal base. At that time, income and corporate taxes did not yet exist and revenues from import tariffs were limited by the unequal treaties. In 1875, the land tax and import tariffs accounted for 85.0 percent and 2.9 percent of all tax revenues, respectively, as shown in Table 3.1. Since this reform meant a tax increase, peasant protests and rebellions broke out across the country (Banno 2007: 173–75).

This rural discontent coincided with the growing dissatisfaction among the former samurai who had failed to obtain jobs in the new government and were experiencing a general decline in their social and economic status. Their discontent exploded in 1876 when the government finally decided to terminate their monthly stipend and to grant them a one-time transfer of interest-bearing national bonds in amounts calculated according to their rank. While a privileged minority of high-ranking samurai received bonds valuable enough to be used for investment purposes, most faced a huge decline in income and a complete loss of privilege. A series of violent rebellions occurred, culminating in the fierce February–September 1877 civil war led by Takamori Saigo, one of the most famous anti-Tokugawa leaders (Gordon 2003: 84).

To mitigate the general social discontent, the government reduced the land tax by 16.7 percent in early 1877. To suppress the armed rebellions, however, it did not hesitate to use coercive power. The problem for the government was that it was not a united entity but was composed of an assortment of anti-Tokugawa leaders who had diverse and often divergent visions for the future (Banno 2001: Chapter 1). One of the biggest differences was over the question of the priority the government ought to give to external military expansion and domestic economic development. Saigo promoted the military option and left the government when he was defeated by others who prioritized industrial promotion to strengthen the national economy.

Another dimension of intra-leadership contention was the timing of the establishment of a publicly elected Diet and the kind of authority to be given to parliamentarians. Some leaders wanted to see a national Diet with power sufficient to control the government. Others hoped to delay the establishment of a Diet and restrict its authority through the prerogatives of the Emperor. By the beginning of the 1880s, the former had lost out to the latter (Banno 2001: 29). But even the most conservative members of the government could not totally neglect the demand to open a Diet for several reasons. First, coercion alone was considered an unproductive means of reducing resistance to government policies. As mentioned above, many Meiji leaders could not claim absolute authority since they came from the lower echelon of the samurai class. Neither had the authority of Emperor been consolidated strongly enough to secure unconditional loyalty from his subjects. Furthermore, due to intra-elite divisions and competition, some of these leaders' former friends and colleagues joined the opposition. It was thought that the establishment of a Diet would dampen the anti-government fervor and weaken those who would opt for armed resistance.

Consequently, in October 1881 the government issued the Imperial Ordinance for the Establishment of a Diet by which the government promised to enact a constitution and organize general elections in nine years (Banno 2007: 238–39). This compromise by the government did not satisfy many opposition forces, who demanded the quick installation of a strong Diet. What made the situation worse was the highly austere economic policy that the government adopted in the early 1880s. The policy was again the result of an intra-governmental dispute which the belt-tightening faction had won. A highly deflationary policy was adopted in an effort to control the inflation resulting from the huge fiscal deficits accumulated during the 1877 civil war. The policy included increases in the municipality land tax and the rice-wine (sake) tax. The privatization of public corporations was implemented in accordance with the same line of policy. These policies, however, aggravated social and political discontent and stoked many violent rebellions by farmers and ex-samurai in the first half of the 1880s, to which the government responded with repressive measures. Fortunately for the government, macroeconomic conditions were stabilized by the mid-1880s. Simultaneously, with the weakening of the radical rebels, people who organized into political parties gained influence among the opposition and sought relatively peaceful means of fighting against the government.

The government fulfilled its promise to enact and promulgate a constitution in February 1889. To the detriment of the opposition forces, the Constitution gave only limited authority to the Diet while granting to the Emperor formal power to control the military and the government. But when the first general election was held in July 1890, opposition parties participated and succeeded in attaining a parliamentary majority. The majority of the parliamentarians were rich farmers and local gentry, because suffrage was determined by the amount of taxes paid. At the time of the first general election, the qualified electorate constituted only 1 percent of the total population (Gordon 2003: 125). In this respect, the new Diet was an elitist institution. However, it counterbalanced the authoritarian government by frequently rejecting its budget proposals and calling for accountability to taxpayers.

Facing intransigence in Diet on the part of political parties, moderate leaders in the government headed by Hirobumi Ito decided to work with them instead of fighting against them (Gordon 2003: 127). In response, the Diet gradually softened its stance toward the government. One of the reasons for its moderation was the decline of tax burdens imposed on the agricultural lands. The income tax and the national business tax were introduced in 1887 and 1896 respectively, enabling non-agricultural businesses to share the tax burdens with the landed elites who accounted for a large proportion of the Diet seats. As shown in Table 3.1, the share of land tax dropped from 85 percent (in 1875) to 32 percent (in 1905) of the central government's tax revenues while income and business taxes increased from 0 to 16.8 percent in the same period.

After a long painful process frequently marked by violent clashes, the Meiji state builders and their opponents attained a compromised equilibrium toward the end of the nineteenth century. The result was a partial democracy in which elections were held and the elected House of Representatives shared the legislative power with the House of Peers. It was partial because suffrage was limited, political freedom restricted, and the elected majority not allowed to assume governmental power.

In short, Japan's weak position in the external power configuration heightened the national sense of crisis and prompted the state building effort. The initiative to build a modern state equipped with centralized state machinery and a growing economy required policies that effectively sacrificed former samurai and peasants. These people, however, did not accept their fate without resistance. Meiji leaders adopted both repressive and cooptive measures just as their opponents resorted to both violent and peaceful resistance. The stakeholders' assessment of the cost of inclusion and the cost of exclusion finally tilted toward the latter, prompting both sides to accept a partial democracy.

The period (from the late 1880s to the 1890s) in which economic spurt became notable under the private entrepreneurship coincided with the period in which electoral politics replaced violent clashes. However, the economic development was too new to be plausibly counted as a firm base for democratization. It was, rather, the contentious politics which had unfolded during the long period of state building that finally resulted in the establishment of a semi-democracy in Meiji Japan. Economic development certainly helped moderate landed elites' opposition against the government by broadening the tax base to the industrial and commercial sectors. However, the stable investment environment indispensable for economic development could only be guaranteed by successful state building, of which compromise among stakeholders after strenuous confrontation (and the resultant partial democratization) was an integral part.

4 Popular upsurge and the Taisho democracy

The period between 1905 and 1932 is known as the era of truly democratic upsurge in prewar Japan. This upsurge, however, was less associated with state building and more related to new distributional and ideational conflicts in a developing economy. The unequal treaties, which had formed the initial motivation of state building, were successfully revised by the new treaties of 1894 and 1911. The 1894 treaties abolished foreign countries' extraterritorial rights while the 1911 treaties allowed Japan to recover tariff autonomy. The new treaties symbolized the completion of the state building endeavor of Meiji Japan. Nevertheless, the successors to the Meiji leaders in the state bureaucracy and the military earnestly pursued the enlargement of military capability so that Japan could pull itself into the ranks of the great powers in the imperialist competition. Consequently, their appetite for state power and budget continued to be strong and sometimes clashed with the aspiration of political parties representing taxpayers, in much the same way as the Meiji state builders had to deal with their opponents.

However, the primary forces that propelled democratization during the first 20 years of the twentieth century were the new social cleavages and political contentions associated with economic development of the nation. As we saw in the previous section, the Japanese economy had entered the era of higher growth during the latter half of the 1880s. Real GDP grew annually by 3.7 percent between 1886 and 1895, 1.7 percent between 1896 and 1905, and 3.6 percent between 1906 and 1915 (see Table 3.2). This expansion of the national economy was led by the secondary sector, which grew by 6.2 percent, 5.2 percent, and 8.2 percent during the same periods. Industrialization was first led by the cotton-spinning sector. The import of cotton yarns was surpassed by domestic production in 1891 and by yarn exports in 1897 (Otsuka *et al.* 1988: 29). In addition, heavy and chemical industries started to expand in the early twentieth century. The ratio of the domestic production of steel to domestic consumption increased from 13.4 percent in 1900–04 to 50.8 percent in 1915–19 and 70.7 percent in 1925–29 (Ando 1975: Table 5.69).

As a result of economic development, the social structure changed. The relative share of "gainful workers" in the primary sector shrank while the ones in the nonagricultural sectors expanded. The latter was 27.5 percent in 1880, 33.9 percent in 1900 and 47.9 percent in 1920.[4] Miscellaneous types of family businesses (retail

Table 3.2 Growth rates in 1934–36 prices (annual average, %)

	GDP	*Agriculture, forestry, and fishery*	*Manufacturing and mining*	*Commerce and services*
1886–95	3.7	2.5	6.2	4.8
1896–1905	1.7	0.8	5.2	1.5
1906–15	3.6	3.3	8.2	1.7
1916–25	4.2	1.3	3.9	4.7

Source: Calculated from Ohkawa and Shinohara (1979), Table A12

shops, taverns, food processors, backstreet workshops) increased in the urban areas. The expansion of modern transportation, manufacturing, commercial and financial sectors was accompanied by the increase of blue-collar workers and white-collar employees. Together with professionals and intellectuals, white-collar employees composed the urban middle strata. Among the blue-collar workers, the formation of modern labor unions and strike activities started to increase in the 1890s. The membership of Yuaikai, the first national labor union in Japan, reached 30,000 in 1919. In the same year, the number of labor strikes numbered 497 (Gordon 2003: 152). The middle-strata people also enhanced their number and influence. They started to play important roles in movements that demanded the improvement of urban living conditions and the enlargement of the franchise. In short, the new social cleavages gave birth to new contentious politics over the distribution of the benefits of development and democracy.

The first important sign of the contention emerged in 1905 in the form of serious mass riots in Tokyo and other urban areas. In September 1905, mobs, composed mostly of urban laborers of various kinds, rioted against the government and burned police stations/boxes, the residence of the Minister of Home Affairs, and a pro-government newspaper company in central Tokyo. Riots spread in many parts of Japan and the government was forced to put Tokyo under martial law to put them down (Narita 2007: 2–7).

The reason for the rebellion was that the government had accepted the US-mediated peace agreement that put an end to the Russo-Japanese war. The agreement did not include indemnity payment by defeated Russia, to which many Japanese believed Japan was entitled, as many citizens had lost family members and borne heavy tax burdens to support the fierce conflict. Political parties and their rich supporters did not like the mob violence, but they could live with it as long as the people's discontent was directed at the conservative government leaders who continued to impose heavy taxes but refused to have a representative government.

Gordon (2003: 130) lists eight additional incidents of mass riots which occurred between 1905 and 1918. The motives varied from opposition against tax increases or price increases to defense of constitutional rights, and to criticism of the government's timid China policy. During the same period, the movement demanding universal suffrage also grew. Some of the riots were in fact associated with this movement. The government, which was still controlled by ageing Meiji leaders and their successors repressed these riots by mobilizing the police force. However, amidst another nationwide riot, this time protesting a sharp rise in the price of rice, the first ever cabinet led by the leader of the largest party and composed mostly of party politicians was allowed to form in 1918. The party cabinet continued in existence until 1932, except for the period between 1922 and 1924. Universal male suffrage was introduced by one of these party governments in 1925, expanding the electorate to 20 percent of the population. Although radical leftist parties were banned by the Internal Security Law, the practice of two political parties competing against each other in free elections was established (Narita 2007: 82–93, 190–98).

Just like the partial democratization during the Meiji era, the democratic upsurge of 1918–32, usually called Taisho Democracy, was characterized by harsh contentions between conservative forces within the military and bureaucracy, on the one hand, and the social forces that attempted to realize their policy preferences through political parties and the Diet, on the other hand. The former accepted the party cabinet and universal suffrage because the latter agreed to ban radical social movements and because the latter's grip on the government was loosened by partisan conflicts and corruptions. Political parties varied in their stances toward the mass movements but they were united in their dislike of any radical movement. Once in power, they did not hesitate to mobilize even the military forces to put down radical labor strikes. Neither did they allow the existence of leftist political parties and mass organizations. Furthermore, because urban voters were unreliable, they sought secure support bases in local communities where landowners and local gentry maintained strong influence among the residents. To do so, parties resorted to clientelistic measures of offering public works or subsidies in exchange for electoral support. Such practice, initiated by the Meiji government in the 1890s to placate local opposition, was now adopted by political parties themselves on a greater scale. Some party politicians also deepened their connections with big business groups called *zaibatsu*. As a result of these clientelistic practices, money politics entered party competition.

The first general election based on male universal suffrage was held in February 1928. This was the heyday of the prewar democracy, or semi-democracy, to be precise. In spite of the sporadic riots in the streets and labor and tenants' disputes, a basically pro-business political stability was maintained and helped foster the industrial and commercial activities of private businesses. The expansion of national wealth in turn helped the government raise fiscal resources which were then used to maintain stable clientelistic ties with local elites.

The practice of democracy, however, did not last long. In 1932, in the face of economic stagnation, fiscal difficulties, and social/political unrest (caused by the Great Depression, the Manchurian incident, and terrorist violence by extreme rightists), political parties handed the cabinet over to conservative leaders supported by bureaucrats and the military. Although parties continued to compete in elections until 1937 and individual politicians were coopted into the cabinet, they never regained premiership.

One of the main reasons why the Taisho Democracy was short-lived is that political parties ruined their reputation among the middle-class and lower-class electorate because of the unprincipled partisan/factional conflicts and corruption scandals that frequently broke out. When the political parties temporarily lost power in 1922 to the conservative forces, public opinion supported the "Defend the Constitution" movement organized by political parties. Such support disappeared in the 1930s (Gordon 2003: 195).

Another reason for the failure of the political party system, and consequently of the prewar democracy, was the fact that the demand for democracy had been almost always accompanied by a nationalist and imperialist fervor. To cite an example, opposition movements during the 1880s were able to survive government repression and reactivate themselves thanks to public perception of moral weakness in the government's posture in renegotiating the unequal treaties. The opposition accused the government of offering "excessive" concessions to the western powers in exchange for their abandonment of extraterritorial rights (Gordon 2003: 90). The riot of 1905, in which the opposition forces took advantage to criticize the government, was also motivated by nationalist indignation against perceived fainthearted government diplomacy. The political parties and the general electorate supported enthusiastically the wars against China (1894–95) and Russia (1904–05), although they were not happy with the related tax burdens. Most of them also supported Japan's imperialist expansion into the Korean Peninsula and China.

Similarly, whenever they could, the successors to the authoritarian legacy of the Meiji era took advantage of wars and imperialist expansion to bolster support among the population and to secure the consent of the party-dominant Diet. Political competition for nationalist credential between autocrats and opponents contributed to deepening people's sense of the nation which had been nurtured by school education and by Japan's external wars. Such sense of nation was easily transmuted into externally aggressive nationalism during the 1930s, when domestic social tensions were especially high and needed a safety valve.

Thanks to the early timing of its state building, Japan was probably the last country among the non-western late modernizers to take advantage of imperialist policies in the pre-World War II period to mitigate the domestic sociopolitical tensions accompanying the state building and economic development processes. Imperialist policy was still an internationally accepted practice at the time, and the power configuration in Asia provided Japan with room for external expansion.

However, nationalism was a double-edged sword for the ruling elites. While it helped them mobilize people's support to their otherwise illegitimate rule, it was also accompanied by people's reciprocal expectation that their sense of national grandeur be continuously satisfied. A successful external adventure needed to be followed by another, a chain that pushed Japan into ultimately devastating wars, first against China (1937) and then the United States (1941).

The alliance between democracy and imperialism led to an unhappy outcome for the former. When the military embarked on adventurous actions abroad, stirring up nationalist or even xenophobic sentiment and arousing in the public a sense of national crisis, political parties and the electorate could not resist the tide and were absorbed into the fervent ultranationalist wave.

In short, prewar democracy once flourished by driving a wedge into the authoritarian Emperor regime, thanks to support from the middle and lower classes who enhanced their influence under rapid economic development. If political parties had been more prudent in managing partisan competition and controlling money politics and if the ultranationalist option had not been available to Japan, political parties might have continued to receive people's support and forced the military/bureaucratic elite to accept further compromise, compromise that might have further strengthened democratic institutions and practices.

5 Postwar reforms and enduring democracy

While Meiji leaders were required to start building a modern state under externally vulnerable conditions, postwar Japanese leaders were forced to start their effort of rebuilding the state under direct foreign occupation. Unlike the Meiji leaders, however, the postwar leaders could count on a capable and centralized bureaucracy from the beginning. This is because the American occupation forces decided to use the existing administrative structures (except for the military and the Ministry of Home Affairs) and their personnel to govern Japan.

The effort at state rebuilding, however, faced difficulties in attaining legitimacy and subsequent stability. Although the populace maintained its respect for the Emperor, his authority had suffered a serious decline due to Japan's defeat in the devastating war. He no longer commanded enough prestige to make the people accept the state in his name. This problem of state legitimacy was closely associated with the ideational and distributional conflicts unleashed during the early postwar years.

On the one hand, defeat in the war and the liberalization reforms introduced by the occupation forces fostered a sudden upsurge of liberal and leftist trends. Many people hated the fact that they had been indoctrinated by the government and the military to believe in the righteousness and invincibility of the totalitarian regime and now demanded a full democracy. The people who dominated the state immediately after the war were, however, conservatives who had deep roots in the prewar regime. In fact, notwithstanding the general state of lethargy, political, bureaucratic, and economic elites (excluding military leaders who had lost prestige and trust) were determined to maintain as many elements of the ancient regime as possible, including the Emperor's sovereignty. For example, Shigeru Yoshida, who served as Prime Minister five times between 1946 and 1954 and is regarded as the central figure in the reconstruction of the postwar state, held the optimistic view that Japan would eventually return to its pre-militarist age (Dower 1979: 277; Kohno 2002: 26).[5] If these elites had been successful in their restoration attempt, the postwar regime would have been one in which a representative government controlled by elected political parties ruled under the sovereignty of the Emperor, suppressing leftist political parties, workers' and tenants' movements, and radical mass media. Under this regime, Japan would have been a semi-democratic state, more democratic than contemporary China or Singapore but as democratic as Malaysia.

In addition to this ideational strife, the immediate postwar years saw numerous and serious distributional conflicts. The war-torn economy could not feed a population which was swelled by millions of civilians and soldiers repatriated from various parts of East Asia. Hundreds starved to death in Tokyo alone. People were constantly hungry and crime was rampant. Many observers have described social conditions at that time with terms such as despondency, psychological shock stemming from defeat and foreign military occupation, despair at the difficulties of everyday life, and absence of vision for the future (Dower 1999: 89; Gordon 2003: 227). Labor disputes and popular demonstrations demanding food were widespread.

These distributional conflicts, however, did not directly affect the process of democratization because the occupation government was determined to implement democracy-promoting reforms, with or without distributional conflicts. On the contrary, as will be seen below, reforms introduced by the American occupation government helped precipitate distributional conflicts. It is true that American aid, which amounted to as much as 66 percent of all imports to Japan between September 1945 and December 1949 (Ando 1975: Table 7.22), helped Japan survive the most difficult postwar years by mitigating tensions stemming from distributional conflicts. It is, however, too hasty to conclude that the remolding of the state from an autocratic to a democratic one in postwar Japan was a successful case of external intervention for state building. For one thing, American assistance was not large enough to temper distributional and ideational conflicts. Radical labor disputes continued to shake Japanese society before and after Japan's recovery of independence in April 1952. After this date, conservative elites had opportunities to reverse the course of democratization and annul American-introduced reforms. If this restoration scenario of the elites did not materialize, it is because drastic transformations of domestic and external structures and people's mindset had changed the cost calculation by the elites, heightening the cost of exclusion while lowering the cost of inclusion.

On the domestic front, a series of democratization reforms launched by the GHQ after October 1945 contributed to changing the power relations among various political and social forces. The Internal Security Law was abolished and mass media and social and political organizations were given full freedom; leaders who were regarded as responsible for the war were expelled from the bureaucracy, political parties, and mass organizations;[6] land reform was implemented; and *zaibatsu* were forcibly dissolved. In addition, and under strong pressure from the GHQ, by October 1946 Shigeru Yoshida's government and the Diet had adopted a new constitution that transferred sovereignty to the people while reducing the Emperor to a mere symbol of the nation. Furthermore, the Constitution's famous Article 9 prohibited the exercise of military power or the threat thereof as a means to solve international disputes (Section 1), renounced military force, and relinquished the right to engage in warfare (Section 2). The combined result of all these reforms was a sharp decline in the power of the prewar (military, industrial and agricultural) elites and an equally rapid increase in the power of the liberal and leftist political parties and labor movements (Bisson [1949] 2005: 44–45).

The land reform and the liberalization of labor regime were especially important in this regard. In 1940, landless tenants occupied 26.8 percent of all rural households. Among the landowning farmers, 75.6 percent held less than 1 hectare each while 0.5 percent owned more than 10 hectares. Thanks to fully-fledged land reform under the GHQ, the share of landless tenants went down to 5.1 percent of all households while independent farmers increased from 31.1 percent to 61.9 percent between 1940 and 1950 (Ando 1975: Table 18, Table 21). In five years, Japanese rural society was transformed into a domain wholly dominated by small independent farmers. These farmers were divided politically. The majority supported conservative parties but a significant number of farmers voted for the Socialist Party because some of the socialist leaders had worked to organize the tenants' movement.

Reforms in labor relations were as profound as the land reform. Workers were granted legal rights to freely organize unions, negotiate contracts with their employers, and engage in strikes. Although in July 1948 the GHQ imposed a law banning civil servants' strikes, workers' space for free activity was enhanced significantly. As a result, the unionization rate, which had been only 3.2 percent in 1945, shot up to 41.5 percent in 1946 and reached 55.8 percent in 1950.[7] Several peak associations of labor unions were organized and re-organized between 1946 and 1955 and they supported the Socialist Party or the Communist Party.

The relative power of labor was strengthened by another GHQ reform which forced the dismantling of large business conglomerates. Labor unions, together with some of the independent farmers and the leftist parties, now emerged as powerful counterbalances to conservative forces (Montgomery 1957: 173). They were so powerful that it would have been highly costly for the conservatives to abrogate these postwar reforms and restore the old authoritarian regime.

The great transformation of the external structure also worked against conservatives' restorationist ambitions. Japan's complete defeat in the war profoundly affected the regional power structure in Asia. The military capability of Japan was largely curtailed by the occupation forces, while China emerged as an influential country and Korea and some Southeast Asian countries gained independence. A militarily expansionist policy abroad would have been extremely difficult and costly, even if Japan had succeeded in heavy rearmament. In short, all these changes rooted in Japan's unconditional surrender made a marriage between democracy and imperialism impossible. Unlike the prewar period, any political force that held governmental power in the postwar period now had to cope with domestic opposition without resorting to nationalist expansionism. Peaceful competition and consensus-building looked to be the sole means available.

Still, some conservative leaders did not give up their attempt to reverse the course. They took advantage of the sense of insecurity brought by the war in the Korean Peninsula and the nationalist anti-American sentiment temporarily aroused by media reports that the 1946 Constitution was "imposed" by foreigners. In an opinion survey conducted by *Yomiuri Newspaper* on April 16, 1952 (12 days before Japan's recovery of sovereignty), 42 percent of the respondents endorsed the necessity of constitutional revision while only 17 percent opposed it.[8] In the same survey, 48 percent agreed that Article 9 should be revised while 39 percent disagreed. An opinion poll by *Mainichi Newspaper* (April 14, 1952) revealed a similar pattern, with 43.2 percent endorsing revision of Article 9 while 26.8 percent opposed it.[9] These conservative leaders demanded Japan's heavy rearmament as a means to free the nation from the Japan-US Security Treaty of 1951 which they regarded as an unequal treaty. Nationalist conservatives sought revision of the Constitution since they considered Article 9 to be a serious obstacle to full-scale rearmament. They also wanted to recover some of the Emperor's prewar prerogatives (Watanabe 2005: 14–16). The conservative movement culminated in the establishment of the Commission on the Constitution, first in 1954 in the ruling Liberal Party and two years later in the Diet (Ruoff 2003: 74–77).

The conservative nationalists' efforts never succeeded, not only because of the transformation of the power balance among political and social forces but also because of the deep ideational transformation that Japan had undergone in the course of the Japanese people's bitter experiences of the war and surrender. Although the conservative parties succeeded in winning the majority seats in the Diet in the consecutive elections (in October 1952, April 1953, February 1955, May 1958, and in November 1960), they never mustered a two-thirds majority (necessary for a constitutional revision) because the opposition parties received the persistent support of the people who disliked constitutional revision, which they regarded as opening the door to the return of militarism.[10]

Furthermore, conservative voters were no longer ardent supporters of the prewar-type authoritarian regime. They shared with the opposition voters a deep aversion to the war and the military after their devastating and disastrous experiences of war and surrender, presumably caused by the military-led totalitarian regime. Heavy rearmament with an inevitable increase in the military's influence could not muster public support.

As shown in the public opinion survey conducted by the Cabinet Office in August 1955, many people still believed that the Constitution had been imposed by General MacArthur but those who regarded the Constitution as "appropriate" for Japan were more than three times the number of those who did not believe so.

The defeat also destroyed the myth held by the people of a sovereign Emperor, although it did not lead to rejection of the emperor system itself. On the one hand, hundreds of thousands people who gathered at the plaza outside the Imperial Palace on the first postwar May Day of 1946 shouted their denunciation of the Emperor and demanded that the emperor system be dismantled. On the other hand, in a poll taken in the early days of 1946, more than 90 percent expressed support for the system (Hara 2008: 154–55). This overwhelming support for the emperor system was reconfirmed in opinion surveys conducted after the recovery of independence. For instance, Table 3.3 demonstrates that 72 percent

Table 3.3 Public opinion survey by the Cabinet Office, August 1955 (%)

	Yes	*No*	*Yes/No*	*Don't know*
Was Constitution imposed by MacArthur?	34	18	14	14
Do you regard the Constitution appropriate?	31	9	28	12
Do you support the constitutional revision?	26	27	20	27
Do you believe that Japan needs the Emperor?	72	18	2	8
Should the Emperor appoint the Prime Minister?	14	71	1	14
Should the Emperor be the national symbol?	60	24	2	14

Source: Cabinet Office (1955)

of the respondents supported the Emperor in 1955. In that same survey, however, the 60 percent who endorsed a "symbolic" Emperor greatly exceeded the number (14 percent) who believed that the Emperor should be granted genuine authority. It is clear that the Japanese citizens who had been loyal subjects of the sovereign Emperor before the war continued to support the emperor system, no longer in its prewar form, but rather in a newly reconfigured one in which the Emperor would function as a symbol rather than a sovereign.

Leftist forces, for their part, needed to work within the institutional democratic framework since few people supported violent methods. The early Meiji years were a legatee of the violent clashes in the final years of the Tokugawa Shogunate. The conflict over state building prolonged such a legacy of violence in the following decades. Even after the centralized state was more or less stabilized, the "strong army" discourse and practice contributed to fomenting a social atmosphere in which the exercise of coercive forces was not unusual. But the devastating experiences of the war dramatically changed people's mindset. They now abhorred violence. Although many people were dissatisfied with their impoverished life conditions, few supported the use of violence as a means of changing the status quo. When the Communist Party of Japan launched an armed struggle in 1951, the party lost public support so rapidly that it was forced to abandon its violent approach in 1955. According to a series of public opinion surveys conducted in the middle of the 1950s (Cabinet Office 1954, 1955 and 1956), the public did not like labor strikes and demonstrations, which were radical and rough in the 1950s. They overwhelmingly and consistently supported electoral politics and rejected the use of violence as a means to improve social conditions. The moderate attitude of the citizens lowered the cost of inclusion on the part of the conservative forces.

By the middle of the 1950s, the postwar democratic state had become firmly established. This, however, placed the conservative forces in a difficult position. To stay in power under a full democracy, they could no longer rely on coercive measures or the Emperor's authority. They had also lost social allies such as landlords and *zaibatsu* families and were now mainly supported by bureaucrats, prewar politicians, and local business people. Unlike their European peers, they could not think of the corporatist cooptation of labor and social democratic parties. The meteoric rise of these forces in postwar Japan as challengers against the status quo was conceived as a threat to be fought against. To compete with the leftist parties, the conservative parties (which unified to be the Liberal Democratic Party in 1955), sought support from local voters such as farmers and small businesses in manufacturing, commerce, service, and construction. In the postwar economy, these were non-competitive, low-productivity sectors which relied on government subsidies and protection for their survival. Fortunately for the conservative government, necessary fiscal resources could be obtained from the rapidly growing economy. Production in the primary and secondary sectors returned to the prewar (1940) level in 1952 and 1955 respectively (Ando 1975: Table 1). The annual GDP growth rates reached 8.9 percent in 1956–60, 9.0 percent in 1961–65, and 10.9 percent in 1966–70 (Yano Tsuneta Kinenkai 2006: Table 3.3, Table 3.13).

How this growth was achieved was once a subject of heated debate. Kaplan's book on Japan (1972) and Johnson's book on the developmental state (Johnson 1982) emphasized the leading role of the state. Their view was severely criticized by both political scientists (e.g. Friedman 1988; Samuels 1987) and economists (Beason and Weinstein 1993; Komiya *et al.* 1988) during the 1980s and 1990s. The critiques pointed out that industrial targeting was grossly incomplete or misdirected and there were many cases of failure of government policies. Today almost every scholar rejects the view that the state steered the national economy to a high-growth path in postwar Japan. However, it would be equally wrong to regard the postwar Japanese state as a useless or laissez-faire state. It did play important roles in three different ways.

First, during the first 15 years, as in the first 15 years of the Meiji government, when the economy was fragile and full of uncertainties, the state provided the market with financial resources by printing money, manipulating interest rates, offering the Bank of Japan credits, aiding the issuance of long-term debentures, and mobilizing postal-saving money. The state also distributed scarce foreign exchange to promising industries not only to facilitate the import of inputs but also to foster the introduction of most modern foreign technologies while excluding foreign companies and merchandise from the Japanese market.

Second, the private institutions which contributed to supporting long-term relations among market players – banks and producers, group companies belonging to different sectors, the management and the labor, big manufacturers and their subcontractors – and consequently helped Japanese companies and workers commit their resources not to short-term profits but for long-term development were originally formed with direct and indirect assistance from the government. For instance, government financial policies were crucial in fomenting close bank-industry relations while the policy to subsidize small and medium-sized enterprises (SMEs) in machinery industries and the lax anti-monopoly policy helped form broad subcontracting networks (O'Brien 1994: 44).

What should be emphasized, however, is that these measures, which aimed at restricting market competition and reducing uncertainty about the future prospect of survival and profitability, never suffocated competition. On the contrary, vigorous competition for investment and production by private enterprises was observed in many leading sectors, sometimes due to intentional government policies, but at other times because of the failure or lax implementation of competition-restricting policies.

Third and most importantly, the state (bureaucracy and the Liberal Democratic Party – LDP) created and maintained pro-business political stability for the long run. The high growth brought abundant fiscal resources to the government. It used the resources to subsidize farmers and other small producers. Their votes helped the LDP win elections consecutively. The pattern was similar to the clientelistic connections between prewar parties and local elites. The resultant stability helped further activate private investment. There was a virtuous circle of stability and growth (Kabashima 2004; Pempel 1998).

The contentious politics under democracy thus led to a long-term equilibrium characterized by a curious mixture of developmental and clientelistic policies. Under conservative rule, the share of the manufacturing sector in GDP expanded from 28.4 percent in 1955 to 33.7 percent in 1965 while the share of the primary sector declined from 19.9 percent to 9.8 percent during the same period (Yano Tsuneta Kinenkai 2006: Table 3.3, Table 3.13). The expanded urban white-collar population, or the "new middle mass" (Murakami 1987: 60), demanded a better quality of life. To respond to the new contentious politics, the LDP government attempted to extend the clientelistic networks to urban consumers by enhancing welfare and housing programs. But when the growth rate slowed down in the 1970s, the pervasive clientelism started to obstruct the functioning of the virtuous circle and, by 1990s, spiraled into a vicious circle of instability and stagnation. But the analysis of this process is beyond the scope of this chapter.

As for the relationship between economic development and democracy in postwar Japan, high economic growth certainly helped the consolidation of the democratic state by providing abundant resources for clientelism. However, the analysis presented above shows that the postwar democracy was already firmly established by the middle of the 1950s, a time when the Japanese economy had barely recovered to its prewar level. No one can say with certainty whether democracy would have survived in Japan if its economy had grown more slowly, but judging from the profound changes in people's mindset and the equally profound changes of internal and external structures, this author believes that the odds would have favored democracy's endurance even under a stagnant economy.

Japan attained Przeworski's point of no return (per capita income of $6,055 at 1985 PPP) in 1968. As the economy developed, Japanese society became more complex and diverse. Social and political powers were distributed more broadly. Asian neighbors strengthened their economic and military power in ways that were comparable or superior to Japan. The cost of de-democratization increased with each passing day. Postwar democracy was consolidated.

6 Conclusion

This chapter has examined 100 years of modern Japanese history in terms of democratization theories. The analysis reconfirmed Tilly's and Acemoglu and Robinson's thesis that democracy is born of contentious politics. Democratization advanced in both prewar and postwar Japan when the cost of exclusion exceeded the cost of inclusion in the calculation of struggling contenders. The nature of contention changed over time. During the Meiji era, state building was the main source of contention while Taisho Democracy and postwar democracy were more closely associated with distributional and ideational conflicts.

The cost calculation was affected by domestic and external structural factors. Domestically, Meiji leaders could not overwhelm their opponents because their origin in lower samurai families did not grant them natural legitimacy and they were divided among themselves over a vision of national development. Government leaders frequently found their former peers allied with discontented social forces. While they successfully demoralized the most radical armed rebels by harsh repression, they eventually accepted the constitutional order in which public policy was not imposed but deliberated and negotiated in the Diet. In the following decades, popular upsurge demanding social and economic improvement and universal suffrage helped political parties enhance their influence vis-à-vis the bureaucratic and military elite and finally attain governmental power. Both the first constitutional regime and Taisho Democracy were not, however, full democracies. They were based on limited franchise and restricted political freedom.

In contrast with these prewar experiences, the postwar regime was a full democracy. The reform policies implemented by the occupation forces drastically transformed the power balance of the social and political forces, opening the way for free political participation by liberal and leftist forces who demanded economic betterment, democracy, and/or socialism. The cost of exclusion jumped up sharply for prewar elites who still dominated the government. The cost of exclusion on the liberal and leftist side was equally high due to the strong abhorrence of violent means prevalent among the citizens who had experienced the unforgettable destruction of war. Democracy was thus solidified by the middle of the 1950s.

The external structure in which Japan was located also affected the power balance of the contenders and consequently their cost calculation. The "weak" diplomacy of the Meiji government concerning the treaty-revision issue and the peace negotiation after the Russo-Japanese War functioned to the advantage of the opposition against the Meiji autocracy. But nationalist sentiments, which had been heightened by the competitive bid for nationalist credentials, played out to the disadvantage of political parties and eventually helped bring about the downfall of Taisho Democracy when the military started to use the strengthened position of Japan in the Asian region for its expansionist adventures. After the defeat and American occupation of Japan, the regional order in Asia totally changed. The military or any autocracy-oriented forces could no longer take advantage of imperialist measures to legitimize their rule. The cost of exclusion became higher as a result.

Notwithstanding the importance of constraints and incentives stemming from domestic and external structures, the timing and nature of democratization and de-democratization, in the final analysis, were shaped by subjective judgment and calculation made by the stakeholders in contention. If Saigo had been smart enough to overwhelm his opponents among his peers in 1873, if the 1877 civil war had ended not in the total victory of the government but in a midway compromise, if Councilor Shigenobu Okuma had succeeded in persuading his colleagues to ease fiscal deficits by foreign bond issuance in 1880, if the radical opponents had adopted more moderate strategies for alliance building in the 1870s and 80s, and if the government had enacted the Constitution earlier and in a different way, the entire cost calculation by the stakeholders would have been different and changed the course of democratization or de-democratization. Similarly, the demise of the Taisho Democracy might have been avoided if the political parties had been more prudent in their partisan, clientelist, and nationalistic activities. Just after Japan's recovery of sovereignty in 1952, the conservative forces could have been bolder in their attempt at the restoration of the ancient regime because the mood of public opinion was rather nationalistic, supportive of constitutional revision, and highly sensitive to Communist threat. In short, the course actually taken by democratization and de-democratization in Japan was neither pre-determined by domestic power relations nor by external relations.

Neither was the relationship between economic development and democratization unidirectional and straightforward in Japan. Economic development creates new social cleavages and new contentious politics, which are potential sources of democratization. However, whether they lead to democracy or not depends on how contending players calculate the cost of exclusion and the cost of inclusion under existing structural conditions. In both prewar and postwar Japan, it would appear that causal relations run from politics to economics, not the other way around. A relatively stable political order under semi-democracy in the prewar period and full democracy after World War II was in place before real economic development started. A basically pro-business political stability greatly facilitated the long-term mobilization of production factors and the consequent economic development.

This chapter argues that the debate on the developmental state misses the most crucial point. A pro-business political order, or night-watch state, or laissez-faire state, for that matter, cannot be presupposed. The existence of such order needs to be explained because many fragile states today suffer precisely from its absence.

Finally, four policy implications based on the Japanese experience are presented here for people engaged in state building, economic development, and democratization today.

First, although political contentions, especially when accompanied by armed clashes, result in many tragedies, including the loss of lives and the delay of economic and social improvement, such contentions should not be regarded as pathological or abnormal phenomena observable only in contemporary fragile states. Almost all countries, including Japan, experienced violent conflicts in the course of state building and modernization. These conflicts even provided the opportunity to enhance democracy, although such development did not unfold automatically. Whether contentious politics bring political stability or even create a democratic order largely depends on the cost calculation of the contenders. This, in turn, is greatly affected by subjectively determined choices and strategies. A person's choice affects the cost calculation of his/her friends and foes and, in turn, his/her own cost re-calculation.

Second, since economic development requires political stability and there is no guarantee that economic development will bring about political stability (either democratic or authoritarian), efforts at state building must be made independent of or in parallel with the effort for economic development. Along with maintaining law and order firmly, an effective state may be able to contribute to fostering a pro-business environment by helping private players take a long-term approach to the use of their resources.

Third, the establishment and consolidation of a more or less democratic political order largely depends on a national consensus reached only after a long and rocky process of conflict and conciliation. It is fundamentally an endogenous process. External forces may contribute to bringing about democracy indirectly by changing the structural and ideational conditions under which the country concerned is situated. The best examples were the US military victory over Japan and the varieties of reforms that Americans introduced after the war. They altered domestic power relations, people's attitude toward violence, and the Asian regional order, thereby affecting the cost calculation in Japan to the advantage of democracy. A word of caution, however, is necessary. The effectiveness of the US intervention was based on the totality of its victory in the war. The mindset of the Japanese people was deeply transformed by the country's unconditional surrender after so much sacrifice and suffering. Furthermore, the conservatives could not prevent the enactment of the new constitution and other pro-democracy reforms because the GHQ had established complete authority over the state. To achieve this level of victory, the United States, itself, paid a high price, losing hundreds of thousands of lives of its own in the war. In the contemporary world where "new war" is the dominant form of armed strife (Kaldor 1999) and public opinion at home is highly sensitive to any loss of life, this kind of total victory can seldom be achieved. Armed groups in the target country are not easily demoralized and political forces are not sufficiently responsive to external demand for quick reforms. External actors who intervene in fragile countries today must accept the reality that their success in remolding them will be limited. It is important to remember that successful state building can be realized only through a lengthy process of conflict and conciliation among local stakeholders.

Fourth, the Japanese experience shows that democracy is not always a bulwark against exclusivist nationalism or ethno/religious xenophobia. Sociopolitical stress stemming from state building, economic development and democratization may induce political forces to adopt these negative identities. External players should not be headlong in their promotion of democracy; they must act carefully and deliberately to avoid an unhappy marriage between democracy and xenophobia.

Notes

1 Only in 1887 did a professional bureaucracy based on meritocratic examinations replace the politically appointed officials who filled government offices (Gordon 2003: 64).

2 Samurai also made up a 2,000-strong police force formed in 1871 to protect the capital city. In 1874, this police force developed into the Metropolitan Police Department under the jurisdiction of the Ministry of Home Affairs. The police force expanded after the 1877 civil war and assumed some of the internal security responsibilities of the military (Katzenstein and Tsujinaka 1991: 35–36).

3 In implementing universal conscription at the town and village levels, the government needed to grant many exemptions to obtain cooperation from residents. The full-scale universal conscription system was established only in 1889 (Ozaki 2005: 72–73).

4 "Gainful workers" are defined as those who have occupations regardless of the length of their working hours (Ohkawa and Shinohara 1979: 243, Table A53).

5 Kijuro Shidehara, the first post-surrender Prime Minister, had served as Foreign Minister and as provisional Prime Minister before the military's influence strengthened in the early 1930s.
6 Yoshida was not among the expelled leaders.
7 The unionization rate went down subsequently to 35.6 percent in 1955 and is less than 20 percent today (Ando 1975: Table 7.36; Yano Tsuneta Kinenkai 2006: Table 2.38).
8 One of the reasons for the strong support for constitutional revision is that citizens had not been informed about the process of the constitutional enactment in which the GHQ had played a decisive role (Kohno 2002: 14). When the information was revealed publicly toward the end of the occupation era, people felt that the Constitution had been imposed upon them by foreigners. The Constitution came to be called the MacArthur Constitution.
9 Another opinion poll, conducted by the Cabinet Office in June–July 1952 with regard to the amnesty given to the purged leaders (including former military officers), showed that the majority of the respondents felt the depurging was acceptable or good and few people saw in it any risk of resurgent militarism (Cabinet Office 1952).
10 One historian argues that it was in 1955, not 1946, that the electorate really voted for the Constitution (Dojidaishi Gakkai 2004: 99).

References

Acemoglu, D. and Robinson, J.A. (2006) *Economic Origins of Dictatorship and Democracy*, Cambridge: Cambridge University Press.

Alexander, G. (2002) *The Sources of Democratic Consolidation*, Ithaca, NY: Cornell University Press.

Ando, Y. (ed.) (1975) *Kindai Nihon Keizaishi Yoran* [*Outline of Economic History of Modern Japan*], Tokyo: University of Tokyo Press.

Banno, J. (2001) *Democracy in Pre-war Japan: Concepts of Government, 1871–1937, Collected Essays*, London: Routledge.

Banno, J. (2007) *Mikan no Meiji Ishin* [*Unfinished Meiji Restoration*], Tokyo: Chikuma Shobo.

Beason, R. and Weinstein, D.E. (1993) "Growth, economies of scale, and targeting in Japan (1955–1990)," Discussion Paper No.1644, Harvard Institute of Economic Research.

Bisson, T.A. ([1949] 2005) *Haisen to Minshuka – GHQ Keizai Bunsekikan no Mita Nihon* [*Prospects for Democracy in Japan*], Tokyo: Keio University Press (in Japanese translation).

Cabinet Office (1952) "Kōshoku Tsuiho ni Kansuru Yoronchosa" ["Public Opinion Survey on the Purge from Public Office"], http://www8.cao.go.jp/survey/s27/S27-06-27-02.html.

Cabinet Office (1954) "Kokumin no Seijiteki Taido (Jiji Mondai) ni Kansuru Yoronchosa" ["Public Opinion Survey on People's Political Attitudes on Current Issues"], http://www8.cao.go.jp/survey/s29/S29-10-29-02.html.

Cabinet Office (1955) "Sengo Jūnen no Kaiko to Tenbo ni Kansuru Yoronchosa" ["Public Opinion Survey on the Recollection of the Postwar Decade and the Prospect of the Future"], http://www8.cao.go.jp/survey/s30/S30-08-30-03.html.

Cabinet Office (1956) "Kenpo ni Kansuru Yoronchosa" ["Public Opinion Survey on the Constitution"], http://www8.cao.go.jp/survey/s31/S32-02-31-13.html.

Dojidaishi Gakkai (Japanese Association for Contemporary Historical Studies) (2004) *Senryo to Demokurashi no Dojidaishi [Contemporary History of Occupation and Democracy]*, Tokyo: Nippon Keizai Hyoronsha.

Dower, J. (1979) *Empire and Aftermath: Yoshida Shigeru and the Japanese Experience, 1878–1954*, Cambridge, MA: Council on East Asian Studies, Harvard University.

Dower, J. (1999) *Embracing Defeat: Japan in the Wake of World War II*, New York: W.W. Norton & Company.

Friedman, D. (1988) *The Misunderstood Miracle: Industrial Development and Political Change in Japan*, Ithaca, NY: Cornell University Press.

Gordon, A. (2003) *A Modern History of Japan: from Tokugawa Times to the Present*, New York: Oxford University Press.

Hara, T. (2008) *Showa Tenno* [*Showa Emperor*], Tokyo: Iwanami Shoten.

Huntington, S.P. (1968) *Political Order in Changing Societies*, New Haven, CT: Yale University Press.

Johnson, C. (1982) *MITI and the Japanese Miracle: the Growth of Industrial Policy, 1925–1975*, Stanford, CA: Stanford University Press.

Kabashima, I. (2004) *Sengo Seiji no Kiseki: Jiminto Shisutemu no Keisei to Henyō* [*Trajectory of Postwar Japan: Formation and Transformation of the LDP System*], Tokyo: Iwanami Shoten.

Kaldor, M. (1999) *New and Old Wars: Organized Violence in a Global World*, Cambridge: Polity Press.

Kaplan, E. (1972) *Japan: The Government-Business Relationship*, Washington, DC: US Department of Commerce.

Katzenstein, P. and Tsujinaka, Y. (1991) *Defending the Japanese State: Structures, Norms and the Political Responses to Terrorism and Violent Social Protest in the 1970s and 1980s*, Ithaca, NY: Cornell University Press.

Kohno, Y. (2002) *Sengo to Koudo Seichou no Shūen – Nihon no Rekishi 24* [*Japanese History, Vol. 24: Postwar and the End of High Economic Growth*], Tokyo: Kodansha.

Komiya, R., Okuno, M., and Suzumura, K. (eds) (1988) *Industrial Policy of Japan*, New York: Academic Press.

Linz, J. and Stepan, A. (1978) *The Breakdown of Democratic Regimes*, Baltimore, MD: Johns Hopkins University Press.

Lipset, S.M. (1959) "Some social requisites of democracy: economic development and political legitimacy," *American Political Science Review*, 53 (1): 69–105.

Lipset, S.M. (1960) *Political Man: The Social Bases of Politics*, Garden City, NY: Doubleday.

Mahoney, J. (2001) *The Legacies of Liberalism: Path Dependence and Political Regimes in Central America*, Baltimore, MD: Johns Hopkins University Press.

Montgomery, J.D. (1957) *Forced to be Free: the Artificial Revolution in Germany and Japan*, Chicago: University of Chicago Press.

Moore, B. (1966) *Social Origins of Dictatorship and Democracy: Lord and Peasant in the Making of the Modern World*, Boston, MA: Beacon Press.

Murakami, Y. (1987) "The Japanese model of political economy," in K. Yamamura and Y. Yasuba (eds) *The Political Economy of Japan, Vol. 1: The Domestic Transformation*, Stanford, CA: Stanford University Press.

Nakamura, T. (1985) *Meiji Taisho-ki no Keizai* [*Economy in the Meiji/Taisho era*], Tokyo: University of Tokyo Press.

Narita, R. (2007) *Taisho Democracy*, Tokyo: Iwanami Shoten (in Japanese).

O'Brien, P. (1994) "Governance systems in steel: the American and Japanese experience," in J.R. Hollingsworth, P. Schmitter and W. Streeck (eds) *Governing Capitalist Economies: Performance and Control of Economic Sectors*, Oxford: Oxford University Press.

O'Donnell, G. (1973) *Modernization and Bureaucratic-Authoritarianism: Studies in South American Politics*, Berkeley, CA: Institute of International Studies.
O'Donnell, G. and Schmitter, P. (1986) *Transition from Authoritarian Rule: Tentative Conclusions about Uncertain Democracy*, Baltimore, MD: Johns Hopkins University Press.
Ohkawa, K. and Shinohara, M. (eds.) (1979) *Patterns of Japanese Economic Development: A Quantitative Appraisal*, New Haven, CT: Yale University Press.
Otsuka, K., Ranis G., and Saxonhouse, G. (1988) *Comparative Technology Choice in Development: The Indian and Japanese Cotton Textile Industries*, Basingstoke: Macmillan.
Ozaki, K. (2005) "Kindai Kokka no Seiritsu – Guntai, Gakko, Eisei" ["Consolidation of the Modern State: Military, Education, and Hygiene"], in Rekishigaku Kenkyukai and Nihonshi Kenkyukai (eds) *Nihonshi Kōza 8 Kindai no Seiritsu* [*Lecture on Japanese History Vol. 8: The Nature of Modern Japan*], Tokyo: University of Tokyo.
Pempel, T. J. (1998) *Regime Shift: Comparative Dynamics of the Japanese Political Economy*, Ithaca, NY: Cornell University Press.
Przeworski, A., Alvarez, M.R., Cheibub, J.A., and Limongi, F. (2000) *Democracy and Development: Political Institutions and Well-being in the World, 1950–1990*, Cambridge: Cambridge University Press.
Rueschemeyer, D., Stephens, E.H., and Stephens, J.D. (1992) *Capitalist Development and Democracy*, Chicago: University of Chicago Press.
Ruoff, K.J. (2003) *The People's Emperor: Democracy and the Japanese Monarchy, 1945–1995*, Cambridge, MA: Harvard University Asia Center.
Samuels, R. (1987) *The Business of the Japanese State: Energy Markets in Comparative and Historical Perspective*, Ithaca, NY: Cornell University Press.
Scott, R. (1959) *Mexican Government in Transition,* Urbana, IL: University of Illinois Press.
Teranishi, J. (2005) *Evolution of the Economic System in Japan*, Cheltenham: Edward Elgar.
Tilly, C. (2004) *Contention and Democracy in Europe, 1650–2000*, Cambridge: Cambridge University Press.
Tilly, C. (2007) *Democracy*, Cambridge: Cambridge University Press.
Watanabe, O. (2005) "Sengo Kokumin Tōgō no Henyō to Shōchō Tennōsei" ["Transformation of Postwar National Integration and the Symbolic Emperor System"], in Rekishigaku Kenkyukai and Nihonshi Kenkyukai (eds) *Nihonshi Kōza 10 Sengo Nihon-ron* [*Lecture on Japanese history Vol. 10: Postwar Japan*], Tokyo: University of Tokyo Press.
Yano Tsuneta Kinenkai (ed.) (2006) *Sūji de Miru Nihon no Hyakunen* [*One Hundred Years of Japan in Figures*], 5th edition, Tokyo: Yano Tsuneta Kinenkai.

4 Changing fortunes: comparing state building and economic development in Indonesia, the Philippines, Thailand, and Malaysia

*Takashi Shiraishi**

1 Introduction

Fifteen years have passed since the collapse of Soeharto's New Order Indonesia in the midst of the economic crisis of 1997–98. In those crisis days many people wondered and worried whether Indonesia would turn into a Yugoslavia, in danger of breaking up owing to ethnic and religious tensions, or a Pakistan, subject to periodic military intervention and the rising jihadist threat, or a Philippines, democratic but with insurgencies simmering in the provinces and a weak and stagnant economy. Nothing of this sort has happened. Instead, Indonesia is now a member of G-20. A politics of economic growth has returned under conditions different from the New Order past. Its political regime has undergone transformation from developmental authoritarianism to decentralized democratic system. Its economy is also back on track. It took six years for its per capita income to reach the pre-crisis 1996 level. But it has grown on average by 5.8 percent a year from 2005 to 2011 and its per capita gross domestic product (GDP) reached USD 3,508 in 2011. In 2012, its economy grew by 6.2 percent.

Nor is it fair to refer to the Philippines as a basket case of flawed democracy and economic stagnation. It is true that after the two successful "People Power" revolutions and an unsuccessful urban underclass revolt, politics has sunk into a morass of electoral politicking dominated by professional politicians and sectoral activists. But the Philippine economy has grown by 4.5 percent a year on average from 1999 to 2011, compared to 3.7 percent a year before the pre-crisis years of 1987 to 1996. In 2012, its economy grew by 6.6 per cent. Its per capita income rose from USD 1,055 in 2000 to USD 2,123 in 2011. By contrast, Thailand and Malaysia, the two often classified as successful developmental states before the crisis with average economic growth rates of 9.5 and 9.1 percent from 1987 to 1996, have seen their economies decelerate to 2.6 percent and 4.4 percent a year respectively from 2007 to 2011 amidst political stalemate and global financial crisis. In 2012, Malaysia registered a full-year growth of 5.6 percent, while Thailand posted a 4.5 percent growth.

The question is why this divergence has happened in the post 1997–98 crisis years. My argument is that it is in part because of the way state power is organized and reorganized in these Southeast Asian countries, as well as the major decisions a given government makes at a time of crisis. But I also argue that it is in part because decisions can have unexpected strategic consequences in a changing world-historical context and because conditions endowed differently – such as population, geography, natural resources, and historical legacies – position countries differently in this globalizing world.

2 Indonesia

Indonesia was hit hard during the 1997–98 crisis. The largest archipelagic country in Southeast Asia, home to a wide variety of ethno-linguistic and religious groups and under a long-staying ageing dictator, Indonesia during the financial crisis – its economy contracted by 13 percent in 1998 alone – also plunged into a deep social and political crisis. Its complexity explains why it took more than half a decade (from 1998 to 2004) for the country to recover, for here we have a case of an economic crisis complicated by social crisis and political instability, both in the center and in the provinces, and a slower recovery trajectory.

The regime transition from developmental authoritarianism to decentralized democracy took place in these years. Major constitutional revisions as well as radical decentralization were introduced. New laws governing government agencies and industrial sectors were enacted. Parliamentary elections were held in 1999, 2004, and 2009 and the first direct presidential elections in 2004 and 2009. Three presidents – B.J. Habibie, Abdurrachman Wahid and Megawati Sukarnoputri – came and went in six years before the first directly elected president, Susilo Bambang Yudhoyono, came to power in 2004. The parliament as well as political parties emerged as key actors in politics alongside the government and the military. Though East Timor opted for independence in 1999, the insurgency in Aceh as well as sectarian conflicts in Maluku and Sulawesi came to an end by the mid-2000s. The Indonesian economy has also got back on track in these years. Although Indonesia in effect lost a decade's worth of growth, its economy has grown on average by 5.8 percent a year from 2005 to 2011 and its per capita income reached USD 3,508 in 2011. Corruption, however, remains endemic. The manufacturing sector is not growing fast enough to satisfy developmentalists. Yet Indonesia's economic performance and political stability have underlined the success of its new politics of economic growth in decentralized democracy. The question is why.

The fall of Soeharto marked the end of an era of developmental authoritarianism that staked its regime stability on national economic development, poverty reduction, the creation of jobs, and the improvement of living standards (Shiraishi 1997). Soeharto fashioned his New Order regime with the state as his power base and the army as its backbone. The regime was centralized, militarized, and authoritarian. Army officers dominated the military and occupied strategic positions in the civilian arm of the state as district chiefs, provincial governors, directors-general and ministers in the name of dual functions. State power was repeatedly impressed upon regime "enemies" – "communists," "separatists" in

East Timor, Aceh, and Papua (formerly Irian Jaya), criminals, labor activists, journalists, and Islamists. The government addressed the question of social divisions along class, ethnic, and religious lines through its politics of stability and economic development: that is, the Soeharto government sought to transform political issues into problems of output and to neutralize social conflict in favor of a consensus on growth, all of which were premised on the "virtue" of political stability which leads to economic development which then leads to rising living standards which in turn leads to further political stability. In effect, the state achieved the "low politics" deemed necessary to national development by barring oppositional groups (whether ethnic, religious, or political) from participation in the political process. Its economic performance – with 7 percent economic growth in 1987–96, for instance – underpinned the efficacy of this politics.

The politics of stability and economic development in combination with the coercive depoliticization and containment of religious, ethnic, and class divisions served Soeharto's authoritarian regime well. Yet it became clear in the 1990s that cracks were appearing in the façade of the New Order state as the regime underwent significant transformation in those years. The change can best be summarized as a shift from a military regime to a personalistic/autocratic regime, because Soeharto, having outlived all the rivals of his generation, emerged as the unrivalled strongman. Army officers, who had served as his personal confidants, dominated the military (Shiraishi 1999). His family members, now grown up and each determined to build his/her own business empire, relied on presidential powers to obtain business opportunities and privileges. Soeharto's lieutenants – his ministers, military commanders, provincial governors, and district chiefs – followed their boss's example. Secret wars went on in East Timor, Aceh and Irian Jaya. Jakarta's control of state powers and resources as well as Javanese domination of the state – the domination of mainly Javanese army officers over military and civilian state agencies, that is – led to a rising demand for local autonomy and the appointment of *putra daerah* (literally, "local sons") in such positions as provincial governors, district chiefs, and mayors. Transmigration, forest exploitation, and the consequent disappearance of living space for local Dayaks in Kalimantan led to widespread ethnic violence against Madurese in East Kalimantan in 1996 (Morishita 2005). Islamic and Islamist forces found more space for political action with the establishment of the Indonesian Muslim Intellectuals Association (ICMI, *Ikatan Cendekiawan Muslim Indonesia*) in 1990.

Indonesia was hit by the currency crisis shortly after Thailand in 1997. Soeharto's declining health deepened the economic crisis, while also turning it into a political crisis. By early 1998, most of the business empires, including those established and owned by Soeharto's relatives and cronies, were bankrupt because they were unable to repay loans in US dollars due to the sharp depreciation of the rupiah. The bankruptcy of business empires had enormous consequences for the state, which had hitherto been funded only in part by the formal budget; its off-budget funding, sourced from state corporations and agencies such as Pertamina and the Logistics Agency (Bulog, Badan Urusan Logistik Nasional) as well as state joint venture businesses with Sino-Indonesian business tycoons and elite family members, were tightly controlled by Soeharto and his lieutenants and had served as huge centrally controlled and directed patronage networks and the main prop of Soeharto's staying power. The crisis, by destroying business empires, also destroyed the informal funding mechanism of the state. It also deepened the social crisis, which manifested itself in increasing unemployment, lootings, disturbances, and rising criminality. Widespread anti-Chinese riots started in January and culminated in May. That same month, the desertion of his allies led to Soeharto's resignation in the wake of massive riots in Jakarta and elsewhere (Ginandjar Kartasasmita 2013; Shiraishi 1999).

Although people had been aware that Indonesia, with its ageing dictator, was coming to a major crossroad, nobody expected the economic crisis to happen, let alone predicted the extent to which the crisis made it impossible for the authoritarian regime to survive intact. B.J. Habibie succeeded Soeharto as President. But he had only a weak presidential mandate and power base. He chose to present himself as a reformer and initiated reform measures that eventually led to the transformation of Indonesia's political system from authoritarianism into decentralized democracy.

The new political system is defined by the constitutional revisions and new laws introduced over the transitional period under Presidents Habibie (1998–99), Abdurrachman Wahid (1999–2002), and Megawati Sukarnoputri (2002–04). The constitutional revisions – which took place incrementally from 1998 to 2003 – reformulated the relationship among the three branches of the state in terms of the division of power. The President and the Vice President, formerly elected by the People's Consultative Assembly (*Majelis Permusyawaratan Rakyat*, MPR), are to be elected directly; the legislature is to consist of the DPR (*Dewan Perwakilan Rakyat*), the Council of People's Representatives and the newly created DPD (*Dewan Perwakilan Daerah*), the Council of Local Representatives; and the MPR, the highest decision-making body under Soeharto which saw the peak of its power in the transitional years under B.J. Habibie and Abdurrachman Wahid, lost much of its powers. While Soeharto controlled the MPR through direct and indirect appointment of its majority members and by extension all the government organs, constitutional revisions in the post-Soeharto era have created a division of powers in which the presidency has to share power with a parliament whose members are directly elected and in which political parties dominate. Elections, both parliamentary and presidential, are to be held every five years and define the national political calendar. Though still powerful, the army no longer dominates politics. The military doctrine of dual functions was scrapped and military officers were withdrawn from the civilian arm of the state. New defense and police laws were enacted. The army domination over the military establishment came to an end. The police was separated from the military (Matsui and Kawamura 2005; Shiraishi 2010).

Free and fair parliamentary elections were held in 1999, 2004, and 2009. Direct presidential elections, which brought Susilo Bambang Yudhoyono to power, took place in 2004 and 2009. Democratization has also gone hand-in-hand with decentralization. The new laws on local autonomy and local finance in 1999 have created local governments, which are no longer accountable to the central government but answer to the local parliament. While Soeharto could in effect appoint provincial governors, district chiefs and mayors, the central government now has to share power with local governments. More powers and resources have also been devolved to local governments, above all district and mayoralty governments at the expense of – and often in tension with – the central and provincial government.

In the new decentralized democratic politics, the parliament (DPR) has emerged as a new power center along with the presidency and the military, and electoral politics has assumed a crucial role in organizing the government. Yet no single party controls the parliament. It is not easy for any president to organize a cabinet to work as a team because any "team" composed of technocrats, professionals, military officers, career bureaucrats, and politicians from different parties is cobbled together not only for the business of governing but also for achieving a majority in the parliament.

Given the new division of power and the effects of decentralization on center-local relations, presidents these days can no longer preside over political life in the way Soeharto did. The government can take policy initiatives to address problems and policy issues only on the basis of an achieved national consensus. But achieving a national consensus under the new democratic dispensation is a big challenge precisely because the era of "low politics" is over, government parties at times act opportunistically with the coming elections in mind, and various social forces are making themselves felt in political processes. For example, the government plan to raise fuel prices (and reduce fuel subsidies) was scuttled by the parliament in 2012 because of the opportunistic opposition of governing coalition member parties. The government has also been unable to revise labor laws because of opposition from labor unions.

But there are important commonalities among those who now dominate local and national politics: the great majority of national and local parliamentary members are predominantly men, born in the areas they represent (*putra daerah*), and highly educated, at least formally. They belong to Indonesia's small but fast expanding urban and rural middle classes, and are represented by such people as business people, professionals, civil servants, military and police officers, religious teachers, and journalists.

The implications are clear. Men with middle-class backgrounds now dominate politics, both national and local. In part a product of Soeharto's politics of stability and development, they emerged as junior partners of the military and bureaucratic elite in the declining years of Soeharto's New Order, but now encompass formerly marginalized (but nonetheless middle-class) groups such as journalists, teachers, and religious leaders. They share in the belief that economic growth is the key to Indonesia's future and are in a position to make this belief a part of the national agenda, even though they do not shy away from calling for populist and protectionist measures in the name of welfare whenever those measures suit their political and economic interests. In his election manifesto, both in 2004 and 2009, Yudhoyono made the achievement of economic growth, along with maintaining national unity, central to his agenda.

Decentralization has also affected the return of this politics in an unexpected way. As noted earlier, decentralization has given real powers and resources to local governments, especially district chiefs and mayors. More than 60 percent of government resources for infrastructural development projects, for instance, are now allocated to district/city and provincial governments. To see how decentralization combined with democratization – above all direct elections of local chiefs – worked, it is useful to examine two provinces with very different sets of social conditions, North Sumatera and Central Java (including the special region of Yogyakarta).

In North Sumatra, which is ethnically and religiously diverse (with 33 percent Javanese, 16 percent Tananuli Bataks, 10 percent Toba Bataks, 8 percent Mandailing Bataks, 6 percent Nias, 5 percent Karo Bataks, 5 percent Malays, 3 percent Angkora Bataks as well as smaller minorities, while 65 percent Muslim, 27 percent Protestant, 5 percent Catholic, and 3 percent Buddhist), the number of districts and cities increased from 19 in 2000 to 26 in 2008. Seventeen small parties (which did not have members in the national parliament) along with seven national parties helped forge governing coalitions that differed in composition and membership from one district to another (on average, about 2.7 small parties in a coalition). In 12 out of 26 districts/cities, governing coalitions were made up with a combination of nationalist parties and Islamic parties; only 4 districts/cities were under control of Islamic/Islamist parties (Shiraishi 2010).

In Central Java, which is ethnically and religiously homogeneous, with 98 percent Javanese and 96 percent Muslim, a different picture obtains. The number of districts and cities has remained the same. A smaller number (2.3 on average) of small parties joined governing coalitions in a smaller number of districts and cities (6 out of 40); in 18 out of 40, a coalition of nationalist parties (PD, Golkar and/or PDIP) with Islamic and Islamist parties, while 6 districts and municipalities came under the governing coalition of Islamic and Islamist parties (Shiraishi 2010).

The implications should be clear enough. In ethnically diverse North Sumatera, ethnic politics thrives, but now it is very much localized and contained in local politics because ethnic groups have ended up creating their own local governments and/or joining governing coalitions. Religious politics has also to some extent come to be contained locally because the areas with a high concentration of pious Muslims have Islamic/Islamist party coalitions under which local governments introduce religious regulations to meet the demands of pious Muslims, while in other districts these religious issues remain muted because the coalition brings together both nationalist and Islamic/Islamist parties (Okamoto 2011).

To put it simply, democratization and decentralization have not only expanded "stakeholders" who benefit directly and indirectly from their control of official positions in the state and the parliament, but also and unexpectedly localized and contained ethnic and religious politics. Politics of identity, once suppressed under Soeharto's New Order, thus thrives now, but mainly as a local issue. National issues are largely framed by, and very much tied to, a politics of economic growth, with the central government deriving its public support and electoral success from its perceived capacity to deliver economic growth, job creation, poverty reduction, and low inflation.

The transformation of the Indonesian technocracy as well as the changing conditions under which technocrats work also needs to be understood in this changing political context. Indonesia was under the management of the International Monetary Fund (IMF) from 1997 to 2003, when drastic institutional changes such as the constitutional revisions, the expansion of local autonomy, and the new laws governing the central bank, state finance, and national planning took place. In fulfillment of IMF conditionality, President Habibie dismantled developmental projects, including the agency for strategic industries he established and managed under Soeharto. The central bank was given its independence from the government. The Law on State Finance requires the government to follow a self-restraining fiscal policy, keeping the annual budget deficit below 3 percent of GDP and the total government bonds issuance below 60 percent of GDP. The law led to the reorganization of the Ministry of Finance and expanded its powers. The power to make fiscal policy and the macroeconomic framework has come under its jurisdiction. The budget, which used to be classified as the routine and the development budget and was under the MOF and the BAPPENAS (National Development Planning Agency) respectively, came under MOF with the elimination of this distinction. BAPPENAS, the "super-ministry" in charge of development in Soeharto's days, lost much of its powers to the MOF and to local governments. Yet, and its importance is still not fully appreciated, the legacy of BAPPENAS as the super-ministry remains: its career officials, now in strategic positions both in the central government and in local governments, form an informal network for economic policy coordination. All these changes signified the shift in government economic policy priority from developmental planning to achieving macroeconomic stability. To put it differently, even though the government policy orientation turns to accelerating economic growth, poverty reduction, and job creation, macroeconomic stability and self-restraining fiscal policy informs its budget-making and restrains proactive government expenditures on such areas as education and infrastructural development (Hill and Shiraishi 2007).

Growth has returned under these circumstances. Prudent macroeconomic management has kept the exchange rate stable and inflation (6 percent in 2007–11) under control. Commodity exports, especially coal and palm oil, have fueled private consumption (60 percent of GDP in 2006–10), thanks to the expansion of coal and palm oil export to China. These exports increased from USD 2,768 million in 2000 to USD 15,693 million in 2010, in which commodity exports constituted 78 percent. Expanding private consumption has driven Indonesia's economic growth by 5.8 percent between 2007–11. The fact that it grew by more than 6 percent a year in those years except in 2008 matters, because it means the economy has created enough jobs for those 2 to 2.5 million people who come to the job market every year. The unemployment rate, which shot up from 4.7 percent in 1997 to 11.2 percent in 2005, came down to 6.8 percent in 2011 (Sato 2011: 19). The manufacturing sector, however, has grown by only 3.7 percent a year between 2006–10, while it did so by 10 percent in 1994–96 before the crisis. Manufacturing exports have also declined from a 59 percent share in exports in 2000 to 41 percent in 2010 (Sato 2011: 118–19). And private investment, both domestic and foreign, has started to show signs of picking up, and because its per capita income is above USD 3,000, Indonesia promises to be a major economy in a few decades.

3 The Philippines

While the 1997–98 East Asian economic crisis constituted a major break in Indonesian politics and economy, it was not the case with the Philippines, which was hit relatively lightly. It was the crisis in the final years of the Marcos dictatorship from 1983 to 1986 and its resolution that had a decisive effect on the way state power is organized and policies are framed.

Calling for revolution from the center, Ferdinand Marcos embarked on fashioning a developmental state in the 1970s with an ambitious industrialization program. The Philippine economy posted a 6.2 percent annual growth rate in the 1970s, but faced a serious balance of payments crisis and increasing political instability in the early 1980s. This was partly because Marcos and his allies relied heavily on foreign loans for financing their developmental projects. The Philippine external debt ballooned from \$5.1 billion in 1976 to \$14.8 billion in 1981. Caught suddenly by international interest rate hikes in 1981, Philippine financial institutions and businesses relied on short-term loans to tide them over. But the economic crunch did not ease and plunged the Philippine state into serious fiscal crisis in 1983–85. The government devalued the peso three times in 1984–85 to discourage imports and capital flight. It imposed tariffs and export taxes to increase revenues. But these efforts did little to alleviate the crisis. The assassination of Benigno Aquino Jr. in 1983 transformed the economic crisis into a political crisis. The killing mobilized many from the upper- and middle-class people for anti-Marcos movement, while invigorating armed communist insurgency in the countryside (Raquiza 2011: 40–41; Shiraishi 2000: 169–71).

Although both were developmentalist, Marcos' New Society differed structurally from Soeharto's New Order. Indonesia's New Order regime was built with the military as its backbone and the regular and monotonous rhythm of seniority-based promotion informed its elite circulation. Military officers, bureaucrats, and technocrats came and went, and in due course their children and relatives built their businesses and emerged as another force for Golkar, Soeharto's electoral machine. In the Philippines, however, power had traditionally resided outside the central state institution. It is dispersed among locally (and provincially) entrenched politicians. Marcos had to rely on provincial and local politicians to build his electoral machine, but he would justify his New Society program as a way to curb the power of the traditional elite, fostering new groups of professionals and entrepreneurs – some of them later branded as "cronies" – who came from outside the ranks of the traditional elite. Although the military constituted a pillar of his New Society, he retained men personally loyal to him in senior strategic positions beyond retirement age and thereby invited the revolt of young turks who chafed at their long-staying (and often corrupt) superiors under Marcos (Shiraishi 2000: 169–71).

Corazon Aquino, who came to power in 1986 in the People Power revolution, faced two strategic tasks. She had to restore democratic rule. She also had to put a battered economy in order. She immediately set out to dismantle authoritarian rule: a new constitution was adopted and the pre-martial law presidential system was restored. She also embarked on clipping state powers for economic development. As Raquiza (2011: 41–42) points out, the catchphrase "crony capitalism" served this purpose well. Aquino attacked corruption under Marcos as the major cause of the economic crisis and expropriated crony enterprises. She reorganized the Department of Trade and Industry in 1987 and abolished the Bureau of Industrial Development, the unit responsible for making industrial policy. She also expanded the scope of trade liberalization by reducing the number of commodities with high tariffs and increasing the number of commodities with low tariffs (Raquiza 2011: 43–44).

This, however, is only part of the story. To understand the contemporary Philippine political economy, it is also important to remember that its English-language educational expansion started earlier and proceeded more steadily than anywhere else in Southeast Asia, and that Marcos made the decision in the crisis years about Filipino workers abroad, now the mainstay of the Philippine economy. In the Philippines, the number of students in higher education for every 100,000 population was 1,808 in 1975, 2,641 in 1980, and 2,760 in 1995 (in contrast, it was 316 in 1975 and 2,096 in 1995 in Thailand) (Hattori *et al.* 2002: 299). This development nurtured educated middle classes in professional, business, and technical professions. But the stunted economic development and the fiscal crisis in the 1980s, coupled with the oil boom in the Middle East and the rapid economic growth experienced by East Asian countries, forced the government to adopt a policy of exporting its labor force. This explains why Filipino labor – which includes an increasing number of middle-class people – has become deterritorialized. In 2002, an estimated 7.4 million Filipinos, constituting about 10 percent of the population and 21 percent of the total labor force, remitted US$7.4 billion or the equivalent of 9 percent of the Philippine gross national product (GNP) for the year. By 2011, the remittances of 9.5 million Filipinos (or roughly 10 percent of the population) working abroad reached US$20 billion (Whaley 2012). It is also said that 22.5 to 35 million Filipinos, or roughly half of the country's population, are directly or indirectly dependent on these remittances. Scholars have also pointed to the increasingly feminized and "domesticated" nature of Filipino overseas work. From 12 percent of deployed workers in 1975, the percentage of female overseas Filipino workers (OFWs) increased to 47 percent in 1987, 58 percent in 1995, and 72 percent in 2001 (Hau 2004). This explains why private consumption drives Philippine GDP growth (72 percent of GDP in 2010) and the Philippine service sector has steadily expanded from 46 percent of GDP in 1993, to 52 percent in 2000, to 55 percent in 2010. It is fueled by the steadily expanding overseas workers' remittances: Philippine net factor income from abroad increased from USD 13.9 billion, 14.7 percent of Philippine GNI, in 2000 to USD 66.3 billion, 24.9 percent, in 2010. Per capita gross national income (GNI) has also increased faster than per capita gross domestic income (GDI) from USD 1,237 in 2000 to USD 2,829 in 2010.

Scholars in the developmental state school label the Philippine state as "anti-developmental" (Bello *et al.* 2004) and lament the decline of the Philippine manufacturing sector whose share went down from 26 percent of GDP in 1980 to 21 percent in 2009 (Raquiza 2011: 19). But given that this is the outcome of policy decisions the Philippine state made under Marcos, it is important to ask about its implications for the Philippines in the wake of his ousting.

Educational expansion and remittances have fuelled the expansion of the service sector, above all retail, banking, real-estate development, and an expanding range of specialist services (business process outsourcing) like accounting, legal services, advertising, computing, and market research, and given rise to new middle classes. Among their most visible segments are the Chinese Filipinos and young, skilled urban workers. As Michael Pinches (1999: 278, 285) notes, Chinese entrepreneurs made substantial inroads into areas formerly controlled by the old mestizo elite and established conglomerates which cater to a wide range of income groups, particularly in the middle-class and lower-income spectrums, and which have in some cases surpassed some of the old rich. A major factor making this and related developments possible was the opening up of citizenship to Filipino Chinese in 1975 (professional occupations were restricted to citizens). In the meantime, a large pool of young, urban, English-speaking workers (61 percent of the population) has provided the manpower for the outsourcing industry. The Philippines is currently the world's leading provider of voice-based outsourcing services – call centers employ some 683,000 people and raked in more than US$11 billion in revenue (Whaley 2012).

The new middle classes have also given rise to new coalition politics in the post-Marcos years, which reveals the extent to which coalition politics accommodates different political forces, including traditional politicians, local bosses, and caciques, as well as social movements, non-governmental organizations (NGOs) and people's organizations (POs). This shifting coalition is created in support of presidential candidates. Coalition forces capture government agencies while being granted their own spheres in which to operate. The diverse and often divergent agendas of these various factions of the coalition mean that the coalition ends up pursuing paradoxical policies and programs. Maintaining the coalition requires that resources be allocated and channelled for this purpose. This delimits the political choices the President makes. The state – although marked by pockets of efficiency – reaches an impasse: its resources, reach, and functions are delimited by coalition politics.

The increasing importance of the overseas workers, their remittances, and the expanding service sector also has implications for the state leadership. In the 2010 presidential election, Benigno "Noynoy" Aquino III coasted to victory to succeed outgoing President Gloria Macapagal Arroyo. It was a race between Aquino and Manuel "Manny" Villar. Aquino is the son of Benigno Aquino, Jr. who was assassinated in 1983 and former President Corazon Aquino and has promised "a clean government." Villar, on the other hand, hails from a slum in Manila and has made his fortune as a real estate developer, building houses affordable for people in the middle-class or lower-income brackets in the capital. In Manila, no large-scale real estate development project is viable without the involvement of relevant officials from top to bottom – from the President to the Mayor to municipal assembly members. For Villar, business and political activities are two sides of the same coin. It is indispensable for him to become a major insider within the inner circle of the Philippine political class as a way of ensuring success in the business sphere. Aquino was born into money, Villar into poverty. But both now have great wealth. Aquino is "clean" and Villar is probably "dirty," but the difference merely results from the fact that Aquino's family has been rich for three generations, while Villar worked his way out of a slum. What is important is to learn *where* the two men have made their fortunes. Aquino represents a traditional group who owns vast farming estates in the Philippines that are not internationally competitive. Villar represents both those who have earned middle-class spending power while working abroad and the emerging group of people who have been able to thrive in tandem with the rise of the middle class in Philippine society. Gathering further momentum in the Philippines is the part of society that includes people like Villar. Aquino triumphed in the presidential election because the death in August 2009 of Cory Aquino reminded voters of the People Power revolution. But the current of the times will not change in the face of increasing urbanization as well as deterritorialization of Filipino labor. Filipinos working abroad have gained a formidable influence in the political and economic affairs of the Philippines and they are expected to continue acquiring power. No matter who assumes the presidency, he or she cannot afford to choose policy options hostile to these workers. At the same time, alleviating poverty, particularly among people in the rural areas in the wake of a shrinking agricultural sector, and providing good education to young Filipinos remain the most important challenges.

4 Thailand

Thailand enjoyed a long period of economic development from the late 1950s to the late 1990s, which culminated in the economic boom in 1987–95 and led to its collapse in 1997–98. This history is well known. Open politics, which the student revolution ushered in, in 1973, and in which small urban middle classes as well as peasants and workers for the first time in Thai history emerged as political forces, was truncated with the counter-revolutionary coup in 1976 and was replaced by half-democracy, so called because the military and bureaucratic elite could no longer ignore urban middle classes when Indochina went communist and thousands of student activists joined the communist insurgency. The military and bureaucratic elite was willing to share power with party politicians and business elites. Although neither Kriangsak Chomanan (Prime Minister, 1977–80) nor Prem Tinsulanonda (Prime Minister, 1980–88) were elected members of the parliament, government stability under their leadership depended on their success in forming and sustaining a governing coalition of political parties as much as obtaining and maintaining the support of the military and bureaucratic elites. In this period of half-democracy, government economic policy remained friendly to business, while parties, run by local bosses, businessmen and professional politicians, dominated party politics, capitalizing on income disparities between Bangkok and the provinces, mobilizing agrarian support with public works and outright vote-buying, and making politics a money-making business (Phongpaichit and Baker 2008a: 13).

The half-democracy reached a turning point when Chatichai Choonhavan led the Thai Nation Party to victory in the 1988 election and became Prime Minister (1988–91). The son of Field Marshal Phin Choonhavan who lost the power struggle with Sarit Thanarat in the late 1950s, Chatichai called for a policy to turn Indochina "from battlefield to a market place." He improved Thai relations with Cambodia and Laos. He promoted trade with Cambodia, Laos, and other countries. He embarked on major infrastructural development projects such as the expansion of the telecommunication network, the development of the Eastern Seaboard of Thailand, and road and rail networks in the Greater Bangkok Area. While the military was the senior partner and political parties the junior under Prem Tinsulanonda, the rise of party politician Chatchai Choonhavan as Prime Minister threatened to relegate the military to a junior partner position. The military under Suchinda struck back and appointed Anan Panyarachun, a diplomat-turned-business leader, Prime Minister. When Suchinda appointed himself as Prime Minister in 1992, however, the opposition galvanized, culminating in a "middle-class revolt" which forced his resignation (Shiraishi 2008; Tamada 2008).

This development, however, did not mean the decline of the military and bureaucratic elite, let alone the arrival of middle-class hegemony. The Thai economy grew by 7 percent annually between 1960 and 1980 and by 8 percent annually between 1987 and 1996. But the development took place mainly in Bangkok and its vicinities and disproportionately benefited the Bangkok middle classes in the making. Denied opportunities for high-school, let alone university, education, peasants and farmers in the provinces either remained in the agricultural sector of declining productivity or migrated to Bangkok as unskilled workers on a short-term contract basis. The Thai agricultural population constituted more than 50 percent of the working population even in the 1990s (while the GDP share of the agricultural sector declined to 11 percent in 1995). Thus resulted a huge and expanding per capita income disparity between the provinces and the Bangkok Metropolitan Area. The per capita regional GDP in Bangkok was nine times larger than that in the northeast, the poorest region with one third of the Thai population in the 1990s. And even in 1988, at the beginning of the boom, Bangkok middle-class people were making four to six times more money than peasants and farmers in the provinces. Yet peasants and farmers dominated the franchise in the institutions of representative democracy.

At elections, their votes were influenced by the bureaucratic power of the army and the Ministry of Interior, and by the money and local influence of local bosses. For the metropolitan business interests, the countryside remained a new and unexplored political frontier.

Thai party politics was thus characterized by shifting coalitions. Coalitions, however, lacked stability because the departure of a coalition partner could bring down the government. The urban-rural division divided parties. In the 1995 elections, for instance, the Thai National Party emerged as the majority party in the provinces, but did not win even a single seat in Bangkok. In the 1996 elections, the New Aspiration Party under Chaovalit Yongchaiyudh emerged victorious, but won only a seat in Bangkok. The major issue in these elections was corruption and vote-buying. Agrarian voters sold their votes because they could not expect to obtain benefits in any other way from electoral politics. But urban middle-class people found it repugnant.

In the mid-1990s, this war was fought in the constitution-making process. The Committee for Constitutional Amendment was composed of university graduates even though university graduates constituted only 2.5 percent of the Thai population aged 20 and above. The parliament dominated by parties and party bosses with agrarian bases opposed constitutional revisions the Committee drafted.

The crisis then hit Thailand in 1997. Thailand had liberalized its financial sector and deregulated foreign exchange controls and capital transactions in the late 1980s and early 1990s. A major turning point came in 1993 when the government established an offshore financial center. Financial inflow turned into flood in 1993–95 when the out-in transactions, which were 27.6 billion baht in 1987, reached 650.4 billion baht in 1995. Money went to the stock market and consumer loans. It also went to real estate development, hotels, and big industrial projects in steel, petrochemicals, and cement. The real estate bubble popped in 1995–96. Financial institutions experienced rapid deterioration in their balance sheets and many of them became insolvent. Thai baht also came under attack in 1995–96. The Thai monetary authority decided to suspend the operation of 16 insolvent financial institutions in June 1997 and to float baht in the foreign exchange market in July. But it was too late: the Thai government went to the IMF for assistance in the same month.

The crisis highlighted the defect of Thai party politics. With the arrival of coalition governments in the 1990s, cabinet posts were distributed to coalition partners in proportion to the parliamentary seats each party controlled. The ascendancy of party politics also undermined Thai technocracy. The Development Planning Agency at the Prime Minister's office, which had once served as the command post for the Thai developmental state, was transformed into a center for the distribution of pork barrels among parties and party politicians, while the central bank had to be careful not to hurt powerful interests with its financial and currency policy. Party bosses who owned coalition parties could veto any policy that might harm their interests, threatening to bolt the coalition (Suehiro forthcoming).

The showdown took place shortly after the Thai government went to the IMF. Prime Minister Chaovalit raised taxes on gasoline and diesel oil as required by the IMF, but retracted the measure when it was opposed by a coalition partner. The government collapsed. Chuan Leekpai replaced Chaovalit as Prime Minister, assembled a Democratic Party-led new coalition government with the strong representation of urban interests, shut down 56 failed financial institutions as required by the IMF, and embarked on structural reforms. Chuan was also successful in passing the constitutional revision, because parties could not afford to vote down constitutional amendment and deepen the economic crisis into a political one. The new constitution required parliamentary members and cabinet ministers to have university degrees, making it hard for local bosses to become parliamentary members and cabinet ministers. It also prohibited parliamentary members from serving as cabinet ministers, making it hard for politicians to make money with public works and corruption. And it made the senate elective, denying the military and bureaucratic elite the parliamentary arena.

The crisis seriously threatened Thai business. In the boom years, "external markets, external finance, foreign partnerships, new technology, and new ideas" were the keys to business profit (Phongpaichit and Baker 2009: 15) In the wake of the crisis, however, foreign capital bought up the wreckage of bankrupt Thai companies. Thai business enthusiasm for globalization turned into nationalism. Business elites were also dismayed with party politics. By the time the crisis hit Thailand in 1997, the government failure to manage the economy had become evident. Business also wanted political reform and government protection (Phongpaichit and Baker 2009: 16–17).

This provided a rare opportunity for Thaksin Shinawatra, a business tycoon turned political entrepreneur, to bridge the urban-rural division. He presented himself to Bangkok business and the middle classes as a CEO who could overcome the crisis with domestic demand-led development, while calling for equitable and autonomous agrarian development in the provinces. His new party, Thai Rak Thai, won a major victory in the 2001 elections. And yet, Thaksin's project ultimately failed, largely because he underestimated the power of the military and bureaucratic elite, the old elite, and the urban middle classes. The middle classes came to fear his "populist" schemes because they threatened to empower the rural masses, to raise the tax demand on the middle classes, and to make the middle classes politically irrelevant. The bureaucracy resented his plans to shift power away from military officers and bureaucrats to businessmen-politicians. And the old elite took fright at Thaksin's brash, new form of public politics and populist leadership. Thaksin was ousted in a coup in the fall of 2006. The junta revised the constitution, intent on protecting bureaucratic power and limiting the power of elected politicians, but in effect ushered in a period of political stalemate, in which any coalition government, whether under Abhisit Vejjajiva-led Democratic Party or Yingluck Shinawatra-led Pheu Thai Party, is haunted by violent street demonstrations, by Thaksin in exile, and by the dying king (Phongpaichit and Baker 2009).

At the heart of the current political stalemate, however, lay the reality that the Thai state with its laws, institutions, and thinking geared to the old era of development, needed to come to terms with the new reality in which its economic dynamism came from exports, spearheaded by the automotive, electrical, electronic, and other technology-based sectors dominated by multinationals, while not a few Thai business families were badly damaged. Both the Crown Property Bureau and the Shinawatra mobile phone empire, which was based on a politically granted concession and defended by Thaksin, survived the crisis thanks to massive rents they could reap. As Pasuk Phongpaichit and Chris Baker point out, the crisis has taught the business elite how important politically generated rents are. In the wake of the crisis, Thaksin called for an ambitious political project "to create a single rent-gathering coalition that included many of the big business families" (Phongpaichit and Baker 2008b: 273). But this project was misconceived, precisely because it did not address the policy issues confronting the Thai state in this era of globalization. Thailand has become a mainland Southeast Asian hub for multinational manufacturing. The government needs to invest in infrastructure and human resources as a host for multinationals. It also needs to encourage competition and assist domestic companies to enhance their capabilities and become more competitive. And given the fact that at the bottom of the political stalemate and the disorder in the 2000s lies the deepening division between the elite and urban middle classes on the one hand and the rural poor on the other, state power has to be reorganized to address the question of social safety nets and income redistribution, and to expand its social base (Phongpaichit and Baker 2008b: 274–77).

5 Malaysia

A plural society par excellence, in which maintaining ethnic peace is considered to be of paramount importance as a condition of national life, Malaysia has been under the National Front (NF) government since the early 1970s. It is a governing coalition of ethnic and regional parties led and dominated by the UMNO, United Malay National Organization, with its stated objectives of "eradication of poverty, irrespective of race" and "restructuring to abolish the identification of race with economic function" (Khoo 2006: 178). Its New Economic Policy (NEP) as well as its successor, National Development Policy (NDP) and New Economic Model (NEM) have been geared in part to achieving these objectives, equated with improving Malay social and economic positions and creating Malay middle classes with state-led economic and educational development, while lulling non-Malays with export-oriented economic growth. Quotas were introduced for Malay employment in business and Malay enrolment in universities. Malay replaced English as the language of choice at the high school and university level. The Malay corporate share of 30 percent was targeted. Public enterprises were established by the government to create a Malay business elite.

The Malaysian political economy was transformed in the 1980s under Prime Minister Mahathir Mohamad (1981–2003). He embarked on building "Malaysia Inc." He shifted his developmental emphasis from the public sector to the private and privatized public corporations to create a Malay business elite. He also embarked on heavy industrialization with the establishment of the HICOM, the Heavy Industries of Malaysia, with technology sourced from Japanese and South Korean firms through joint ventures. The government also liberalized the investment regime in the mid-1980s. Limits on foreign equity ownership were removed and fresh investment incentives offered. These measures coincided with moves by Japanese and other East Asian multinationals to relocate their production bases in the wake of the 1985 Plaza Accord. A wave of investment drove the rapid economic growth in the boom years from the late 1980s to 1997 (Khoo 2006: 182–83).

Though ethnic divisions remained the most important divisions in Malaysian politics, the rise of Malay and non-Malay middle classes made its effect felt in Malaysian politics. In the first place, the UMNO became more business-oriented. Its traditional social bases were among peasants and farmers, civil servants, and schoolteachers. In the 1981 party congress, for instance, 40 percent of delegates were schoolteachers. By the late 1980s, however, business executives and managers emerged as a major force in the party. In the 1987 party congress, 25 percent of delegates were business executives and managers, while 19 percent were schoolteachers and 23 percent civil servants, even though only 1.4 percent of the Malay working population was classified as executives and managers even in 1990 (Torii 2001).

The UMNO also became business-oriented in another sense in the same years. With the establishment of Fleet Holdings as its business arm, the party went into business in a major way, investing in food processing, hotels, and real estate development. Its branches followed suit. Politically connected Malay, non-Malay and interethnic conglomerates arose in such sectors as banking, resource exploitation, construction, property and real estate, tourism, utilities, and selected import-substituting industries (Khoo 2006: 184).

Mahathir's privatization policy and the BOT scheme he introduced for infrastructural development projects (such as the North-South highway) also worked for the UMNO's business orientation. The UMNO leadership distributed business opportunities to its supporters. To obtain business in public works, government-funded development projects, and BOT projects, business executives and managers joined the party to control important positions in the party organization at the state, branch, and district levels. To get elected to important party positions, they invested in election campaigns, and once elected, they tried to recoup their investment, if necessary, establishing new UMNO firms and demanding the government and the party distribute more business opportunities to UMNO members and business entities.

In the second place, Islamic revival among the rising Malay middle class deeply affected the UMNO. Not only Malay- and Arabic-educated, but also and more significantly the increasing number of English-educated Malays have come to follow the straitlaced, Arab-type Islam. The UMNO leadership tried to coopt Islamic revivalist forces. Anwar Ibrahim, ABIM (Angkatan Belia Islam Malaysia, Malaysia Islamic Youth Movement) chairman, joined the UMNO, ran successfully for parliament in the early 1980s, was awarded a cabinet post, and rose in the party hierarchy to become Deputy Prime Minister in 1993.

The UMNO in the 1980s and 1990s thus presented itself to the Malay community as the guardian of Malay economic interests and Malay Islamic identity. The UMNO leadership under Mahathir and Anwar Ibrahim in 1993–98 embodied this double guardianship. In 1991, Mahathir started the NDP, announcing Vision 2020 and setting the goal that Malaysia join the group of advanced industrial countries by 2020 with the 7 percent annual growth for the coming 20 years and the nation-building based on Malaysian national consciousness. The NDP emphasized growth, while retaining the NEP's ethnic considerations. Government policies welcomed the multinationals and portfolio investment, while relying on the conglomerates as the vanguard of Malaysia Inc. (Khoo 2006: 186). In a symbolic move, the government deregulated and liberalized the university educational system and approved the establishment of private universities for non-Malay students in the mid-1990s. The government also institutionalized policy consultation mechanisms with the private sector, in part represented by Chinese entrepreneurs.

It was the 1997–98 economic crisis that threatened the survival of conglomerates and almost wrecked the UMNO and the UMNO-dominated NF regime. Anwar Ibrahim, together with his former ABIM activists and business executives and entrepreneurs, rose in the UMNO in the 1990s. But it was Mahathir who had the final say in the distribution of business opportunities. This set the stage for the power struggle between Prime Minister Mahathir and his deputy, Anwar Ibrahim, in the crisis years of 1997 and 1998. The crisis depreciated the currency, radically reduced stock market valuations and sent the economy into recession. The conglomerates were threatened because their dependence on external borrowing and stock market capitalization exposed them to bloated loan repayments, plunging asset values, and imminent insolvency. Yet the IMF insisted on higher interest rates, austerity, market liberalization, financial sector reform, and good governance, in effect dismantling Malaysia Inc. (Khoo 2006: 187).

Mahathir and Anwar had different positions on how to deal with the crisis. Anwar called for the fiscal austerity and criticized cronyism; Mahathir opted for economic stimulus and wanted to bail out troubled Malay firms and banks. When the crisis spread to Malaysia, Anwar announced a strategic plan for the economic and fiscal stabilization in 1997 to overcome the crisis with a high interest rate and tight fiscal policy package. This put a brake on the economy and not a few firms and banks ran into trouble. Mahathir established the National Economic Action Council (NEAC) in January 1998 in the Prime Minister's office and looked for ways to stimulate the economy with the promotion of foreign and Chinese capital investment.

It was in this context that Anwar mounted an attack on Mahathir at the UMNO party congress in 1998. The UMNO Youth spearheaded as anti-Mahathir force in support of Anwar and attacked the Malay-first policy as "crony economy"; Anwar, however, was unsuccessful in ousting Mahathir as UMNO President. Mahathir took the economic policy-making into his own hands. In September 1998, the government announced the introduction of capital control and the fixed foreign exchange rate system. Anwar was ousted as Deputy Prime Minister and Finance Minister. He was arrested, tried twice for sodomy, and sentenced to imprisonment. The capital controls presaged a regime of reflating the economy, relaxing monetary policy, and resuscitating local business. The Japanese government also came to his rescue with the Miyazawa plan (Shiraishi 2005). By late 1999, trade surpluses had built up the country's reserves and the economy began to emerge from recession. Mahathir saved strategic economic sectors and conglomerates by domestic initiative. The Anwar Ibrahim affair divided Malays and led to the unprecedented loss of Malay support for the UMNO in the 1999 election, even though the NF electoral victory left policy direction in Mahathir's hands (Khoo 2006: 189–90).

Post-Mahathir Malaysia is thus bequeathed with the UMNO-led NEP status quo legacy. But the alienation of the Malay electorate over the Anwar affair and the stagnation of NEP restructuring haunt the UMNO-led NF government. This was demonstrated in the 2008 and 2013 elections. As with all previous general elections, the UMNO-led coalition won the parliamentary election. But the NF could not maintain the two-thirds majority.

As Mohamed Ariff, a leading Malaysian economist, bluntly says (2012: 17), Malaysia is now in search of a new economic model with which to reposition itself in the global economy. Income inequality has widened since the crisis with the Gini coefficient rising for all ethnic groups. Its potential growth rate has shrunk from 7.5 percent in the late 1980s to 5.5 percent now, jeopardizing the goal of making Malaysia a developed country by 2020 (Ariff 2012: 17–23). Frustration with the NDP manifests itself in a serious brain-drain. Foreign direct investment (FDI) has also trickled in very slowly in recent years – at 1 percent a year in 2006–09 – a far cry from the 9 percent growth seen before the crisis (Ariff 2012: 21) Yet trapped in the post-crisis political impasse, the policy drift in the name of "the second best strategy" (to cite a leading Malaysian technocrat in interview, 2007) to give due consideration to ethnic peace in effect protects Malaysia's strategic economic sectors and conglomerates.

6 Conclusion

Although scholars can endlessly fret about whether a particular state can be classified as a "developmental state" or not and concern themselves with arguing over the features that characterize such a state, the idea of the "developmental state" itself – an idea equated with state-led industrial development – has long informed, if not overshadowed, our understanding of East Asian and Southeast Asian political economies. More importantly, this idea of the developmental state has informed the strategy of state building and economic development and the ways in which state power was variously organized to achieve their stated purposes in Marcos's New Society, Soeharto's New Order, the Thai bureaucratic state and the UMNO-led and NEP-driven NF regime in Malaysia. This is not surprising. Legatees of colonial (or in the case of Thailand, semi-colonial) state building and economic processes, these states began to redefine their national projects in the 1960s by turning from the objectives of achieving national independence to those of nation building. In the context of the Cold War years, these states adopted anti-communist nation building from above, in often coercive ways. All the states staked their legitimacy on a politics of economic growth, and tried to meet the challenges of state building, economic development and nation building with the state apparatus serving as backbone and deploying state resources strategically.

Drawing on lessons learned from other countries (notably neighbors like Japan, Korea, Taiwan, and Singapore, which underwent rapid economic development and which were lumped together by some scholars as "developmental states"), these states set the development of the manufacturing sector as the central objective of national industrial development and identified technocracy, industrial development, and national education as the crucial elements of their respective nation-building projects. The Thai business-politician and cabinet minister, Boonchu Rojanastien, for example, unsuccessfully called for the creation of "Thailand, Inc." in the early 1980s, while Mahathir proved more successful in fashioning a "Malaysia, Inc."

Yet the overall performances of these countries have differed from each other and, more importantly for the purpose of this chapter, from one era to another. Malaysia and Thailand, two Southeast Asian countries that were touted as Tiger Economies in the pre-crisis years, are now mired in political stalemate and register less impressive economic performance in the post-crisis era, while Indonesia, which was once called a "failing state" in the wake of the 1997–98 crisis, and the Philippines, the so-called "sick man of Asia," are now back on the track of economic growth (with some measure of political stability). Thailand and Malaysia are, in a sense, trapped in the formula of their own success, and the particular configuration of power in these countries, now firmly embedded in the middle-class society their past success has created, has made it difficult to break out of the impasse in which they now find themselves. This formula, which had served both countries well in the era of export-led industrialization when Japanese and other East Asian multinational companies moved their production facilities abroad, especially in Southeast Asia and coastal regions of China, for global market places, works less well in a time when China has emerged as a global workshop offering stiff competition to many manufacturing sectors in Southeast Asia. Indonesia's growth is fuelled by commodity exports and by fast expanding domestic consumption. The Philippine economy is driven by the remittances of its deterritorialized labor force and by the competitive advantage of its human capital.

It is now time, then, to ask how useful the idea of a developmental state is, both as a concept and as a state objective. The problem with this concept is that it is too fixated on manufacturing and manufacture-led economic growth and on the idea of a strong state equated with a strong bureaucracy. Running through this concept is the dream of national autonomy based on the state's ability to manage transnational flows and movements, to maximize a country's position in the world economy, and exercise sovereignty in foreign relations. What began as an heuristic description of Japan's postwar emergence as an economic power (Johnson 1982) became both an analytical model and a grand-strategic prescription. In this sense, scholarly analysis became public discussion and public policy.

But to understand the political economy and state building of countries like Indonesia and the Philippines, the idea of the developmental state is not particularly useful and often invites the wrong questions. While scholars accept the inevitability of attending to specific historical and material contexts in order to account for differences in economic performance and political stability among countries, global and regional contexts and contingencies are still treated as secondary factors that are invoked mainly to explain why countries fail to live up to the ideal or prescription of a successful developmental state. There is no single prescription for successful state building and economic development. Countries like Indonesia and the Philippines did not set out to flout the prescription, but rather figured out their own formulas in the course of having to deal with very pressing crises. Yet, interestingly, the purpose of politics remains the same, both in Indonesia and the Philippines as well as in Malaysia and Thailand: maintaining national unity and domestic peace, while achieving economic growth, creating jobs, and improving the standard of living. What has changed is the set of conditions under which this politics of economic growth or politics of productivity can be successfully pursued. If the state being built once looked developmental, it was because politics made it developmental: the idea of development remained anchored in a limited understanding of "value," that is, "value" could only be created through "productive" activities, mainly in the primary and secondary sectors, with an expanding national market that is clearly demarcated from the so-called "world market."

But those days are over. National economies are now deeply integrated into larger regional and global economies, as evident in the regional and transnational production chains, international labor migration, brain circulation (rather than simply brain-drain), and the outsourcing of services. The key to economic development may no longer rest on a single, one-fits-all model of industrialization based on a strong manufacturing sector. Instead, positioning one's economy within a larger regional and global system which evolves along with changing dynamics in comparative advantages among developed and developing countries, and training one's people to take advantage of opportunities available in this system, is becoming far more important (see Chapters 9 and 10). Manufacturing industries in Thailand and Malaysia need technological and managerial upgrading to survive in the increasingly competitive global and regional markets. But this can happen only if and when serious political stalemate is overcome and the government embarks on revamping the old formula of economic development and social control. In contrast, political contentions are now sufficiently contained in Indonesia and the Philippines not to obstruct the smooth functioning of their respective leading economic sectors: natural resource development in Indonesia, Filipino labor abroad, and back office business services in the Philippines.

Although economic growth remains the purpose of politics, the state's capacity to deliver on its promise depends on how state power is organized and deployed, who runs the state institutions, what kind of resources both state and society can mobilize, the kind of investment a country makes in its people, and the complex political and economic processes that inform their decisions and operations.

Note

* The author would like to thank Caroline Sy Hau and Khoo Boo Teik for very useful comments and suggestions.

References

Ariff, M. (2012) "Preface," in H. Hill, T.S. Yean, and R.H.M. Zin (eds) *Malaysia's Development Challenges: Graduating from the Middle*, London: Routledge.

Bello, W.F., deGuzman, M., Malig, M.L., and Docena, H. (2004) *The Anti-Development State: The Political Economy of Permanent Crisis in the Philippines*, London: Zed Books.

Ginandjar Kartasasmita (2013) *Managing Indonesia's Transformation: An Oral Hisotry*, Singapore: World Scientific Pulbishing.

Hau, C.S. (2004) *On the Subject of the Nation: Filipino Writing from 1981 to 2003*, Manila: Ateneo de Manila University Press.

Hattori, T., Funatsu T., and Torii T. (eds) (2002) *Ajia Chukan-so no Seisei to Tokushitu* [*The Formation of Asian Middle Strata and Their Features*], Tokyo: Ajia Keizai Kenkyusho.

Hill, H. and Shiraishi, T. (2007) "Indonesia After the Asian Crisis," *Asian Economic Policy Review*, 2 (1): 123–41.

Johnson, C. (1982) *MITI and the Japanese Miracle: The Growth of Industrial Policy 1925–1975*, Stanford, CA: Stanford University Press.

Khoo, B.T. (2006) "Malaysia: balancing development and power," in G. Rodan, K. Hewison, and R. Robison (eds.) *The Political Economy of South-East Asia: Markets, Power and Contestation*, Melbourne: Oxford University Press.

Matsui, K. and Kawamura, K. (2005) *Indoneshia Sosenkyo to Shinseiken no Shido: Megawati kara Yudoyono e* [*Indonesia's General Elections and the Start of a New Administration: From Megawati to Yudhoyono*], Tokyo: Akashi Shoten.

Morishita, A. (2005) "Suharuto Taisei Hokai-go no Indoneshia: Nishi, Chugu, Higashi Karimantan no Riken wo Nigiru no wa Dou Itta Hitotachi ka?" ["Local politics in Post-Suharto Indonesia: Who Controls Local Resources in West, Central and East Kalimantan?"], Ph.D. Dissertation, Kyoto University.

Okamoto, M. (2011) "Minshuka shita Ta Minzoku Kokka Indonesia ni okeru antei no Politics" ["Politics of stability in democratized multi-ethnic state of Indonesia"], Ph.D. dissertation, Kyoto University.

Phongpaichit, P. and Baker, C. (2008a) "Thailand under Thaksin: a regional and international perspective," in T. Shiraishi and P. Phongpaichit (eds) *The Rise of Middle Classes in Southeast Asia*, Kyoto: Kyoto University Press and Trans Pacific Press.

Phongpaichit, P. and Baker, C. (2008b) "Conclusion," in P. Phongpaichit and C. Baker (eds), *Thai Capital: After the 1997 Crisis*, Chiang Mai: Silkworm Books.

Phongpaichit, P. and Baker, C. (2009) *Thaksin*, Chiang Mai: Silkworm Books.

Pinches, M. (1999) "Entrepreneurship, consumption, ethnicity and national identity in the making of the Philippines' new rich," in M. Pinches (ed.) *Culture and Privelege in Capitalist Asia*, London: Routledge.

Raquiza, A.R. (2011) *State Structure, Policy Formation, and Economic Development in Southeast Asia: The Political Economy of Thailand and the Philippines*, New York: Routledge.

Sato, Y. (2011) *Keizai Taikoku Indonesia: 21-Seiki no Seicho Joken* [*Economic Power Indonesia: Conditions for Growth in the 21st Century*], Tokyo: Chuo Koron Shinsha.

Shiraishi, T. (1997) *Sukarno to Suharto: Idai naru Indonesia wo mezashite* [*Sukarno and Suharto: Toward Great Indonesia*], Tokyo: Iwanami Shoten.

Shiraishi, T. (1999) *Hokai: Indonesia wa doko he iku* [*Whither Indonesia?*], Tokyo: NTT Shuppan.

Shiraishi, T. (2000) *Umi no Teikoku* [*Empires of the Seas*], Tokyo: Chuo Koron Shinsha.

Shiraishi, T. (2005) "The Asian crisis reconsidered," in P.N. Abinales, I. Noboru, and T. Akio (eds) *Dislocating Nation-States: Globalization in Asia and Africa*, Kyoto: Kyoto University Press.

Shiraishi, T. (2008) "Introduction: the rise of middle classes in Southeast Asia," in T. Shiraishi and P. Phongpaichit (eds), *The Rise of Middle Classes in Southeast Asia*, Kyoto: Kyoto University Press.

Shiraishi, T. (2010) "Indonesia ni oite Keizai Seicho no Seiji wa ikani shite fukkatsu shit aka" ["How has the politics of economic growth come back in Indonesia?"], in K. Otsukaand T. Shiraishi (eds) *Kokka to Keizai Hatten* [*State and Economic Development*], Tokyo: Toyo Keizai Shinposha.

Suehiro, A. (forthcoming) "Technocracy and thaksinocracy in Thailand: reforms of the public sector and the budget system under the Thaksin government," in T. Shiraishi, K.B. Teik, and T.E. Tadem (eds) *Politics of Technocracy in Southeast Asia*, Singapore: Institute for Southeast Asian Studies.

Tamada, Y. (2008) "Democracy and the middle class in Thailand: the uprising of May 1992," in T. Shiraishi and P. Phongpaichit (eds) *The Rise of Middle Classes in Southeast Asia*, Kyoto: Kyoto University Press and Trans Pacific Press.

Torii, T. (2001) "Malaysia no Kaihatsu Senryaku to Seji Hendo" ["Developmental strategy and political change in Malaysia"], in Susumu Yamakage and Akira Suehoro (eds) *Ajia Seiji Keizai Ron: Ajia no naka no Nihon wo mezashite [Essays on Asian Political Economy: Toward Japan in Asia]*, Tokyo: NTT Shuppan.

Whaley, F. (2012) "A youthful populace helps make the Philippines an economic bright spot in Asia," *New York Times*, 27 August, http://www.nytimes.com/2012/08/28/business/global/philippine-economy-set-to-become-as ias-newest-bright-spot.html?_r=2&pagewanted=all.

5 The evolution of land policy in African state building

Shinichi Takeuchi

1 Introduction

There is a broad consensus among the international community that building a functional state is one of the most critical concerns for today's Sub-Saharan Africa.[1] On the one hand, researchers as well as practitioners agree that the dysfunctional state (or state failure) has brought about political insecurity and serious armed conflicts (Holsti 1996; Rotberg 2004; Zartman 1995). Therefore, donors regard state building as "the central objective" in their assistance to overcome fragile situations (OECD 2007). On the other hand, against the backdrop of severe criticism against the "Washington Consensus," the role of the state in economic development has been widely recognized since the 1990s. This is the reason why the international financial institutions have emphasized the importance of good governance for economic development (World Bank 1989, 1993, 2001). Projects of state building in Africa have attracted wide attention, exactly because Africa's predicaments, including civil wars and economic crises, have been often attributed to the dysfunctional states.

According to recent arguments, a functional state is supposed to be based on a constructive state–society relation (OECD 2007, 2011). The primary role of the state is considered to be the provision of basic services, of which the maintenance of social order is the most important one; the service provisions will determine popular attitudes towards the state. In response to the positive (or negative) attitude of the society, the state may (or may not) change behaviors. If the state is responsive enough to change its behaviors in taking popular aspirations into account, the state–society relation is regarded as constructive, and the process of state building will be stable in the long run.

If we problematize African states and seek a constructive state–society relationship, it is indispensable to look back at their historical trajectories and understand how the present states as well as the state–society relationship have been formed. On this point, one of the most salient features of the African states is their exogenous origin. Besides a few exceptions, the origins of current African states can be found in the arbitrary territorial demarcations by European colonial forces. For many of them, the Berlin Conference held in 1884–85 was the decisive point for starting their state building. Since the imposition by the external powers at the beginning of the colonial period, African states have struggled to control territories as well as to incorporate society.

These efforts have been clearly reflected in the state policies as well as practices with regard to land. Controlling land is by definition inseparable from controlling territory. Moreover, land has close relations with the society, as it is indispensable for people's living. This is particularly true in agrarian societies like those in Africa, where the overwhelming majority of people have critically depended on land for their subsistence. Attempts to control these societies have been, therefore, directly reflected in land policies.

In focusing on land policies, this chapter attempts to shed light on changes in and continuities of state–society relations and examines the challenges of state building in Africa. It begins by tracing a history of state intervention on land as well as societal reactions against it from the pre-colonial to the post-colonial period. After presenting a rough picture of the historical development of state intervention in land, the chapter focuses on the case of Rwanda. As a country that has actively adopted policies securing land tenure, Rwanda tends to be regarded as a showcase for land tenure reform, but detailed examination of the socio-political background reveals serious challenges for policy objectives.

2 State and land in pre-colonial Africa

In comparison with pre-modern Europe and Japan, land played quite a different role in pre-colonial African states. In the former regions, political domination was deeply connected with the control of land, on which intensive agriculture flourished in densely populated areas. Land was the basis of state building, because the national revenue depended heavily on agriculture. The relationship between political authority and land was considerably different in pre-colonial Africa. The difference was clearly indicated in the proportion of land to population. In Africa, the population was extremely scarce and land was highly abundant. In 1750, when Japan, Europe, and China had 78.3 persons, 26.9 persons, and 22.2 persons, respectively, Africa had only 2.7 persons (Herbst 2000: 16). This implied the easy availability of land in Africa and, therefore, frequent changes of residence. These conditions greatly affected the meaning of territorial domination. Controlling land was not crucial for establishing political authority in cases where inhabitants could easily flee whenever they were not satisfied with their ruler.

Another important feature was the weight of kinship. While pre-colonial Africa was overwhelmingly rural and agrarian like other pre-modern societies, its conspicuous feature was a predominance of the principle of kinship. Lineage networks based on familial ties were by far the most important compared with other networks, such as clientship, existing in pre-colonial Africa (Coquery-Vidrovitch 1982: 67). The weight of familial ties logically implied the substantial autonomy of rural communities vis-à-vis the state. In addition, the level of technologies available for political authorities also constrained their territorial control. Rulers in pre-colonial Africa were extremely short of infrastructure to broadcast power. When Fanti leaders in what is now Ghana approved the so-called Mankessim Constitution to formalize their Confederation in 1871, one of its primary goals was "to make good and substantial roads" (Herbst 2000: 42).

In sum, African pre-colonial states lacked the capability to formally establish control over a large territory beyond the center of the polity. Their territory was generally small, as shown, for example, in pre-colonial kingdoms in the Great Lakes region, two of which later became Rwanda and Burundi (Ogot 1984). Even in cases where the claimed territories were considerably large, like the empire of Mali or Songhay, their ability to extract resources under ruled areas was deemed quite limited, as the state revenue depended mainly on long distance trade rather than agriculture (Cissoko 1984). It was on this basis that Coquery-Vidrovitch (1969: 77) pointed out, in arguing about the "African mode of production," the "absence of a true despotism aiming at a direct exploitation of the peasant class." Although judging whether African pre-colonial states had constructive state–society relations or not is beyond the scope of this chapter, it is safe to say that, in comparison with states in later periods, they had only limited capabilities to seize and extract resources from society, thereby leaving the latter ample room for autonomy.

3 Land in African colonial states

African colonial state and its change

In his seminal work, Crawford Young divided the colonial period into two stages according to the nature of African colonial states. The first was the period of constructing "Bula Matari." Translated as "breaker of rocks," Bula Matari was originally a nickname for Henry Morton Stanley, an American explorer who brought to light the whole course of the Congo River and, in collaboration with the ambitious Belgian King Leopold II, opened the way to the establishment of the Congo Free State. While the nickname spread over the regions through which Stanley passed, Bula Matari subsequently came to represent the newly established Congo Free State, with connotations of the intrusive, alien, crushing, and ruthless nature of its rule (Young 1994: 1).

Following the conquest of the African continent in the relatively short period between the end of the nineteenth century and the beginning of the twentieth, European powers set up, in haste, a shape of the state, with special emphasis on building hegemony and ensuring fiscal self-sufficiency. After crushing African resistance, systems for collecting the revenue through the head tax, requisitioning labor, and punishing those who refused to obey were quickly installed. As the metaphor of Bula Matari described, the rule was harsh and oppressive.

The end of World War I marked the second stage of colonial rule in Africa. Being armed with more effective administration and more sophisticated ideology than those in the previous period, the colonial state in this stage came to be rationalized and routinized. An important change, in this context, was that an idea of "development" appeared in the doctrine of the colonial state (Young 1994:

150). Although the independence of African colonies was out of the question for European countries at this stage, the principle of promoting the "well-being and development" of indigenous peoples came to be gradually accepted as an international norm following the conclusion of the Covenant of the League of Nations.[2] Development was also promoted from the viewpoint of fiscal self-sufficiency, as it would contribute to state revenue. In this context, African farmers were considered as the main actors for development, and their cash crop production was enhanced by the colonial authorities, though white farmers hampered it in the settler colonies such as South Africa and Kenya for fear of the competition (Mosley 1983).

Land policy under the colonial state

The evolution of land policy reflected the above-mentioned metamorphosis of African colonial states. During the period of Bula Matari, the land policy was characterized by despoliation, through which vast lands were transferred from Africans to the colonial states, white settlers, and private chartered companies. In the settler colonies, the systematic appropriation of land started in the very early stage. In the colony of Natal, which was proclaimed a British colony in 1843, the colonial government forced Africans to dwell in the native "locations" (i.e., reserves). By 1864, there were 42 locations with 2 million acres out of the total colonial area of 12.5 million acres. Legally, the rest of the colony was either owned by whites or held by the government as unassigned Crown lands (Thompson 1990: 97). In those days, Africans numbered at the lowest reckoning more than 300,000, while the Europeans, who numbered less than 20,000, owned most of the best land (de Kiewiet 1937: 188). It was in fact a clear precursor to the notorious Native Land Act in 1913, by which all Africans were obliged to reside in the reserves accounting for only 7 percent of the total national territory. In the case of Kenya, although it was in the inter-war period that the number of European immigrants to the so-called White Highlands markedly increased,[3] huge tracts of land had been alienated under the Crown Lands Ordinance of 1902 for leases of 99 years (Meek 1968: 79).

While the number of European settlers was limited in the French and Belgian colonies, the spoliation of land was also severe and systematic. The concept of "vacant lands without owner" ("*terres vacantes et sans maître*") was utilized for this purpose. The model of this policy could be found in the Congo Free State. The Ordinance of 1 July 1885, which was promulgated just after the creation of the country, claimed all "vacant" lands to be the property of the state. Due to this Ordinance, the overwhelming part of the territory was formally transferred to the hands of the colonial government, and then granted to chartered companies for concession. The same system was adopted in the French Equatorial Africa. At the end of the nineteenth century, almost all the territory of the French Congo (present Republic of Congo, Gabon, and Central African Republic) was divided among 40 big concession companies (Coquery-Vidrovitch 1972). While French West Africa did not see such a massive transfer of land through concession companies, it was due to the resistance mounted by French merchants, who had already developed their own activities and feared the entry of rival companies into the market.

Since the inter-war period, on a parallel with the change of colonial policy in general, the protection of African land rights came to be emphasized under the "indigenous policy." Although arguments for the protection of African rights as well as criticism against the massive land spoliation had not been unknown,[4] the inter-war period saw a systematic change in colonial land policies, in recognizing and formalizing customary laws for managing lands in rural areas.

In French colonies, the move was accelerated due to the total failure of the previous development policy depending heavily on chartered companies. The concept of "vacant land" was abandoned, and attempts were made to activate African customary laws by codifying them. For instance, three volumes of customary codes ("*les grands coutumiers*") were published in French West Africa (Comité d'études historiques et scientifiques de l'Afrique occidentale française 1939). In British colonies, customary powers were institutionalized in the colonial governance system. The Native Authorities were organized as a body representing traditional indigenous authorities, and they were officially allowed to exercise a wide range of customary powers (Hailey 1957: 414). In this system of "indirect rule," traditional chiefs were considered to be indispensable elements for the social stability of colonies. They had often to be "found" or "created" in some African societies that did not have a centralized political structure. The policy implied that African "tribes" were supposed to be in an organized state, each with its own territory, customs, and leadership (Mamdani 1996: 81). Although customary laws were not codified in the British colonies, the chiefs' judgments were respected and backed by the colonial authority, thus considerably reinforcing their personal power in comparison with the pre-colonial period. That was the reason why Mamdani (1996) called the system "decentralized despotism."

State control over society

Two characteristics can be identified with regard to the state–society relationship in the colonial period. Coercion and oppression were the first feature. Following the conquest, it was imperative for the colonial state to control the African societies and bring order. For this reason, a coercive system to provide security and to extract resources was rapidly established. The extraction heavily depended on a flat-rate poll tax (or hut tax) and labor requisition, particularly in the early stage of the colonial period. The Bula Matari had the capability to seize individual Africans and force them into paying taxes and providing labor. In this context, Africans were deprived of enormous amounts of land by force as well as by law. However, unlike pre-capitalist Europe and Japan, where the land tax or tributes of agricultural products was a critical component of state revenue, colonial authorities in Africa could not directly rob African farmers of their agricultural products. The introduction of a land tax was impossible in a society where the overwhelming majority of people depended on shifting cultivation.

Secondly, the state–society relationship was indirect and multiple. The colonial state established the relationship with African societies through the intermediation of "tribes." Under the indirect rule, "tribes" were indispensable means of territorial administration and were reorganized for this purpose. As typically shown in the Native Authorities in British colonies, African chiefs were institutionalized within the colonial governance, and were delegated considerable power from the colonial state. Their function was similar to "agencies for the provision of what are usually described as Local Government services" (Hailey 1957: 416). On the assumption that the group shared a common custom, chiefs of the "agencies" were provided with not only political but also administrative and judicial power over members. The legal pluralism thus became a prerequisite for the system[5] because, in addition to the statutory law, each "tribe" or the Native Authority was provided with its own customary law.

It is also important to note that, as agencies for the local government services, "tribes" were strictly connected to a territory. The colonial authority delegated the power to each Native Authority to rule over a defined territory. The territory had to be clear for the agencies to control people through such activities as communicating administrative orders, providing technical services, adjudicating conflicts, and so on. The Native Authorities, therefore, connected "tribes" to clearly defined territories, of which people was severely constrained from leaving. As a consequence of the indirect rule, the territorial adherence of each ethnic group was considerably reinforced and the ethnic difference came to be inevitably emphasized (Feder and Noronha 1987).

4 Post-colonial African states and land

Post-colonial African states

Independence did not automatically establish constructive state–society relationships in Africa. Rather, post-colonial African states have attracted attention because of the predicaments they face. In other words, Africa's recent difficulties, such as civil wars and economic crises, have been regarded as the results of the state dysfunction (Bayart 1993; Sandbrook 1985). The arguments can be roughly distinguished into two groups. On the one hand, scholars focused on a sharp contrast between "the empirical and the juridical in statehood" (Jackson and Rosberg 1982a). The independence of African countries could be attributed to the change of international norms rather than to maturity with regard to political economy as the sovereign state.[6] The emergence of the "quasi-states" (Jackson 1990) was an inevitable consequence of the mass-production of sovereign states. On the other hand, the nature of state governance has particularly attracted academic interest. In this context, the personal and patrimonial characters of governance under the one-party rule have been pointed out (Chabal and Daloz 1999; Jackson and Rosberg 1982b; Médard 1982). These studies stress the continuity of the nature of the state–society relationship in post-colonial African states with those in the pre-colonial and the colonial period.

Although the historical continuity has been an important feature characterizing post-colonial African states, the huge impacts that the end of the Cold War had on their nature should not be ignored. During the Cold War era, the oppressive and patrimonial nature of African states was tacitly endorsed and even protected by the major international powers, as both the western and the eastern blocs supported these problematic countries in favor of their allied politics. While the superpowers were quite eager to hold their allied countries in their own camps, tacit permission was given to the dubious nature of African states. The end of the Cold War induced drastic changes in the attitude of the western countries. As the eastern bloc disappeared, the West had no need to take the Cold War logics into account. Consequently, they instead put forward a new demand for democratization for African countries, as a condition of official development assistance. The demand produced dramatic effects in African countries, suffering from serious financial shortage because of protracted economic crises. Although the influence of African social movements for democratization should not be underestimated, it seems safe to say that the conditionality of aid was the main reason why the number of one-party states, which had accounted for two-thirds of all African countries at the end of the 1980s, rapidly decreased and finally disappeared in a few years (Bratton and van de Walle 1997; Clapham 1996).

Needless to say, the abolition of one-party rule did not automatically result in democratization in the true sense of the word. In fact, Africa saw, in the 1990s, the spread of democratic institutions and the frequent outbreak of serious armed conflicts at the same time (Takeuchi 2007). In quite a few among the countries introducing democratic systems, democracy has been fictitious, in the sense that a number of devices invalidating civil liberties have been maintained for the sake of rulers. However, it is also true that there are countries that have positively transformed the state–society relationship in the same period; Ghana and Benin have successfully promoted democracy to date. In sum, the end of the Cold War has clearly activated contentious politics in Africa (Tarrow and Tilly 2007).

Land policy until the 1980s

While newly independent African countries adopted a variety of land policies, common features were observable among them: the state hegemony over land was legally intact, or even strengthened, after independence. From the legal point of view, lands in African colonies could be categorized into three types: (1) registered lands ensuring private property rights mainly for white settlers; (2) national lands, over which the colonial state had assumed full and direct authority for the disposition; and (3) customary lands, over which reorganized indigenous institutions such as the Native Authorities were delegated the power to control. In settler colonies and South Africa,[7] a relatively small number of settlers occupied vast areas under their private property rights. For many of the newly independent African countries, however, the establishment of private property rights was not the policy priority. For example, in Côte d'Ivoire, although lawmakers adopted a new land law in 1963, which aimed at promoting the establishment of private property rights, the president F. Houphouët-Boigny relied on his prerogatives to suspend the promulgation (Ley 1972: 28). African leaders were generally not eager to rapidly introduce private property rights over customary lands, for fear that it would provoke social confusion.

The reasons why post-colonial states strengthened their legal control over land were multiple. Firstly, the scope of the state control was enlarged due to the effect of independence. In Burundi, customary lands were simply incorporated into the national land just before independence (Kolhagen 2010), thereby providing the state with the role of trustee of customary lands. Secondly, the resource nationalism had a significant impact, particularly in the 1960s and 1970s. The basic idea of the former Zairian land law in 1973 was that the state should have the supreme right over the whole national territory as well as the underground mineral resources. Thirdly, the socialist ideology contributed to reinforcing national control over land. Not only the Marxist-Leninist countries like Angola and Ethiopia, but also African socialist regimes like Tanzania, fiercely opposed the promotion of private property rights, which were supposed to exacerbate the economic gap among nationals.

New African states actively intervened in rural societies under the banner of modernization and development, though the results tended to be disappointing. Socialist countries were particularly eager to modernize rural areas. Adopting African socialism under J. Nyerere, Tanzania undertook endeavors to promote rural development. Following the Arusha Declaration in 1967, considerable efforts were made for villagization. The construction of Ujamaa villages was regarded as the first step to achieve African socialism. This stage should be succeeded by the formation of collective farms, which finally ought to be the sole agricultural production unit (Nyerere 1968). In reality, however, the construction of collective farms was confronted with strong resistance, and was officially abandoned in the 1980s. Mozambique was another country which sought to implement a radical policy of rural development. In this Marxist-Leninist country, the program of voluntary agricultural collectivization was an important pillar of socialist policy. The aim of the program has been to gather the dispersed rural population into centralized settlements – known as "communal villages" – and to increase productivity through state farms and cooperatives. Despite advances in the areas of health, education, habitation, and poplar political participation, the strategy could not achieve economic success. State farms as well as cooperatives performed poorly, thus leading to the serious decline of agricultural production. Within eight years of independence, the government was obliged to abandon the state-centered rural development strategy (Roesch 1984).

Some countries initiated land redistribution policies at the early stage after independence, though the consequences were rather ambiguous. Kenya was one such country. Following the negotiation for independence, the government purchased large-scale farms from white farmers willing to sell their properties to redistribute them to African small farmers. The resettlement schemes were implemented mainly from the 1960s to the 1970s, and more than 66,000 African families became beneficiaries (Abrams 1979: 19). However, the redistributed areas were only a limited part of the former white farms, of which the majority was transferred to Africans without being dismantled or remained intact in the hands of Europeans (Leys 1974). While the resettlement has arguably contributed to the growth of agricultural production (Green 1987), it brought about antagonism between settlers and original inhabitants, as many agriculturalist Kikuyu gained the lands and settled in the pastoralist Kalenjin area (see Chapter 6).[8]

Ethiopia was another country adopting radical policy reforms. The socialist revolution in 1974 caused considerable changes in rural society. The overlord system was dismantled and their properties were nationalized; the lands were redistributed to small-scale farmers and landless people; and rural modernization policies, including villagization and resettlement programs, were implemented. The consequences of the radical land reform in the 1970s were, however, disappointing. The general assessment was that the reform had little or no effect on the improvement of productivity. Moreover, it did not change the basic attitude of the Ethiopian state towards rural society, in the sense that "a command and control approach continues to dominate agricultural policy" (Abegaz 2004: 321). Although traditional leaders were eliminated in the course of the revolution, the hierarchical state–society relations were generally maintained, as they were only replaced by young party cadres under the socialist regime (Clapham 1988).

After independence, African post-colonial states strengthened legal control over land, and actively intervened in rural communities. This often resulted in marked changes in rural landscapes. However, with regard to state–society relations, independent African states had a clear continuity with their precursors, as they maintained hegemonic control over society. Even if the states were able to impose policies and change the landscape, they did not succeed in getting the expected results of increasing agricultural productivity. In stark contrast to Asian countries with the experience of the "green revolution," African agriculture has suffered from continuous stagnation. Also, the states did not succeed in extracting resources directly from agricultural producers. In abolishing the poll tax and labor requisition,[9] post-colonial African states reduced their capacity to take resources out of rural society. According to G. Hyden's well-known term, the state in Africa failed in "capturing" its peasants (Hyden 1980).

Land policies and land problems after the 1990s

Since the end of the Cold War, many African countries have launched land reform. Factors contributing to the wave of land reform are multiple.[10] Political changes were the most important driving force. In former settler colonies in Southern Africa, Zimbabwe and Namibia gained independence in 1980 and 1989, respectively, and the African National Congress took power in 1994 in South Africa and abolished apartheid. Land reform was one of the top priorities for these countries. Considering grave social injustice due to the massive land appropriation by white settlers and colonial authorities, it was quite natural that the newly established African-led governments stressed the importance of land reform.

With regard to the land distribution progamme, many countries have adopted the "willing buyer, willing seller" principle, under which property rights of white settlers are ensured and only the area that was "willingly" sold can be redistributed to Africans. While the principle has contributed to preventing the drastic outflow of white farmers and social confusion, it has made the progress of land reforms extremely slow, thus making their fruits intangible for the majority of citizens. It was mainly for this reason that Zimbabwe abandoned the principle and adopted a more radical method of land redistribution (Fast Track Land Reform Programme) in the late 1990s.[11] Assessments of the policy change have been highly controversial as well as polarized. Supporters have praised its effects of activating small-scale African farmers, while opponents have emphasized the incidental violence against white farmers and nepotism regarding land acquisition (Cliffe *et al.* 2011; Pilossof 2012). The "willing buyer, willing seller" principle has been severely criticized also in South Africa, in which the prevailing opinion has been that land reform has so far failed in producing expected results (James 2007; Republic of South Africa 2012).

Although it is understandable that the Southern African governments have been quite eager to obtain tangible results from reform, land redistribution tends to always be controversial. In addition to the simple fact that transforming a socio-economic distortion that has been formed since the colonization requires a long time, the policy assessment itself may be problematic. As the land redistribution may affect social values relating to land in various ways, policy assessments are likely to be polarized according to political stances with regard to which value should be prioritized. In South Africa, serious debates have continued between those who aim at restoring social identity and social justice through the land distribution and those who prioritize economic efficiency and agricultural development (Leyshon 2009).

Southern African countries are not the only place where land reform policies have been implemented. Land tenure reforms without land redistribution have been actively carried out in Africa since the 1990s, as more than 20 countries have revised or newly enacted land laws for this purpose (Alden-Wily 2003). As mentioned above, political liberalization in the same period has formed an important background to this trend. In addition, an ideological change in land and property rights should be pointed out. Through influential studies like those by North (1981) and de Soto (1989), the key role of property rights for economic development has been widely recognized. In this context, against the backdrop of a broad consensus on the importance of customary land rights and that of state intervention for their protection (Ostrom 1990; Platteau 1996), recent land laws tend to officially recognize and protect customary land rights, though the concrete measures taken have considerably varied (Alden-Wily 2011; Deininger and Binswanger 2001). For instance, Tanzania enacted in 1999 the Village Land Act, which was characterized by the cardinal decentralization of land administration. The law designated the Village Council, a local body composed of 25 elected adult members of a village, as a land manager in charge of tasks including managing lands in accordance with the customary law of the area, issuing certificates of customary title, and adjudicating land disputes among villagers.

The recent wave of land (tenure) reforms, aiming at ensuring small farmers' land rights, has been generated in the context of democratization as well as increasing land shortages due to various reasons including rapid population increase.[12] Can the policies provide land tenure security for the majority of rural inhabitants? Can they consequently promote economic development, as theorists of new institutional economics advocate? Considering the short period since the implementation of new land laws, it may be too early to assess the results of recent land tenure reforms. For a better understanding of the attempts as well as their challenges, an in-depth case study would be helpful.[13] In the next section, recent land policies in Rwanda and their background are analyzed. Rwanda has made serious efforts towards systematic land registration for several years, and will complete the provision of land certificates for all over its territory. We will explore the background of this first experience in Africa and examine its effects and challenges.

5 Rwanda's post-conflict state building and the land

Rwanda is a tiny country in Central Africa. With 10 million people living in an area smaller than Belgium, it is one of the most densely populated countries in Africa. The population is composed of three ethnic groups: the Hutu comprises the overwhelming majority (more than 80 percent), while the Tutsi is a minority, and the Twa is an extremely small group of hunter-gatherers comprising around 1 percent. The three groups share a language (kinyarwanda) and a religions (Christianity and Islam), and live in mixture in the hilly country. While the distinction of and hierarchical relations among the groups can be traced back to the pre-colonial period, they were formalized and considerably strengthened as a consequence of the colonial administration,[14] thereby provoking resentment among the discriminated majority, Hutu, and causing violent ethnic clashes at the last stage of the colonial period. The clashes resulted in the collapse of the Tutsi-led political system and the massive outflow of Tutsi refugees to neighboring countries.[15] It was their second generation who organized a Tutsi-led rebel group, the Rwandan Patriotic Front (RPF), and invaded the homeland in 1990. Ethnic antagonism in the civil war finally resulted in mass killing, in which at least 500,000 Tutsis were slaughtered in 1994 (Straus 2006). The war came to an end with the RPF's total victory, and consequently massive numbers of Tutsi refugees, who had been obliged to stay abroad for decades, returned to the homeland.

Winning the war, the RPF carried out a series of radical interventions in relation to land. Firstly, the massive number of Tutsi returnees were provided with parcels of land for dwelling and cultivation. Under a policy called "land sharing" (Musahara and Huggins 2005), Hutu inhabitants were ordered to give up a half of their lands and provide them to returnees without compensation. Secondly, women's inheritance rights for land were officially recognized in 1999. This was a drastic change from Rwandan customary land tenure, in which women had virtually no rights regarding the inheritance of land. Thirdly, following the adoption of the new land law in 2005, Rwanda has made serious efforts towards land tenure reform (Sagashya 2012). The new land law, emphasizing rational and productive land use, made land registration obligatory.[16] A policy of systematic land registration has been in place since the late 2000s with the help of international donors. As a consequence, the demarcation of land plots has been completed throughout the territory, and certificates had been distributed for about half of the plots as of June 2012.[17] This makes Rwanda the first African country that has completed land registration throughout the territory. Positive effects of the land registration including increases in investment have been reported (Ali *et al.* 2011).

With the policy providing lands for returnees, guaranteeing women's land rights, and promoting land registration, will Rwanda successfully establish land tenure security and reduce land conflicts? The effects of the land registration should be deliberately examined taking the whole background information into account. Three points are particularly important in this regard. The first one is related to the arrangement of registration. In Rwanda, registering a land plot under the name of an extended family member is officially recognized. Such a system of registration has enabled the postponement of dealing with the problem of inheritance among family members that is yet to be completed or where there is a dispute over the division. Without this arrangement, it is certain that an innumerable number of land conflicts would have erupted, as contention about inheritance among family members is the most frequent pattern of Rwandan land dispute (Lankhorst and Veldman 2009). However, this arrangement may exert an unintended effect in combination with another regulation, namely that prohibiting dividing land that is equivalent to or less than 1ha.[18] This regulation makes the official division of land very difficult because the majority of land parcels are already less than 1ha.[19] As it is virtually impossible to ban farmers from dividing their lands for inheritance, the division will surely continue informally. Consequently, the gap between the registered records and the reality of land tenure will be widened. Over time, the informally divided land plots may turn into something similar to the previous customary lands, in which land conflicts among right-holders would be quite likely to break out. It may be unlikely that land registration contributes to reducing land disputes among family members.

Secondly, the hegemonic nature of the state–society relationship did not change in comparison with the previous regime. The victory of the RPF in 1994 led to the collapse of the Hutu-led political regime and the establishment of the Tutsi-led regime. Although the RPF government introduced democratic political institutions, its rule has been generally considered as authoritarian.[20] With regard to land, such a characteristic is well reflected in the policy of land consolidation, which is defined as "a procedure of putting together small lots of land in order to manage the land and use it in an efficient uniform manner so that the land may give more productivity (*sic*)."[21] Under this policy, farmers are requested to plant the same crops, such as maize and rice, in designated areas. Although the policy may be advantageous for farmers possessing relatively large plots, those who have only a tiny plot tend to prefer to cultivate a variety of products for subsistence. However, their demands to plant crops that they want have always been rejected. Despite the official statement that it is local farmers who choose the crops to be planted, agricultural officers in the local administration determine them and give no other choice to farmers.

The third point is connected to Rwandan political stability. While the "land sharing" policy is radical and coercive, it has not triggered massive resistance to date. The fundamental reason that Hutu inhabitants have accepted the policy is that the RPF's rule has been strong enough to enforce it. Based on military might, the former rebel group has maintained a virtual monopoly of state power in the post-conflict period and has so far succeeded in suppressing the discontents (Beswick 2010; Reyntjens 2011). Although the returnees' land rights were officially recognized by the 2005 land law and through the process of registration, they are essentially fragile in the sense that they are basically underpinned by the RPF's coercive power. It is foreseeable that resentment of the Hutu farmers will erupt in the future whenever RPF rule is destabilized. Property rights guaranteed by enforcement are fundamentally fragile.

Rwanda's post-conflict land policies such as the provision of land for returnees and land registration agree with international trends. Securing land rights for returnees has been strongly emphasized in the recent literature on peace-building.[22] There is also no doubt that land registration is one of the most effective tools to ensure land rights. However, historical backgrounds should be taken into account for the in-depth understanding of a policy. The case study clearly shows that Rwanda's recent land policies have been considerably framed following the historical path. The policy of "land sharing" was adopted exactly because the RPF has the same ethnic affiliation with the Tutsi returnees and it won the war. One may speculate that the RPF took advantage of the new land law and land registration to formalize returnees' land rights. While it is difficult to prove such a speculation, Rwandans understand the post-conflict land policies in this context.

Rwanda is not a special case. As political philosophers including Hobbes and Locke have argued, property rights need to be endorsed and protected by a political authority, which is, in the contemporary world, the state. It is, therefore, not surprising that property rights tend to be fragile when political order is unstable and that they tend to be biased in favor of state power-holders.[23] In other words, the stability of property rights depends essentially on the nature of the state–society relationship. Post-conflict Rwanda has so far ensured land rights in building a strong state capable of imposing rules on society. What is unclear, however, is how far such a rule, based on military power and enforcement, will be sustainable. The long-term stability of property rights would require a sustainable state–society relationship, in which political actors share the rule in order that political power struggles do not turn into serious political violence. The real challenge for Rwanda, therefore, will be to transform the nature of the state–society relationship so as to ensure long-term political stability.

6 Land tenure security in Africa

Since the end of nineteenth century, when modern states were established in Africa by European powers, Africans have made tremendous efforts to transform the imposed states into their own states, with which they can enter into the social contract. After more than 100 years since then, both African states and their societies have considerably changed. On the one hand, independence and democratization after the end of the Cold War have made African states more responsive to societies. As a result, official land policies have shifted from spoliation to the protection of Africans' rights. On the other hand, in stark contrast with the African societies of 100 years ago, it is totally impossible today to generalize about them being land abundant. Due to various reasons including rapid population growth, frequent outbreaks of armed conflict, and the rising market pressure caused by the heightened demand for foods and bio-energies, African land has become increasingly scarce.

While independence and democratization have contributed to the normalization of the African state–society relationship, land tenure security has not been ensured for many Africans, particularly for small-scale farmers. Rather, because of the eruption of land conflicts and enormous land grabs in rural areas (Anseeuw and Alden 2010; Deininger and Byerlee 2011), their land tenure security tends to be more jeopardized than ever. To tackle the crises, it is of course important to take legal and institutional measures including the enactment of appropriate land laws and the promotion of land registration, for which the international community should provide assistance. However, it should be remembered that, as this chapter shows, the long-term security of land and property rights requires a sustainable state–society relationship. Considering Africa's turbulent past, which is filled with severe experiences such as colonization, dictatorship, and a series of armed conflicts, a long period of time might be needed before political actors agree to prevent internal violence, and until people really feel that their land rights are secured.

Notes

1 The focus of this chapter is on Sub-Saharan Africa. Hereinafter, "Africa" refers substantially to Sub-Saharan Africa.
2 Article 22 of the Covenant stressed this point, in stipulating "there should be applied the principle that the well-being and development of such peoples [indigenous people in colonies] form a sacred trust of civilisation and that securities for the performance of this trust should be embodied in this Covenant."
3 The term White Highlands refers to an area located in the uplands in central Kenya. Because of good soil and temperate weather conditions, the British East Africa colony, founded in 1905, encouraged British immigration into the area.
4 King Leopold's atrocity in the Congo was fiercely denounced in the UK and the US at the beginning of the twentieth century (Morel 1906).
5 On legal pluralism, see for example Moore (1973) and Griffiths (1986).
6 One of the landmarks was the "Declaration on the granting of independence to colonial countries and peoples," a resolution adopted by the United Nations General Assembly at its fifteenth Session on 14 December 1960 (A/RES/1514(XV)).
7 South Africa's independence in 1910 exerted no influence on the colonial nature of the country. It rather accelerated the racial segregation and thus resulted in the enactment of the Native Land Act in 1913. It was only after the abolition of the apartheid policy that the country initiated the land reform.

8 On this point, see for example Africa Watch (1993) and Hornsby (2012).
9 As a symbol of oppression, African new leaders were eager to deny, at least verbally, the colonial state and its administration system.
10 The recent surge of land right reform has been marked not only in Africa; rather, it is a worldwide phenomenon (Borras *et al.* 2007; Lipton 2009).
11 It should also be noted that the UK government's virtual refusal of assistance for land reform was an important background of this policy change.
12 In 2008, the average population density in 48 African countries was 33.8 persons per square kilometer, while the figures considerably vary from Mauritius (622 persons) to Namibia (2.6 persons). The number might be considered to be modest, as it is not far from that in Europe in the eighteenth century. The average ratio of population to arable land in the same African countries in the same year was, however, considerably high, as it amounted to 395.4 persons per square kilometer (calculated from data in World Bank 2011). Africa can no longer be generalized as a land-abundant continent.
13 As a recent attempt of this kind, see Holden *et al.* (2013).
14 As to the Rwandan ethnic groups and their transformation, see Newbury (1988).
15 This political process has been referred to as the "social revolution." See Lemarchand (1970) for details.
16 Organic Law No.08/2005 of 14/07/2005, Determining the Use and Management of Land in Rwanda, article 30. See Pottier (2006) for an assessment of the law.
17 Interview with the Deputy Director-General of the Rwanda National Resource Authority on 1 October 2012.
18 Article 20 of the 2005 land law.
19 According to official statistics, the average farmland per household was 0.76ha; the average number of farm fields per household was four; and the proportion of households owning more than 1ha accounted for 20 percent (Republic of Rwanda 2010: 36).
20 International assessments such as the "Freedom in the World" and the "Worldwide Governance Indicators" have continuously pointed out that political rights and civil liberties have been tightly restricted in Rwanda. See their website for details.
21 Article 2 of the 2005 land law.
22 See the Pinheiro Principles (UN 2005) as well as Leckie (2008).
23 This is what Hobbes described in his classical work, *Leviathan*, particularly in Chapters 15 and 24. On this point, see also Fitzpatrick (2006).

References

Abegaz, B. (2004) "Escaping Ethiopia's poverty trap: the case for a second agrarian reform," *Journal of Modern African Studies*, 42 (3): 313–42.

Abrams, P.D. (1979) *Kenya's Land Resettlement Story: How 66,000 African Families Were Settled on 1,325 Large Scale European Owned Farms*, Nairobi: Challenge Publishers and Distributors.

Africa Watch (1993) *Divide and Rule: State-Sponsored Ethnic Violence in Kenya*, New York: Human Rights Watch.

Alden-Wily, L. (2003) *Governance and Land Relations: A Review of Decentralisation of Land Administration and Management in Africa*, London: International Institute for Environment and Development.

Alden-Wily, L. (2011) "'The law is to blame': the vulnerable status of common property rights in Sub-Saharan Africa," *Development and Change*, 42 (3): 733–57.

Ali, D.A., Deininger, K., and Goldstein, M. (2011) "Environmental and gender impacts of land tenure regularization in Africa: pilot evidence from Rwanda," Policy Research Working Paper 5765, Washington DC: World Bank.

Anseeuw, W. and Alden, C. (eds) (2010) *The Struggle over Land in Africa: Conflicts, Politics and Change*, Cape Town: HSRC Press.

Bayart, J.F. (1993) *The State in Africa: The Politics of the Belly*, New York: Longman.

Beswick, D. (2010) "Managing dissent in a post-genocide environment: the challenge of political space in Rwanda," *Development and Change*, 41 (2): 225–51.

Borras, S.M. Jr., Kay, C., and Akram-Lodhi, A.H. (2007) "Agrarian reform and rural development: historical overview and current issues," in A.H. Akram-Lodhi, S. M. Borras Jr., and C. Kay (eds) *Land, Poverty and Livelihoods in an Era of Globalization: Perspectives from Developing and Transition Countries*, Abingdon: Routledge.

Bratton, M. and van de Walle, N. (1997) *Democratic Experiments in Africa: Regime Transitions in Comparative Perspective*, Cambridge: Cambridge University Press.

Chabal, P. and Daloz, J.P. (1999) *Africa Works: Disorder as Political Instrument*, Oxford: James Currey.

Cissoko, S.M. (1984) "The Songhay from the 12th to the 16th Century," in D.T. Niane (ed.) *General History of Africa IV: Africa from the Twelfth to the Sixteenth Century*, Paris: UNESCO.

Clapham, C. (1988) *Transformation and Continuity in Revolutionary Ethiopia*, Cambridge: Cambridge University Press.

Clapham, C. (1996) *Africa and the International System: The Politics of State Survival*, Cambridge: Cambridge University Press.

Cliffe, L., Jocelyn, A., Ben, C., and Rudo, G. (2011) "An overview of fast track land reform in Zimbabwe: editorial introduction," *Journal of Peasant Studies*, 38 (5): 907–38.

Comité d'études historiques et scientifiques de l'Afrique occidentale française (1939) *Coutumiers Juridiques de l'Afrique Occidentale Française*, Vols 1–3, Paris: Larose.

Coquery-Vidrovitch, C. (1969) "Recherche sur un mode de production africain," *La Pensée*, 144: 61–78.

Coquery-Vidrovitch, C. (1972) *Le Congo: au Temps des Grandes Compagnies Concessionnaires*, 1898–1930, Paris: Mouton & Co.

Coquery-Vidrovitch, C. (1982) "Le régime foncier rural en Afrique noire," in E. Le Bris, E. Le Roy, and F. Leimdorfer (eds) *Enjeux Fonciers en Afrique Noire*, Paris: Karthala.

de Kiewiet, C.W. (1937) *The Imperial Factor in South Africa: A Study in Politics and Economics*, Cambridge: Cambridge University Press.

de Soto, H. (1989) *The Other Path: The Invisible Revolution in the Third World*, New York: Harper & Row.

Deininger, K. and Binswanger, H. (2001) "The evolution of the World Bank's land policy," in A. de Janvry, G. Gordillo, J.P. Platteau, and E. Sadoulet (eds) *Access to Land, Rural Poverty, and Public Action*, Oxford: Oxford University Press.

Deininger, K. and Byerlee, D. (eds) (2011) *Rising Global Interest in Farmland: Can it Yield Sustainable and Equitable Benefits?* Washington, DC: The World Bank.

Feder, G. and Noronha, R. (1987) "Land rights systems and agricultural development in Sub-Saharan Africa," *World Bank Research Observer*, 2 (2): 143–69.

Fitzpatrick, D. (2006) "Evolution and chaos in property rights systems: the third world tragedy of contested access," *Yale Law Journal*, 115: 996–1048.

Green, J.K. (1987) "Evaluating the impact of consolidation of holdings, individualization of tenure, and registration of title: lessons from Kenya," *LTC Paper* 129, Land Tenure Center.

Griffiths, J. (1986) "What is legal pluralism?" *Journal of Legal Pluralism and Unofficial Law*, 1 (24): 1–55.

Hailey, L. (1957) *An African Survey: A Study of Problems Arising in Africa South of Sahara* (revised 1956), London: Oxford University Press.

Herbst, J. (2000) *States and Power in Africa: Comparative Lessons in Authority and Control*, Princeton, NJ: Princeton University Press.

Holden, S., Otsuka, K., and Deininger, K. (eds.) (2013) *Land Reforms in Asia and Africa: Assessing Impacts on Poverty and Natural Resource Management*, Badsingstoke: Palgrave Macmillan.

Holsti, K.J. (1996) *The State, War, and the State of War*, Cambridge: Cambridge University Press.

Hornsby, C. (2012) *Kenya: A History Since Independence*, London: I.B. Tauris.

Hyden, G. (1980) *Beyond Ujamaa in Tanzania: Underdevelopment and an Uncaptured Peasantry*, London: Heinemann.

Jackson, R.H. (1990) *Quasi-state: Sovereignty, International Relations and the Third World*, Cambridge: Cambridge University Press.

Jackson, R.H. and Rosberg, C.G. (1982a) "Why Africa's weak states persist: the empirical and the juridical in statehood," *World Politics*, 35 (1): 1–24.

Jackson, R.H. and Rosberg, C.G. (1982b) *Personal Rule in Black Africa: Prince, Autocrat, Prophet, Tyrant*, Berkeley, CA: University of California Press.

James, D. (2007) *Gaining Ground: "Rights" and "Property" in South African Land Reform*, Abingdon: Routledge-Cavendish.

Kolhagen, D. (2010) "Vers un nouveau code foncier au Burundi?" in S. Marysse, F. Reyntjens, and S. Vandeginste (eds) *L'Afrique des Grands Lacs, Annuaire 2009–2010*, Paris: L'Harmattan.

Lankhorst, M. and Veldman, M. (2009) *La proximité de la justice au Rwanda: rapport socio-juridique sur les modes de gestion des conflits fonciers*, RCN Justice & Démocratie.

Leckie, S. (ed.) (2008) *Housing, Land, and Property Rights in Post-Conflict United Nations and Other Peace Operations: A Comparative Survey and Proposal for Reform*, Cambridge: Cambridge University Press.

Lemarchand, R. (1970) *Rwanda and Burundi*, London: Pall Mall Press.

Ley, A. (1972) *Le Régime Domanial et Foncier et le Développement Economique de la Côte d'Ivoire*, Paris: Librairies Générale de Droit et de Jurisprudence.

Leys, C. (1974) *Underdevelopment in Kenya: The Political Economy of Neo-Colonialism 1964–1971*, Berkeley, CA: University of California Press.

Leyshon, D.J. (2009) "Land reform, restitution and entitlement in post-apartheid South Africa," *Journal of Southern African Studies*, 35 (3): 755–68.

Lipton, M. (2009) *Land Reform in Developing Countries: Property Rights and Property Wrongs*, Abingdon: Routledge.

Mamdani, M. (1996) *Citizen and Subject: Contemporary Africa and the Legacy of Late Colonialism*, Princeton, NJ: Princeton University Press.

Médard, J.F. (1982) "The underdeveloped state in tropical Africa: political clientelism or neo-patrimonialism," in C. Clapham (ed.) *Private Patronage and Public Power: Political Clientelism in the Modern State*, London: Frances Pinter.

Meek, C.K. (1968) *Land Law and Custom in the Colonies*, 5th edition, London: Frank Cass.

Moore, S.F. (1973) "Law and social change: the semi-autonomous social field as an appropriate subject of study," *Law & Society Review*, 7 (4): 19–46.

Morel, E.D. (1906) *Red Rubber: The Story of the Rubber Slave Trade Flourishing on the Congo in the Year of Grace*, New York: The Nassau Print.

Mosley, P. (1983) *The Settler Economies: Studies in the Economic History of Kenya and Southern Rhodesia, 1900–1963*, Cambridge: Cambridge University Press.

Musahara, H. and Huggins, C. (2005) "Land reform, land scarcity and post-conflict reconstruction: a case study of Rwanda," in C. Huggins and J. Clover (eds) *From the Ground Up: Land Rights, Conflict and Peace in Sub-Saharan Africa*, Pretoria: Institute for Security Studies.

Newbury, C. (1988) *The Cohesion of Oppression: Clientship and Ethnicity in Rwanda, 1860–1960*, New York: Columbia University Press.

North, D.C. (1981) *Structure and Change in Economic History*, New York: W.W. Norton.

Nyerere, J. (1968) *Ujamaa-essays on socialism*, Dar es Salaam: Oxford University Press.

OECD (2007) *Principles for Good International Engagement in Fragile States & Situations*, Paris: OECD.

OECD (2011) *Supporting Statebuilding in Situations of Conflict and Fragility: Policy Guidance*, Paris: OECD.

Ogot, B.A. (1984) "The Great Lakes region," in D.T. Niane (ed.) *General History of Africa IV: Africa from the Twelfth to the Sixteenth Century*, Paris: UNESCO.

Ostrom, E. (1990) *Governing the Commons: The Evolution of Institutions for Collective Action*, Cambridge: Cambridge University Press.

Pilossof, R. (2012) "'The future is bright' versus 'the future is bleak': a comparison of recent documentaries on land reform in Zimbabwe," *Journal of Southern African Studies*, 38 (4): 1007–11.

Platteau, J.P. (1996) "The evolutionary theory of land rights as applied to Sub-Saharan Africa: a critical assessment," *Development and Change*, 27: 29–86.

Pottier, J. (2006) "Land reform for peace? Rwanda's 2005 land law in context," *Journal of Agrarian Change*, 6 (4): 509–37.

Republic of Rwanda (2010) *National Agricultural Survey 2008*, Kigali.

Republic of South Africa (Department of Rural Development and Land Reform) (2012) *Midterm Review of the Department of Rural Development and Land Reform*, Pretoria.

Reyntjens, F. (2011) "Constructing the truth, dealing with dissent, domesticating the world: governance in post-genocide Rwanda," *African Affairs*, 110 (438): 1–34.

Roesch, O. (1984) "Peasants and Collective agriculture in Mozambique," in J. Barker (ed.) *The Politics of Agriculture in Tropical Africa*, Beverly Hills, CA: Sage.

Rotberg, R.I. (ed.) (2004) *When States Fail: Causes and Consequences*, Princeton, NJ: Princeton University Press.

Sagashya, D. (2012) "Rwanda: reforming land administration to enhance the investment environment," in X. Shen and X. Sun (eds) *Untying the Land Knot: Making Equitable, Efficient, and Sustainable Use of Industrial and Commercial Land*, Washington, DC: The World Bank.

Sandbrook, R. (1985) *The Politics of Africa's Economic Stagnation*, Cambridge: Cambridge University Press.

Straus, S. (2006) *The Order of Genocide: Race, Power, and War in Rwanda*, Ithaca, NY: Cornell University Press.

Takeuchi, S. (2007) "Political liberalization or armed conflicts? Political changes in post-cold war Africa," *Developing Economies*, 45 (2): 172–93.

Tarrow, S. and Tilly, C. (2007) "Contentious politics and social movements," in C. Boix and S.C. Stokes (eds) *The Oxford Handbook of Comparative Politics*, Oxford: Oxford University Press.

Thompson, L. (1990) *A History of South Africa*, New Haven, CT: Yale University Press.

UN (United Nations, Economic and Social Council, Commission on Human Rights) (2005) *Economic, Social and Cultural Rights, Housing and Property Restitution in the Context of the Return of Refugees and Internally Displaced Persons,* Final Report of the Special Rapporteur, Paulo Sérgio Pinheiro, principles on housing and property restitution for refugees and displaced persons. (E/CN.4/Sub.2/2005/17).

World Bank (1989) *From Crisis to Sustainable Growth – Sub-Saharan Africa: A Long-Term Perspective Study*, Washington, DC: World Bank.

World Bank (1993) *The East Asian Miracle: Economic Growth and Public Policy*, Oxford: Oxford University Press.

World Bank (2001) *World Development Report: Building Institutions for Markets* (*World Development Report* 2002), Washington, DC: World Bank.

World Bank (2011) *Africa Development Indicators 2011*, Washington, DC: World Bank.

Young, C. (1994) *The African Colonial State in Comparative Perspective*, New Haven, CT: Yale University Press.

Zartman, I.W. (ed.) (1995) *Collapsed States: The Disintegration and Restoration of Legitimate Authority*, Boulder, CO: Lynne Rienner Publishers.

Part II

State failures and successes

6 Land disputes and post-election violence in Kenya

Takashi Yamano and Yuki Tanaka

1 Introduction

Following the Kenyan presidential election in December 2007, people who were not satisfied with the election results resorted to violence. Attacks targeting certain ethnic groups induced revenge attacks, resulting in over two months of civil unrest throughout the country. Almost 1,000 people were reported killed and around 500,000 were internally displaced due to the post-election violence (PEV) (Human Rights Watch 2008). Many experts had anticipated election-related ethnic conflicts would occur in Kenya because ethnic clashes have become a common phenomenon during and after presidential elections since 1992 when the first election under the multi-party system was held (Kimenyi and Ndung'u 2005).

Although the trigger of the violence was clearly the presidential election in 2007, there are various hypotheses as to its root causes. The first hypothesis is that the violence was caused by conflicts among ethnic groups. The 2007 presidential election was in essence a contest between the incumbent President Kibaki, a Kikuyu, and the opposition candidate Odinga, of Luo origin, each of whom involved different ethnic groups to form a coalition for the election campaign. One of the central issues during the election was devolution or decentralization.[1] On the one hand, Odinga represented the voice of the smaller ethnic groups that had felt marginalized by the central government and yearned for devolution of power. On the other hand, President Kibaki represented the largest ethnic group, the Kikuyu, and others who favored a strong centralized system (Gibson and Long 2009; Nguyen 2007). Thus, PEV can be considered as part of the power struggle between these two groups. Another hypothesis is that the violence was motivated by land conflicts. Rift Valley Province, where the violence occurred most prevalently, is also a land that was once controlled largely by the white settlers during the British colonial era but then re-allocated to indigenous people and immigrants at independence. Therefore, the seeds of land conflict existed between the indigenous Kalenjin and Maasai people and the immigrants, notably the Kikuyu since independence (Kimenyi and Ndung'u 2005). This is distributional and ethnic conflicts associated with the new state building that leads to contentious politics according to our analytical framework discussed in Chapter 1 (see particularly Figure 1.1). If the root cause of the violence is the deprivation of land from the original owners by the white settlers and then by the immigrants, then the risk of future incidence of violence will never be abated unless the land dispute or political contentions arising from it are resolved. If it is solely about the devolution of political power, then the devolution will abate future conflicts and contribute to political stability. To prevent incidences similar to the 2007 PEV, and ensure political stability for economic development, it is vital that the root cause of the violence is identified and relevant policies are put in place.

As was reviewed in Chapter 5, conflict arising from insecure land rights has become a major issue in state building in Sub-Saharan Africa (SSA), where the value of land has been rising due to rapid population growth. The case of Kenya is particularly relevant because of prolonged land disputes due to the failure to establish secure land rights. The purpose of this chapter is to explore whether and how insecure land rights and PEV are related by using household-level panel data. Prior to the 2007 PEV, about 800 rural households in the central and western regions of Kenya were interviewed twice in a panel survey (Yamano *et al.* 2011). Then, in March 2009 we re-interviewed 275 households that were part of the panel survey and were originally located in Rift Valley Province and the adjacent Nyanza Province. If they were still internally displaced at the time of the 2009 interview, we found and interviewed them at their relocated areas. As a result, we found that about 10 percent of the household members had been victims of violence, 11 percent were internally displaced, and 23 percent hosted at least one internally displaced person. In the analyses below, we estimate the determinants of becoming a victim, being displaced, and hosting displaced people to identify the root causes of the 2007 PEV.

The organization of this chapter is as follows: First, Section 2 explains the background to the 2007 presidential election and the violence that ensued as well as its relation to land disputes; in Section 3, data and simple descriptive statistics are introduced; in Section 4, the regression model and variables are explained; Section 5 discusses the results; and the last section concludes with policy implications.

2 History of violence in Kenya

The 2007 presidential election and PEV

In the presidential election that was held on December 27, 2007, the main contestants were the incumbent President Kibaki and candidate Odinga. These two candidates had previously cooperated under the National Rainbow Coalition (NARC) and, in the presidential election in 2002, together won against candidate Kenyatta who was backed by the then Moi administration. Within NARC, the following agreements had been reached as conditions for appointing Kibaki as a presidential candidate for the 2002 election (Tsuda 2010): (1) divide the cabinet posts equally between the Democratic Party (DP) group which was led by Kibaki and the other group which was led by Odinga; (2) set up a new constitution and devolve to the Prime Minister part of the authority that the President held under the existing constitution; and (3) support Odinga to be elected as the Prime Minister.

However, as the new government was formed, the process of cabinet formation and constitutional reform faced constant delay, and the relationship between the camps under NARC started to fall apart. The existing constitution, which had been written at the time of independence from the British, gives the Kenyan President significant power, initially designed to overcome obstacles for state building. During the presidential campaign for the 2002 election, NARC pleaded to devolve certain presidential power to other posts and regional governments. However, the "new" constitution proposal, which was drafted under the close supervision of the newly elected President Kibaki, failed to devolve much presidential power. The draft was eventually vetoed by the disillusioned public in the referendum of 2005, greatly undermining public support for President Kibaki. Meanwhile, Odinga newly formed the Orange Democratic Movement (ODM) and continued to gain support throughout the country by setting up the Pentagon, a political partnership among regional politicians from not only Nyanza Province where he comes from but also from the Western, Rift Valley, Eastern, and Coastal Provinces. The significance of this partnership was that it was not those politicians in the Central Province where capital Nairobi is situated, but the regional provinces that strongly desired political decentralization, who agreed to side with Odinga.

Against this background, the two former allies contested for the presidency in the 2007 election. Furthermore, the two candidates represented not only their own ethnic groups, but also other ethnic groups that were pulled into each camp, thus polarizing political support along ethnic lines. The resulting voting pattern as surveyed in an exit poll, described in Gibson and Long (2009), is shown in the Appendix to this chapter, Table 6.A1 (see p. 135). The countrywide exit poll randomly selected polling stations and surveyed 5,495 randomly selected voters. The sampling was proportionate to population size in each region. According to this exit poll, 94 percent of Kikuyu voters voted for Kibaki (who is Kikuyu), 98 percent of Luo voters voted for Odinga (Luo), and 86 percent of Kamba voters voted for the third candidate Musyoka (Kamba). None of the candidates can reach a simple majority from their own ethnic group as Kikuyu, Luo, and Kamba make up only 23 percent, 13 percent, and 10 percent respectively of the population.[2] The candidates needed support from other ethnic groups. For example, both Kibaki and Odinga fielded a Vice President candidate from the Luhya tribe, the largest among the remaining ethnic groups, in order to attract Luhya votes (Gibson and Long 2009). As a result, 75 percent of the Luhya voted for Odinga and 23 percent for Kibaki. Odinga, in addition, succeeded in acquiring regional support and gained 88 percent of votes from the Kalenjin people, to which the previous President Moi belonged. Among other smaller ethnic groups, the Kisii and Maasai took a neutral stand.

Under this intense competition, the exit poll predicted Odinga to be slightly in the lead for the presidential seat. The exit poll suggested that Odinga had won the seat, registering 46.1 percent of total votes against Kibaki's 40.2 percent. Allowing for a sampling error of ±1.32 percentage points, Odinga's victory could be established with statistical significance. In fact, in the parliamentary election that was conducted at the same time as the presidential election, Odinga's ODM won against President Kibaki's Party of National Unity (PNU) by a large margin. However, on the evening of December 30, three days after the voting, the Electoral Commission of Kenya (ECK) reported that Kibaki had won 46.4 percent and Odinga 44.1 percent of the total votes (see Appendix Table 6.A1). Immediately after this announcement, violence broke out in the Nairobi slums and other major cities and soon developed into a series of attacks throughout the country, quickly worsening public order that was not to be restored for over two months (Commission of Inquiry on Post Election Violence 2008; Human Right Watch 2008).

Initially, the main targets of the violence were the Kikuyu people, to which President Kibaki belonged. They were attacked in various places including the Kibera Slum of Nairobi, the city of Kisumu of Nyanza Province, and locations in Coastal Province that are inhabited by Kikuyu and Luo people. In Rift Valley Province, not only spontaneous attacks but also more systematic raids, mainly organized by groups of Kalenjin origin, occurred (Commission of Inquiry on Post Election Violence 2008). The difference between the violence that occurred in Rift Valley and other places was that the politicians in Rift Valley were reported to deliberately fuel the land dispute between the different ethnic groups and appeal to the discontent of the people who had been deprived of land in order to win more public support during the election campaign. Human Rights Watch (2008) reported that several Kalenjin politicians spread rumours to make their people believe that once ODM occupied the presidential office, they would be able to make the Kikuyu leave the province and would redistribute the land among indigenous ethnic groups. Thus, in this particular province, the violence could be said to be highly related to land dispute, resulting in violence of a more serious scale and consequence. The following sub-section describes the land issue in the Rift Valley in more detail.

Violence and land dispute

At independence from the British rule, the new Kenyan government redistributed land that had been previously controlled by white settlers. The fact that part of the lands were then given to immigrants is often cited as a cause of the land conflict in the Rift Valley Province (Daudeline 2002; Kimenyi and Ndung'u 2005). Before colonization, land was managed by communities and allocated to households as seen fit by them. No land certificates were issued, but the user rights were recognized and protected as such by community members. Ignoring the existence of such unwritten land rights, the colonial government appropriated the most fertile plots of land in Kenya that amounted to 2.8 million hectares and gave them to white settlers (Kimenyi and Ndung'u 2005). The Kikuyu people, who had lived in populated Central Province, moved to relatively large-scale farms in the Rift Valley High Highlands as farm workers. The Luo and Luhya that had inhabited the Western Province also emigrated to the Rift Valley in pursuit of better employment.

The situation became more complex in Rift Valley when, at independence, the land redistribution program covered not only the Kalenjin people, who were indigenous to the land, but extended to the Kikuyu, Luo, and Luhya people who had moved there as farm labor.[3] There is also a view that the Kikuyu people were given preferential treatment in the redistribution due to the ethnic attachment of the first President Kenyatta and many other Kikuyu officers who occupied high posts in the government. Obviously, new state building created ethnic conflicts. In the early days of independence, however, when land was in relative abundance and when people had high hopes for economic growth, land issue was not considered a serious problem, as elsewhere in SSA (see Chapter 5). As the economy remained stagnant and the expanding rural population halved the per capita landholding from 0.46 hectares in 1960 to 0.23 hectares in 1990 (Jayne *et al.* 2003), increased demand for land led to more frequent land-related disputes.

Nonetheless, violence as a physical expression of discontent from such land disputes became discernible only after almost 30 years following independence in 1963. The first incident of violence between ethnic groups was reported in the year prior to the 1992 presidential election. Following this, violence has been repeatedly reported at every presidential election. Kimenyi and Ndung'u (2005) report the causes and consequences of the conflicts prior to 2007 in our sample districts of Rift Valley and Nyanza Provinces (see Appendix, Table 6.A2, pp. 135–136). They show that violence happened just before and after the presidential elections, was more prevalent in regions where a high percentage of land is allocated to immigrants, and has occurred between the indigenous and immigrant ethnic groups. Apart from Rift Valley Province, violence has occurred in slums around Nairobi and the coastal areas where immigrants live in significant numbers. Yet, another common characteristic of these places is that various ethnic groups live side by side and that the fear or feeling of antagonism towards the "other" ethnic group may escalate very quickly during election campaigns that are highly tuned along ethnic lines. In this sense, some argue that the violent clashes between the ethnic groups during the PEV was nothing more than a political contest, and that land disputes are rather irrelevant.[4] If such a view is a true reflection of the PEV, then the root cause of the problem will not be weeded away even if land disputes are resolved. Instead, political resolution should be sought. In order to identify the root cause of the PEV and draw relevant policy implications, we need to identify factors underlying the PEV.

3 Data and descriptive statistics

In this chapter, we use panel data of 295 households from Rift Valley and Nyanza Provinces in Kenya (see Table 6.1). These households are sub-samples of 800 households that participated in the 2004 and 2007 surveys as part of the Research on Poverty, Environment, and Agricultural Technology Project

Table 6.1 Ethnicity of sampled households[a]

Province district	*Sample size*	*Ethnic composition of sample households*						*Voting difference (Gap)*[b]
		Kikuyu	*Maasai*	*Kisii*	*Luhya*	*Kalenjin*	*Other*	
	(A)	*(B)*	*(C)*	*(D)*	*(E)*	*(F)*	*(G)*	*(H)*
	Number	*%*	*%*	*%*	*%*	*%*	*%*	*% point*
Rift Valley								
Nakuru	138	75		1	3	18	2	50.7
Nandi	46				15	85		–71.3
Narok	17	12	88					–34.4
Nyanza								
Kisii	61			100				–7.2
Nyamira	33			97	3			12.1
Total	295	36	5	32	4	22	1	

Notes: [a] The ethnic groups that had relatively strong support for President Kibaki are shown towards the left, and those for candidate Odinga towards the right.

[b] Average figure. For estimation method, refer to the main text. The figure is a subtraction of percentage points that candidate Odinga gained from those gained by President Kibaki. Therefore, a positive number indicates support for Kibaki and a negative number shows support for Odinga.

(RePEAT).[5] In March 2009, about 15 months after the onset of PEV, we targeted 311 sample households who were located in Rift Valley Province, where the violence occurred most prevalently, and in two districts in the adjacent Nyanza Province. The five districts surveyed in March 2009 are the following: Nakuru, Nandi, and Narok in Rift Valley Province, and Kisii and Nyamira in Nyanza Province. To reduce the attrition rate, we traced households that had been displaced by the PEV and were living away from their original locations. As a result, out of the 311 targeted sample households, we re-interviewed 295 households, and thus the attrition rate was 5.1 percent. Although the attrition rate was small and we did not find any systematic patterns in the attrition, it is still possible that the attrition occurred because of the PEV to some extent. If we had been able to interview those who were missed, we might have found larger impacts of the PEV on the sample households. Thus, the results here should be treated as conservative estimates. We include households in Nyanza for comparison to the households in Rift Valley Province. However, violence was experienced in Nyanza Province too, as we discuss in the following sections. At the same time, not all the households were affected by the PEV even in Rift Valley Province. There is heterogeneity regarding the scale of damage among districts as well as among households within a district. The original panel data did not anticipate the PEV, but were collected for analyses on agricultural production and poverty in Kenya. Nonetheless, the 2004 survey asked a relevant question on whether sample households were concerned about future land conflicts. This and related issues with land conflicts were analyzed in Yamano and Deininger (2009).

We show ethnic compositions of sampled households in Table 6.1. To highlight the relationship between the ethnic and political affiliations, the ethnic groups are ordered in such a way that the leftmost is the group that supported Kibaki most in the presidential election. In Nakuru, 75 percent of the sampled households are Kikuyu who supported Kibaki and 18 percent are Kalenjin who supported Odinga. As we have already discussed, clashes had occurred between the two ethnic groups in Nakuru District in the past. However, households from the two ethnic groups do not necessarily live in the same community. In our sample, too, it is rather rare to see more than one ethnicity in a community. Therefore, it is more realistic to think of this mix of ethnicity in Nakuru as a mix of different ethnic communities in the district. In the other two districts in the Rift Valley, there was more than one ethnic group that supported the same candidate but to different degrees. In Nandi District, Kalenjin, who mainly supported Odinga, live with Luhya, who partly supported him. In Narok District, Kikuyu, who supported Kibaki, live with Maasai, who partly supported him. Thus, in all three districts, there are multiple ethnic groups, but the kind and degree of political affiliation is different from district to district, making the task of measuring the degree of political confrontation difficult.

One of the appropriate measures of political confrontation may be the percentage of votes gained by each candidate in each district in the 2007 presidential election. The previous studies have argued that violence is more likely to happen in close contests because close contests increase absolute numbers of unsatisfied voters, and it is therefore easier to enlist militiamen to fight for their cause (Collier *et al.* 2009). In fact, at the national level, the 2007 presidential election was a close contest, as shown in Table 6.A1. On the other hand, however, we know from newspaper articles and reports that a higher level of violence occurred toward Kibaki supporters. This may suggest that the larger the difference between percentages of votes gained by President Kibaki and candidate Odinga, the higher the sense of political confrontation between the peoples within the district, and the higher the probability that violence will occur as a result. Thus, to test the hypothesis, we estimated the relationship between the voting difference and the probability of violence in the regression models.

At the local constituency level, Weis (2008) reports the official results of the 2007 presidential election. By using the data, we matched each of our sample communities with the nearest constituency and took the difference between the percentage vote gained by president Kibaki and by candidate Odinga:

$$Gap_i = \hat{S}_i^{Kibaki} - \hat{S}_i^{Odinga}$$

By using this equation, we measured the degree of political confrontation in each sample community. In other words, if this figure is a positive number, then it means that community i supported president Kibaki, and if it is a negative number, then it means that community i supported candidate Odinga. In Table 6.1, we present the results from the above calculations for each district. In Nakuru District, where there is a large Kikuyu population, Kibaki has 50.7 percentage points above candidate Odinga. In other districts, except Nyamira, Odinga won more votes than Kibaki. The differences are especially large in Nandi and Narok at 71 and 34 percentage points, respectively. In Kisii and Nyamira, the differences are much smaller.

Table 6.2 shows the proportion of household members that were directly affected by the PEV: 11 percent of male members and 9 percent of female members answered to have been victims. Noteworthy is that 18 percent of men in Nakuru district answered to have experienced violence during the PEV. One feature of this particular PEV is that even in Kisii, Nyanza Province, where incidences of violence were few and far between in the past, 7 percent of men and 5 percent of women were victims of violence. This suggests the sheer scale of the PEV.

As for displacement, 23 percent of households in Nakuru District were displaced. In other places, only 1 household was displaced in Nandi District. Of the 33 households that were displaced, 13 of them took refuge in relatives' homes, 8 in rented houses, 5 in their own houses in other locations, 4 in housing or camps provided by the government, and 3 in other places. Furthermore, 11 households had not yet returned to their original home as of March 2009, or 15 months after the violence. As we have already discussed in a previous section, Nakuru District is the area where land-related conflicts had occurred in the past.

Among our samples, 22.5 percent of households have hosted at least one displaced person since the 2007 PEV. The average hosting period is 17.2 person-months for the entire sample. The person-months are calculated by adding the total months of all internally displaced persons (IDPs) who stayed with hosts. The average person-months is over 26 in Nakuru District, where the proportion of hosting households is the largest at 26 percent. As for the relationship of the hosted person to the hosting household head, 42 percent is own relative, 10 percent is wife's relative, 14 percent is other relatives, and 34 percent is non-relative. In the two districts in Nyanza Province, around 20 percent of households also hosted IDPs. Since we did not find any displaced households in our sample in Nyanza, we speculate that the reason for the high proportion of hosting households there is that they accommodated people who fled from the neighboring Rift Valley areas.

4 Hypotheses and estimation models

Hypotheses on the causes of violence

As we discussed in the previous section, there are several hypotheses on the root causes of PEV. In this chapter, we classify them into three hypotheses:

Hypothesis 1: politically driven violence
Hypothesis 2: violence driven by the land issues
Hypothesis 3: opportunistic criminal activities

Table 6.2 Percentage of victimized individual and displaced households

Province district	*Victimized individuals*		*Displaced households*		*Hosting households*		*Internally displaced persons*	
	Male (A)	*Female* (B)	*Percentage* (C)	*Period*[a] (D)	*Percentage* (E)	*Period*[b] (F)	*Ratio*[d] (G)	*Period*[e] (H)
	%	%	%	*Months*	%	*Months*	%	*Months*
Rift Valley								
Nakuru	18.4	17.8	23.2	7.5[c]	26.0	26.5	15.2	5.4
Nandi	2.4	1.9	2.2	15	9.5	6.9	3.7	2.9
Narok	2.0	1.3	0	–	16.3	20.0	9.0	2.4
Nyanza								
Kisii	7.2	5.0	0	–	22.6	4.3	5.0	2.0
Nyamira	5.4	2.4	0	–	22.2	5.2	5.1	2.5
Total	10.6	9.2	11.2	7.7	22.5	17.2	9.0	4.5

Notes: [a] Average period of displacement among displaced households.

[b] Average period of hosting among hosting households. This figure is the person-months figure, i.e. if the household hosted two people for three months, it is counted as six months.

[c] Among 33 households that were displaced, 30 percent or 11 households still lived away from home as of March 2009 (15 months after the start of the violence). The survey was conducted at their place of refuge.

[d] Ratio of internally displaced persons to sampled number of household members in the district shown as a percentage of the latter.

[e] Average period of internally displaced persons staying in the hosting households.

If Hypothesis 1 explains the root cause of the violence, we should find that our respondents from certain ethnic groups have a higher probability of experiencing violence regardless of their characteristics, except for basic observables such as age and gender. Human Rights Watch (2008) reports that people were attacked by a mob after showing their IDs and being identified as members of targeted ethnic groups. If such ethnic antipathy is the root cause, then people from the targeted ethnic groups could be attacked more in areas where the voting was closely fought than in areas where one candidate or his political party dominates. Thus, we should find the likelihood of violence peaks when the voting gap is close to zero.

If Hypothesis 2 explains the root cause, on the other hand, factors that are related to land holdings affect violence, in addition to the factors that affect violence under Hypothesis 1. The ownership of official land titles is especially relevant as it may help temporarily displaced people reclaim their land after returning to their home. If they do not own official land titles, it would be difficult to assert their land rights in communities that are hostile to them. Kenya has one of the most advanced land titling programs in SSA. Yamano *et al.* (2009), for instance, found that their sample households had land titles on 72 percent of their plots in Central and Western Kenya. There are, however, those households who do not own land titles and are afraid of eviction in Kenya. Yamano and Deininger (2009), who studied the 2004 survey data that are part of our panel data, found that about 10 percent of the land conflicts were over eviction and use rights, which are more likely to be related to ethnic conflicts. The remaining 90 percent of the land conflicts were about boundaries, inheritance, and land sales. These conflicts were mostly among neighbors and relatives, mostly within the same ethnic group. Therefore, in this chapter, we create two dummy variables: one for households who were concerned about land conflicts over eviction or use rights at the time of the 2004 survey and another for households who were concerned about land conflicts over boundaries, inheritance, and land sales. In addition to these variables, we also include variables on land size and years of settlement. If Hypothesis 2 is valid, then these land-related variables should have a strong influence on the violence.

Lastly, if the PEV was simply conducted by opportunistic criminals, then the mobs would have targeted wealthy households. The mobs may use factors that are related to Hypotheses 1 and 2 to cover up their greedy objectives. Thus, we may still find the variables that are related to Hypotheses 1 and 2 significant. But in addition, we should find wealth-related variables to have a strong influence on the violence.

Note that the hypotheses in this chapter are not mutually exclusive. The estimation results may not help us identify only one hypothesis over the other two hypotheses. This is a major limitation of this study but may reflect the reality of the violence that took place in Kenya in 2009. However, by examining the results closely, we hope that we can obtain a better understanding of the root causes of the violence and, hence, draw specific policy implications to prevent future violence in Kenya and other countries. For instance, if the independent variables that are related to Hypothesis 3 are not statistically significant, we can eliminate this hypothesis. Similarly, if the land-related variables are not statistically significant, we can eliminate Hypothesis 2.

Estimation models

To test these hypotheses, we estimate the following model on the probability of experiencing violence at the individual level:

$$\Pr(v_{ij} = 1) = f(P_{ij}, L_{ij}, A_{ij}, H_{ij})$$

where v_{ij} is a dummy variable of individual i, who is a member of household j, that takes 1 if the person has experienced any violence related to the PEV. P_{ij} is a set of variables that are related to political conflicts. L_{ij} is a set of land-related variables, and A_{ij} is a set of variables, such as the total asset value and the per capita expenditure in 2004, that indicate initial household wealth before the PEV. Finally, H_{ij} is a set of basic individual and household characteristics that are not included in P_{ij}, L_{ij}, or A_{ij}. If Hypothesis 1 is the root cause of the violence, then we should find P_{ij} to be significant factors on the violence but not L_{ij} or A_{ij}. If Hypothesis 2 is the root cause, then we should find L_{ij} to be significant factors, but we are unable to draw any direct predictions on P_{ij}. The political turmoil may provide an environment for people to engage in violence originally rooted in land issues. On A_{ij}, we should not find them significant once we control for land size. Nonetheless, our focus remains on L_{ij} for Hypothesis 2: we should find L_{ij}, such as land title and concerns over land conflicts, insignificant for the other two hypotheses. If Hypothesis 3 is the root cause, then we should find A_{ij} to be significant factors. Again the political turmoil may provide an environment for mobs to engage in opportunistic violence. Thus, we may find P_{ij} to be significant but not L_{ij}. As we discussed in the previous section, these hypotheses are not mutually exclusive. Especially, it is difficult to exclude Hypothesis 1 while supporting Hypothesis 2 or 3. We discuss more on this issue in the Conclusion.

In addition to the determinants of the probability of experiencing violence during the PEV, we also investigate the determinants of internal displacement and hosting of IDPs. In the 2009 survey, we asked the respondents if their household had been internally displaced and, if yes, how many months they were displaced for. We also asked the respondents to list any IDPs that their household hosted. On each of the hosted IDP, we asked about age, gender, relationship to the hosting household, and months he or she stayed at the household. From the list, we calculated the total person-months that the IDPs were hosted by the household. Thus, we use the months of the internal displacement by the household themselves and the total person-months of hosting IDPs as two dependent variables. Because the 2009 survey was conducted approximately 15 months after the PEV, the dependent variables are doubly-bounded at zero and 15 months. Therefore, we estimate the following using a double-bounded Tobit model:

$$y_{ij} = \begin{cases} 15 & if \;\; y_{ij}^* > 15 \\ y_{ij}^* & if \;\; 15 > y_{ij}^* > 0 \\ 0 & otherwise \end{cases}$$

$$where \;\; y_{ij}^* = f(P_{ij}, L_{ij}, A_{ij}, H_{ij})$$

The independent variables are as defined above.

Explanatory variables

The set of variables on political conflicts include ethnicity dummy variables, the difference between the estimated percentage vote between President Kibaki and candidate Odinga at the community level, as we describe in Section 3. If this difference is positive, it suggests that the community supports President Kibaki. Because Table 6.2 shows that districts that voted for Kibaki have high percentages of victims, we expect to find a positive coefficient on this variable. It is not clear, however, if it remains positive and statistically significant after controlling for other variables, such as ethnic dummies. If it remains positive and statistically significant, then it suggests that among people who have similar characteristics, such as ethnicity, those in areas that supported President Kibaki are more likely to experience violence.

In addition to these variables, we also include the average distance to the nearest two towns, measured at the household level, as an indicator for access to the political offices in towns. This variable is calculated using GPS information of the sample households and digitized road maps.

People who live close to urban areas, where political activities are more active, may be more likely to experience violence than people who live in remote rural areas. For instance, political activists who gather at offices in cities or towns may get violently excited, participating in a political rally or watching TV news, and engage in violent activities. The political offices may hold machetes and other tools that could be used as weapons. In contrast, however, it could be safer for mobs to engage in violent activities in remote hidden areas that are far away from the eyes of the police and other outsiders. Deininger (2003) found, for instance, that the probability of violence is higher in remote rural areas than rural areas that are close to urban areas.

The land-related variables include, as explained before, a dummy variable that takes 1 if the sample household owns land titles on any of their plots, a dummy variable that takes 1 if the sample household was concerned about future land conflicts in 2004 over eviction or use rights, and a dummy variable that indicates if the respondent was concerned about a land conflict over boundaries, inheritance, and land sales. We also include the land size and the number of years that the sample households have lived in the area. If the root cause of the violence lies in the grievances of indigenous farmers whose land was taken away by the white settlers and then by the immigrants, the most likely target would be new settlers who are not members of indigenous ethnic groups, are new to the area, and do not have official land titles. To represent household wealth, we use the per capita consumption and the number of cattle. The per capita consumption is obtained from the 2004 survey to represent household wealth before the presidential election in 2007. If the violence was driven by purely opportunistic criminal motives, however, mobs may not have detailed wealth information about the victims. They may use some observable wealth indicators to decide on targets. Thus, we also include the number of cattle owned as an indicator of observable assets. Finally, we include age and education of the individuals in the models in estimating the determinants of the violence at the individual level.

On the determinants of the displacement and hosting of displaced people at the household level, we include demographic variables (the number of male adults over 40 years old, the number of male members below 40, the number of female adults over 40, and the number of female members below 40), the age of household head, and a dummy variable for female-headed households.

5 Results

In Table 6.3, we present the results on the determinants of the violence at the individual level. First, we only include ethnic dummies to compare the results across ethnic groups. According to this table, Kikuyu people have about a

Table 6.3 Probability of being a victim of PEV (probit model)[a]

	(A)	*(B)*
Ethnic and political affiliation[b]		
Kikuyu	0.174***	0.108***
	(8.72)	(5.67)
Luhya	0.155***	0.177***
	(4.51)	(4.67)
Kisii	0.047***	0.413***
	(2.66)	(7.23)
Maasai	–0.038	–0.030
	(–1.20)	(–1.43)
Other	0.063	–0.040**
	(1.07)	(–2.04)
Nyanza Province (=1)		–0.172***
		(–7.74)
Voting difference: Kibaki–Odinga[c]		0.0329**
		(2.42)
Voting difference squared		–0.166***
		(–9.04)

(Continued)

Table 6.3 (Continued)

	(A)	*(B)*
Distance to nearest town (minutes)		0.615***
		(8.24)
Distance to nearest town (squared)		–0.331***
		(–7.11)
Land-related variables (L_{ij})		
Land title (=1)[d]		–0.038***
		(–3.49)
Concerned over land use or eviction (=1)[d]		0.0310*
		(1.84)
Concerned over other land dispute (=1)[e]		–0.005
		(–0.47)
Owned land size (acre)		–0.001
		(–0.92)
Years of settlement		0.000
		(0.67)
Household wealth variables (A_{ij})		
Per capita consumption[f]		–0.000
		(–0.03)
Number of cattle		–0.001
		(–0.83)
Individual and household characteristics (H_{ij})		
Age		0.002**
		(2.51)
Age squared		–0.000**
		(–2.00)
Female (=1)		–0.010
		(–1.29)
Years of schooling		–0.001
		(–0.70)
Urban (=1)		0.053***
		(3.24)
Sample size	2,802	2,619

Notes: [a] Numbers in parentheses are z-statistics. *, **, and *** indicate the 10, 5, and 1 percent levels of significance, respectively. The coefficients represent the marginal changes in probability.

[b] The base ethnic dummy is Kalenjin.

[c] "Voting difference" is the difference in proportion of votes gained by each candidate at the location level.

[d] "Land title" dummy is 1 if at least one of the plots of land used by the household is titled.

[e] "Concerned over land use or eviction" dummy takes 1 if the household head has ever been concerned about land dispute with non-relatives regarding eviction or use rights. "Concerned over other land dispute" dummy takes 1 if the household head has ever been concerned about any other land dispute with non-relatives or relatives.

[f] "Per capita consumption" data is taken from 2004 survey, in US dollars.

17 percentage point higher probability of being victimized than Karenjin people, who are the base group. Because President Kibaki is Kikuyu and the PEV was initially targeted the Kibaki supporters, and because Kikuyu people are minority settlers in Rift Valley, this result is as expected. What is not expected is that Luhya people have a 15.5 percentage point higher probability of being victimized than the Kalenjin people. As we discussed in Section 2, about three-quarters of the Luhya people as a whole ethnic group voted for Odinga. Thus, if the violence was driven purely by the results of the presidential election, Luhya should not be targeted at this high level. But they are also settlers in the Rift Valley who had been targeted in past conflicts, and the Luhya population is smaller than the Kikuyu population in Rift Valley. Thus, they might have been an easy target in this area.

Next, we add variables that are related to political confrontation, land issues, and household wealth, in addition to basic individual and household characteristics. The voting difference between President Kibaki and candidate Odinga is highly significant. The results suggest that the probability of the violence is higher in areas that supported President Kibaki, but as the difference becomes bigger, favoring for President Kibaki, the probability declines. According to the results, the peak of the violence is at the 10 percentage point difference, favoring for Kibaki. Thus, the result is consistent with the view held by previous studies that violence occurs in close contests (Collier *et al.* 2009). Since our result shows that there is a statistically significant correlation between political confrontation and the probability of experiencing violence even after controlling for ethnicity, the result supports Hypothesis 1.

Regarding the distance to urban centers, the probability is higher in remote areas: as the average distance to the nearest two towns increases, the probability of being victimized increases. This suggests either that the Kikuyu and Luhya people live away from towns or that the mobs conducted violence in remote areas to avoid the police, which is under the influence of the Kibaki administration.

On the land-related variables, we find that the land title protects the potential victims. Individuals whose household owns land titles have a lower probability, by 3.8 percentage points, of becoming victims than individuals without land titles. This indicates that the PEV was targeted at those people who do not have secure land titles. This result supports Hypothesis 2 that the violence is related to land conflict. Farmers without land titles were probably targeted by other farmers who disagreed with their land usage. In addition, those who have been concerned over eviction or land use rights have a 3.1 percentage point higher probability of being the victim than those who have not had such concerns. As expected, concerns over other reasons against relatives and neighbors are not related to the violence. Regarding household wealth, we do not find any evidence that wealthy households were targeted: the per capita consumption level in 2004 does not have any impact on the violence nor does the number of cattle. Thus, the results show little support for the opportunistic crime hypothesis.

Next, we present the results on the determinants of the length of internal displacement (see Table 6.4). Consistent with the results on the determinants of violence, the voting difference between the two candidates has a positive impact, with a decreasing size of the marginal impact as the voting difference increases, on the length of internal displacement. In the community that supported Kibaki, the respondents were internally displaced for a longer period than households in the community that supported Odinga. We also find that households with victims have a longer displacement period than those who do not have victims. Interestingly, we find that the ownership of the land title has a positive impact on the displacement. This may suggest that the households with land titles feel confident in reclaiming their land even if they flee. In contrast, those households who do not have land titles may feel insecure leaving their land because it would be difficult for them to reclaim it without land titles once they flee. As for household wealth, the per capita consumption level affects the length of displacement positively. The positive correlation between displacement and wealth may be due to the relative facility of being away from home longer rather than as a result of being chased away by looters.

Table 6.4 Length of displacement and hosting periods (probit model)[a]

	Period of displacement *(A)*	*Period of hosting* *(B)*
Ethnic and Political Affiliation (P_{ij})[b]		
Kikuyu	2.963	–2.791
	(0.50)	(–0.34)
Other	–3.767	–3.993
	(–0.52)	(–0.45)
Nyanza Province (=1)		15.45
		(1.22)
Voting difference[c]	5.661	10.17
	(0.99)	(1.23)
Voting difference squared	–20.27***	32.52***
	(–2.62)	(2.74)
Distance to nearest town (minutes)	60.94	–20.33
	(1.48)	(–0.52)
Distance to nearest town (squared)	–34.17	15.52
	(–1.26)	(0.66)
Household with at least one victim (=1)	16.65***	6.625
	(3.61)	(1.15)
Land-related variables (L_{ij})		
Land title (=1)[d]	8.678*	–11.67*
	(1.73)	(–1.82)
Concerned over land use or eviction (=1)[e]	2.190	9.992
	(0.41)	(1.17)

	Period of displacement (A)	*Period of hosting* (B)
Concerned over other land dispute (=1)[f]	1.076	−1.207
	(0.25)	(−0.20)
Owned land size (acre)	−0.004	−0.330
	(−0.01)	(−0.64)
Years of settlement	0.103	−0.035
	(0.83)	(−0.23)
Household wealth variables (A_{ij})		
Per capita consumption[e]	0.027**	0.053***
	(2.32)	(3.46)
Number of cattle	−0.138	0.706
	(−0.20)	(0.96)
Individual and household characteristics (H_{ij})		
Number of men aged 40 and over	−4.307	0.987
	(−0.78)	(0.14)
Number of men aged less than 40	−0.832	−0.670
	(−0.55)	(−0.30)
Number of women aged 40 and over	0.410	−1.051
	(0.10)	(−0.15)
Number of women aged less than 40	0.250	1.030
	(0.17)	(0.45)
Age of household head	−0.044	0.461**
	(−0.27)	(2.00)
Female-headed household (=1)	−1.213	4.864
	(−0.22)	(0.63)
Constant	−47.16**	−56.22**
	(−2.41)	(−2.39)
Sample size	190	270

Notes: [a] Numbers in parentheses are z-statistics. *, **, and *** indicate the 10, 5, and 1 percent levels of significance, respectively. The coefficients represent the marginal changes in probability.

[b] The base ethnic dummy is Kalenjin.

[c] "Voting difference" is the difference in proportion of votes gained by each candidate at the location level.

[d] "Land title" dummy is 1 if at least one of the plots of land used by the household is titled.

[e] "Concerned over land use or eviction" dummy takes 1 if the household head has ever been concerned about land dispute with non-relatives regarding eviction or use rights. "Concerned over other land dispute" dummy takes 1 if the household head has ever been concerned about any other land dispute with non-relatives or relatives.

[f] "Per capita consumption" data is taken from 2004 survey, expressed in US dollars.

Because internally displaced people escaped from the politically hot conflicts zones, we find that the households hosted displaced people in and out of the conflict areas. The voting difference and the distance variables, which are important determinants of the violence and displacement, have no impact on the hosting. The results also indicate that richer households with older household heads have hosted displaced people. This is probably because hosting displaced people incurs extra cost and possibly requires more patience and experience that only comes with age.

6 Conclusion

Violence may erupt again in Kenya in the future, unless political contention is resolved. After two months of PEV in 2008, Odinga, with other members of his party, joined the Kibaki government to form a joint government and are discussing the draft proposal for the new constitution.[6] The results in this study suggest that the deprivation of indigenous land by the white settlers followed by re-allocation of part of the land to immigrants is one of the root causes and that people without land titles were more likely to be victimized by the PEV than those who have land titles. We suspect that the mobs who attacked the victims who do not have land titles were hoping to obtain land from the victims. The victims would have a hard time reclaiming ownership of their land without official land titles once they had been chased away by the mobs. Thus, to prevent future conflicts, the Kenyan government needs to solve the land issue first. As the results in this study suggest, land title is a strong tool to protect the property rights of owners, even in times of armed conflict. Thus, the government should further assure the property rights of land titles. As Yamano and Deininger (2009) showed, landholding households often neglect updating land titles even after the deaths of the registered owners. The government should encourage land title holders to update them as necessary and non-holders to obtain new titles. However, the government should be careful not to create new conflicts by issuing land titles where disputes over land ownership are not settled. It may be a better idea to let regional offices, that have more accurate information on the situation on ground, settle disputes over land ownership.

It must be recognized that the ethnic confrontations are caused originally by land issues. There is therefore no exaggeration to argue that establishing a secure land ownership system is the foundation for state building geared towards economic development in Kenya. Since the value of land continues to increase in the course of development, insecure land ownership is bound to create social, economic, and political instability, which puts a brake on sustainable economic development. Since land tenure is often insecure in SSA (Holden *et al.* 2009; Stein *et al.* 2013), establishing a fair, secure, and commonly agreeable land ownership system is a major challenge facing many governments in this region.

The degree of land conflict could be eased through land market transactions. As the land sales markets in Kenya, as opposed to land rental markets, are among the most active in SSA (Yamano *et al.* 2009), land sales allow those who want to use land to have access to it without land disputes. It is not clear, however, if the land markets in Kenya still function effectively after PEV and without land title. Landowners may have become reluctant to sell land after PEV. This is an important research topic for the future, and the government should remove such fears from the land markets, if it aims to sustain agriculture-based economic development.

Appendix

Table 6.A1 2007 Presidential election: exit poll and ECK results[a]

Ethnicity	*Main candidates*			*Percentage of total voters*
	Kibaki (Kikuyu) (A)	*Odinga (Luo) (B)*	*Musyoka (Kamba) (C)*	*(D)*
	%	%	%	%
Exit poll				
Kikuyu	94.2	4.1	1.7	23.1
Luo	1.7	97.8	0.4	12.8
Kamba	10.1	3.8	86.1	10.0
Luhya	23.4	74.7	1.9	12.8
Kalenjin	9.3	88.0	2.7	10.0
Kisii	40.4	57.0	2.6	6.4
Mijikenda	23.7	72.0	4.3	3.9
Maasai	41.6	56.0	2.0	1.9
Meru	88.0	5.8	6.2	4.8
Total	40.2	46.1	10.2	100
ECK result				
Total	46.4	44.1	8.9	

Source: Gibson and Long (2009)

Note: [a] Sample size for the exit poll is 5,495. Multi-stage cluster sampling proportionate to population size is used with random selection of polling centers and respondents.

Table 6.A2 Characteristics of sampled districts and causes of past conflicts

Province district	*Percentage of alienated land (A)*	*Causes of past conflicts (B)*
	%	
Rift Valley		
Nakuru	59.0	1991–92, 96–97: conflict between Kalenjin community and immigrants (Kikuyu, Kisii, Luo, Luhya and Kamba). Over 1,500 people killed, 300,000 displaced. Many non-Kalenjin that were displaced from Molo and Olenguruone in 1991–92 had not returned to the farms by 1999. Some have sold or leased the farms to the Kalenjin. The clashes in Njoro were also on the farms.

(Continued)

Table 6.A2 (Continued)

Province district	*Percentage of alienated land (A)*	*Causes of past conflicts (B)*
Nandi	23.9	1991–92: the Nandi against other tribes. Deaths, displacement. One of the earlier examples is the clashes over the land titles on Mitetei Farm. The majority of non-Nandi (non-Kalenjin) shareholders claim to have been driven out before land titles were officially given to the remaining shareholders, most of whom were of Nandi origin. Other clashes were reported to be mainly politically motivated by KANU leaders.
Narok	39.0	1991, 93, 97, 2001: dispute between Maasai and Kisii/ Kikuyu tribes over grazing/agricultural land. Over 50 people killed, 30,000 displaced.
Nyanza		
Kisii	0	None

Sources: Kimenyi and Ndung'u (2005), Akiwumi Judicial Commission of Inquiry on Tribal Clashes (1999)

Notes

1 There are three broad categories of decentralization: devolution, delegation, and deconcentration (Sasaoka 2005). The so-called decentralization policies that have been implemented in Kenya in the past (such as the District Focus for Rural Development or Local Authority Transfer Fund) are mainly financial decentralization resulting in mere "deconcentration." It is often observed that political devolution, therefore, has not yet been achieved in Kenya (Crook 2003; Sasaoka 2005).

2 Ethnic composition of the entire population and that of Table 6.A1 may not be exactly the same as recent censuses do not report ethnic composition. However, as the sampling is carried out randomly proportionate to population size in each region, we can say that they are largely comparable.

3 Whether Kalenjin people actually controlled the land before colonization is questionable. The name, "Kalenjin," itself is said to be a dialect version of the opening words of a radio broadcast speech that called for volunteers to fight in World War II, "I tell you, I tell you," in Rift Valley region (Collier 2009: 69).

4 For instance, Member of Parliament Ruto from Rift Valley is reported to have said: "The issue of the PEV is not land . . . Kikuyus always sit on the land and the only problem is at the end of 5 years. It is all politics. Land is just an excuse" (Commission of Inquiry on Post Election Violence 2008).

5 RePEAT is funded by GRIPS's "21st Century COE" and "Global COE" projects (Yamano *et al.* 2011) Questionnaires and other detailed information can be obtained at http://www3.grips.ac.jp/~21coe/j/index.html. The data are available for research purposes.

6 On November 17, 2009, a committee of domestic and foreign experts submitted a new proposal for a new constitution. Although it is expected that the new proposal will transfer some power from the President to the Prime Minister, and from the central government to the regional offices (Committee of Experts on Constitutional Review 2009), others worry that minority groups could be marginalized by the regional offices.

References

Akiwumi Judicial Commission of Inquiry on Tribal Clashes. (1999) *Report of the Judicial Commission Appointed to Inquire Into Tribal Clashes in Kenya: Rift Valley*, www.scribd.com/doc/2204752/Akiwumi-Report-Rift-Valley-Province.

Collier, P. (2009) *Wars, Guns, and Votes: Democracy in Dangerous Places*, New York: Happer Collins.

Collier, P., Hoeffler, A. and Rohner, D. (2009) "Beyond greed and grievance: feasibility and civil war," *Oxford Economic Papers*, 61 (1): 1–27.

Commission of Inquiry on Post Election Violence (Waki Commission) (2008) *Waki Report*. Nairobi: Government of Kenya.

Committee of Experts on Constitutional Review (2009, November 17) *Harmonized Draft Constitution of Kenya*, www.coekenya.go.ke.

Crook, R.C. (2003) "Decentralization and poverty reduction in Africa: the politics of local-central relations," *Public Administration and Development*, 23 (1): 77–88.

Daudeline, J. (2002) "Land as a source of conflict and in post-conflict settlement," World Bank Regional Workshop on Land Issues in Africa and the Middle East, April 29–May 2, Kampala, Uganda.

Deininger, K. (2003) "Causes and consequences of civil strife: micro-level evidence from Uganda," *Oxford Economic Papers*, 55: 579–606.

Gibson, C.C. and Long, J.D. (2009) "The presidential and parliamentary elections in Kenya, December 2007," *Electoral Studies*, 28: 492–517.

Holden, S., Otsuka, K., and Place, F. (eds) (2009) *The Emergence of Land Markets in Africa: Assessing the Impacts on Poverty, Equity, and Efficiency*, Baltimore, MD: Resources for the Future.

Human Rights Watch (2008) *Ballots to Bullets: Organized Political Violence and Kenya's Crisis of Governance*, http://hrw.org/reports/2008/kenya0308.

Jayne, T.S., Yamano, T., Weber, M.T., Tschirley, D., Benfica, R., Chapoto, A., and Zulu, B. (2003) "Smallholder income and land distribution in Africa: implications for poverty reduction strategies," *Food Policy*, 28: 253–75.

Kimenyi, M.S. and Ndung'u, N.S. (2005) "Sporadic ethnic violence: why has Kenya not experienced a full-blown civil war?" in P. Collier and N. Sambanis (eds) *Understanding Civil War, Vol. 1: Africa*, Washington, DC: World Bank.

Nguyen, K. (2007, December 24) "Kenyan presidential campaigns wrap up with rallies," Reuters, http://www.reuters.com.

Sasaoka, Y. (2005) "Higashi Africa ni okeru chiho bunkenka ni tsuite" ["Decentralization in East African countries"], FASID Discussion Paper on Development Assistance, 7.

Stein, H., Otsuka, K., and Deininger, K. (eds) (2013) *Land Tenure Reforms in Asia and Africa: Assessing Impacts on Poverty and Natural Resource Management*, Basingstoke: Palgrave Macmillan.

Tsuda, M. (2010) "The experience of the National Rainbow Coalition (NARC): political parties in Kenya from 1991 to 2007," IDE Discussion Paper, No. 222.

Weis, T. (2008) "The results of the 2007 Kenya general elections," *Journal of Eastern African Studies*, 2 (2): 1–41.

Yamano, T. and Deininger, K. (2009) "Land conflicts among rural households: evidence from Kenya," in S.T. Holden, K. Otsuka, and F. Place (eds) *The Emergence of Land Markets in Africa: Impacts on Poverty, Equity, and Efficiency*, Washington, DC: Resource for the Future.

Yamano, T., Place, F.M., Nyangena, W., Wanjiku, J., and Otsuka, K. (2009) "Efficiency and equity impacts of land market in Kenya," in S.T. Holden, K. Otsuka, and F. Place (eds) *The Emergence of Land Markets in Africa: Impacts on Poverty, Equity, and Efficiency*, Washington, DC: Resource for the Future.

Yamano, T., Otsuka, K., and Place, F. (eds) (2011) *Emerging Development of Agriculture in East Africa: Markets, Soil, and Innovations*, Amsterdam: Springer.

7 Fiscal decentralization and development outcomes in India

*Kaliappa Kalirajan and Keijiro Otsuka**

1 Introduction

One of the central questions in development economics is why some countries have remained poor for a long period of time, even though the general policy approaches to combat poverty are well understood by policymakers around the world. A corollary to the above question is why a similar package of policies differs in efficacy across countries. Similarly, an identical set of policies differs in effectiveness across provinces or states within a country.[1] Drawing on the Post-Washington Consensus, it may be argued that the inability to achieve similar results from policy packages across states is due to the constraints posed by country-specific institutional or political factors. One of the major institutional factors directly involved in the delivery of public services and in implementing development policies is the degree of decentralization. Therefore, a key to enhancing the efficacy of policies lies in a better understanding of the extent and process through which various forms of decentralization contribute to development.

What do we understand by decentralization? Decentralization can best be understood as a political process in the sense of the devolution of resources, tasks and decision-making power to democratically elected lower-level authorities, which are largely or wholly independent of central government (World Bank 2000). It is rational to argue that decentralization facilitates time-specific and location-specific knowledge to implement policies that influence people's welfare. Decentralization in political, fiscal, and economic systems affects development outcomes in a number of ways. First, decentralized provision of social and physical infrastructures should correspond with the diverse demand conditions in different regions and match their resource endowments better than central provision. Even with regard to the provision of quasi-public goods, identification of target groups of beneficiaries is easier and implementation of policies more effective when undertaken by decentralized governmental units (Ostrom *et al.* 1993). Thus, even when there is some controversy over the redistributive role of sub-central governments, their desirability in implementing poverty alleviation policies is generally agreed upon (Brown and Oates 1987; Ladd and Doolittle 1982; Pauly 1973).

Second, competition among sub-central jurisdictions may promote innovations and enhance productivity. At the same time, as the decentralized governmental units function within a large nationwide unified market free from impediments to the movement of factors and products, it can provide a congenial environment for the efficient functioning of the market economy. Thus, drawing on the decentralization theorem introduced by Oates (1972), in an ideal decentralized system, existing resources will be allocated to yield the maximum possible output (locating on the production possibility frontiers) and the competitive environment, including inter-governmental competition, will be conducive for technological progress (shift in the frontier).

Third, and possibly most importantly, decentralization contributes to social, political, and economic stability as minority groups in the nation as a whole are often majority groups in the regions, and they can influence the policy for their benefit under the decentralized regime. Thus, political decentralization can be a fundamental institution by which the state or the central government can mitigate political contentions arising from inter-group conflicts, as is argued in Chapter 1.

In reality, the possibility of decentralization failing to overcome regional and local dimensions of poverty and inequality (Prudhomme 1995; Rodden 2002) may not be ruled out, mainly because the decision-making power on local developmental initiatives is often highly dependent on state bureaucracy. Further, decentralization may increase the probability of empowering local elites in capturing a larger share of public resources at the cost of the poor (Dreze and Sen 1996).

With the recent developments in the political arena, with a coalition government at the center, and different regional parties who are mostly partners of the coalition, the case study of the Indian experience of decentralization provides an important context for understanding the ways in which decentralization can influence overall socioeconomic welfare. The government of India passed a series of constitutional reforms in 1993 to democratize and empower local administrative institutions beyond the two tiers of the center and the states in the third tier of local governance that has been divided into three layers of district, sub-district and village, in terms of the 73rd Constitutional amendment. Since then, the experiences of different states with respect to decentralization has varied a lot. Though the literature on federalism explains the economic gains from decentralized decision-making and related issues (Rao and Singh 2003), there are very few empirical studies examining the causal relationship between decentralization and development outcomes. Much of the demonstrated gains are in the nature of assertions or qualitative statements. This study attempts to analyse and quantify the impact of decentralization in India on its social infrastructure that needs to be supplied by governments as it is not optimally provided by the private sector, and on rural development where about 70 percent of the population live.

The following section discusses some important issues concerning fiscal decentralization in India. The next section examines the measures of spatial disparity in social infrastructure development across states. The following section analyses the impact of decentralization on social infrastructure and on rural development. A final section brings out the overall conclusions of this study.

2 Fiscal decentralization in India – major issues[2]

The degree of decentralization or local autonomy depends on the Constitutional assignment and practices and conventions developed over the years. The basic framework of inter-governmental relationships in the Indian federation is given by the Constitutional assignment of functions and sources of finance. The seventh schedule to the Constitution of India specifies the union list (the exclusive domain of the central government), the state list (the exclusive domain of the state governments), and the concurrent list where both levels have joint jurisdiction.

An important feature of the Constitutional assignments in India is the centripetal bias in the assignment of powers. First, almost all broad-based taxes, with the sole exception of the sales tax, are assigned to the central government. Second, effectively, states do not have independent borrowing powers. When a state is indebted to the center, it must seek the center's permission to borrow. As all the states are indebted to the center, their market borrowing is determined by the Union Ministry of Finance in consultation with the Planning Commission and the Reserve Bank of India. Also the states cannot incur overdrafts with the Reserve Bank of India for more than 10 continuous working days. The Constitution not only assigns overwhelming powers to the central government due to the adoption of planned development strategy, but also has overriding powers in the event of a conflict in a concurrent jurisdiction.

Another reason for centralization has been the failure to specify the powers and functions of governmental units below the state level, until the 73rd Constitutional amendment was given effect. With the 1993 Constitutional amendment, however, it is mandatory to have a uniform system of local self-government (*Panchayati Raj*) throughout the country and the eleventh schedule specifies a list of 29 development actitvities to be carried out by the local bodies in rural areas concurrently with the state governments. The amendment also provides for regular elections to these *Panchayats* and objective methods of devolution of resources by appointing State Finance Commissions. At present, these amendments are being implemented gradually in many states. For example, among the South Indian states, Karnataka and Kerala have decentralized their local governance effectively by providing responsibilities to rural local bodies for all 29 development activities, not only through legislation, but also through actual implementation.

The above discussion brings out two important features. First, the potential economic and political benefits of decentralization in the Indian federation could not be achieved due to the centripetal bias in the constitution and the centralization of economic powers due to planning and other developments. Second, there has been a significant inter-state variation in the degree of decentralization and other institutional situations. This has impacted differently on states. Therefore, the analysis of different states should lead to a better understanding of the economic dynamics of decentralization.

Another important feature of the Indian fiscal federalism is that states have been assigned expenditure responsibilities far in excess of their revenue resources.

In particular, the Constitution assigns predominant responsibility for building social and physical infrastructure for rural development to the states. Also, being closer to the people, the states have to cater to the needs of the poor much more responsively than the central government. Furthermore, the capacity to raise revenues varies widely among the states. Variation in per capita income, even among the 14 general category states, is almost 1:4. General purpose transfers are required to offset these vertical and horizontal imbalances. Additionally, for services with a high degree of inter-state spillovers or those in the nature of merit goods, specific purpose transfers are necessary to ensure availability of certain minimum levels.

In India, both general purpose and specific transfers are given, but their design and implementation leave much to be desired. The Finance Commission, a statutory institution, and the Planning Commission, give general purpose transfers, but neither has been able to design the transfers to offset the fiscal disadvantages of the states with low revenue capacity and high unit cost of providing public services (Rao *et al.* 1998). In fact, the two agencies have sometimes worked at cross purposes. The bulk of the transfers given by both agencies is on the basis of general economic indicators and is not targeted to offset fiscal disadvantages of states with low revenue capacity and high unit cost of public services. The practice of filling projected budgetary gaps by the Finance Commission has created disincentives for prudent fiscal management. Thus, the general purpose transfers have not served the objectives of either equity or efficiency to the desired extent.

3 Is there spatial disparity in social infrastructure development?

As the major objective of decentralization is to provide easy access to local public goods that improve social infrastructure, we first examine the status of some of the indicators of social infrastructure across states. An effective functioning of decentralization across states is expected not to widen spatial disparity in social infrastructure development. We adopt the measure of weighted coefficient of variation to examine the trends in spatial balance in the basic social development indicators: infant mortality rate (IMR), life expectancy at birth (LE), literacy rate (LR), telecom density per thousand population (TD), and per capita electricity consumption (EC) in kwh. The results are given in Tables 7.1 and 7.2. The trends clearly show that there is a reduction in disparity in LR, and LE. In the case of IMR, the trends are less clear (see Table 7.1). The trends in infrastructure development, which include TD and EC, also show a general improvement, particularly in recent times (see Table 7.2).

Thus, there has been an improvement in recent times in four out of the five development indicators considered, and the progress appears to be more spatially balanced than before, recognizing the importance of decentralization. The movement towards more equitable levels of performance in recent times amidst rising development indicates that there are factors facilitating spatially

Table 7.1 The pace of development and spatial balance in development: selected human development indicators[a]

Year	*Life expectancy at birth*		*Year*	*Infant mortality rate*[b]		*Year*	*Literacy rate*	
	Average	*CV*		*Average*	*CV*		*Average*	*CV*
1983	60.2	0.740	1971	121	0.057	1971	32.8	0.083
1988	61.1	0.730	1976	123	0.065	1981	42.2	0.066
1990	59.2	0.754	1981	107	0.068	1991	51.2	0.058
1991	59.7	0.747	1986	95	0.069	2001	63.9	0.037
1993	60.5	0.738	1991	77	0.071	2002	64.2	0.032
1995	61.2	0.730	1994	53	0.124			
1999	62.1	0.720	1998	66	0.067			
2000	62.3	0.718	2005	54	0.068			
2001	62.5	0.716	2006	62	0.082			
2003	63.0	0.711						

Notes: [a] The coefficient of variation is calculated over data for 15 major states of India. The CV is estimated as a weighted measure using population shares of the states as weights.

[b] Per 1,000 people.

Table 7.2 The pace of development and spatial balance in development: selected infrastructural development indicators[a]

Year	*Telecom density (% population)*		*Year*	*Electricity consumption (kwh)*	
	Average	*CV*		*Average (per capita)*	*CV*
1980	0.38	0.335	1975	97	0.116
1985	0.40	0.166	1980	121	0.132
1987	0.47	0.172	1983	150	0.134
1988	0.48	0.172	1985	168	0.130
1989	0.52	0.173	1987	196	0.135
1990	0.55	0.167	1990	232	0.129
1991	0.62	0.165	1991	247	0.124
1992	0.71	0.160	1992	263	0.127
1993	0.83	0.159	1993	288	0.120
1994	1.00	0.161	1994	306	0.123
1995	1.20	0.163	1996	336	0.124
1998	1.68	0.128	2002	359	0.160
1999	2.37	0.150	2004	387	0.152
2000	2.68	0.150	2006	396	0.149
2003	4.24	0.156			
2004	5.69	0.162			
2006	10.74	0.125			
2007	15.85	0.114			

Note: [a] See notes to Table 7.1.

equitable social development. Which are the factors contributing to such equitable development? Is decentralization a significant contributing factor? Answers to these questions are attempted in the following pages.

4 Factors facilitating spatially equitable development

The central government intends to ensure equal access to basic services such as primary education, primary health care, and infrastructure such as roads, drinking water, electricity, and communication services across states. According to the third column of Table 7.3, states' own revenue barely accounts for 40 percent of their total revenue, which implies that transfers and grants from the center to states are quite important. States spend on average more than 50 percent of expenditure on revenue expenditure, which is recurrent expenditure to generate benefits in the current period including many basic services. However, the last column in Table 7.3 shows that states could finance their revenue expenditures by their own revenues only by about 56 percent. Therefore, the Centre shares some of its revenues from sources such as income tax with the states. Fiscal

Table 7.3 Trends in shares of state's own revenue and revenue expenditures (%)

Year	*State's total revenue to total expenditure*	*State's own revenue to total revenue*[a]	*State's revenue expenditure to total expenditure*[b]	*State's own revenue to state's revenue expenditure*
1990–91	77.2	35.2	54.6	53.1
1995–96	81.3	39.2	57.0	58.6
1999–2000	69.3	38.6	56.4	49.8
2000–01	72.3	37.8	56.0	48.6
2001–02	72.6	40.2	56.9	50.0
2002–03	72.8	38.3	54.3	56.0
2003–04	71.9	37.5	56.3	53.8
2004–05	77.4	38.1	56.3	60.1
2005–06	83.2	37.1	56.6	56.1

Source: in Rao *et al.* (2008), Table 7

Notes: [a] State's total revenue is the sum of state's own revenue (i.e., tax and non-tax revenue), state's share in central taxes, which is transferred from the center, and grants from the center.

[b] State's total expenditure consists of state's capital expenditure and state's revenue expenditure. The former refers to expenditures incurred on capital (assets) items, which generate income in the future and not in the current period, whereas the latter refers to recurrent expenditures, which generate benefits in the current period.

decentralization or autonomy of a state is given by the extent to which it is able to finance its public expenditure from the revenue sources assigned to it. Thus, one measure of decentralization will be the share of a state's own revenue in its expenditures. However, as the statutory transfers are mandated in the Constitution and given on the basis of recommendation by the Finance Commission, an independent constitutional body, the revenue from shared taxes and statutory grants can be considered on par with that of the states' own revenues. We can, therefore, use the ratio of states' total revenue to states' total expenditure, shown in the second column in Table 7.3 as an appropriate indicator of fiscal decentralization index.

The norms for allocation of resources from the center to states are mostly "formula"-based, which depends on factors such as population without any distinction between scheduled tribes (STs), who are the economically weakest section of the population, and the non-ST population.[3] There are two main institutions that are constitutionally created every five years by the President of India to transfer resources from the center to states: the Finance Commission and Planning Commission. Both institutions first fix the total amount of tax revenues that need to be transferred from the center to the states, which is called "vertical transfer," and then distributes the allocated amount to the states, which is called "horizontal transfer," using different formulas. The Planning Commission also does specific-purpose transfers for various central schemes implemented by different ministries of the central government without using any formula, which are called "non-statutory" transfers (Rao and Chelliah 1995). Table 7.4 shows the vertical transfer from the center to the states over the years, which indicates the overall transfer of about 38 percent of center's revenues to the states. The formula used for horizontal transfer by the XII Finance Commission covering the period 2005–10 is also given in Table 7.4 along with the Planning Commission's Gadgil-Mukherjee formula used in the X Plan (2002–07).[4] The Gadgil formula that is binding for the Planning Commission need not have any sanctity for the Finance Commission (Rao 2005).[5]

Has the instrument of decentralization worked in achieving spatial equitable distribution in social infrastructure development in the Indian context? We now examine this dimension of reform policy.

5 Disparities in state government expenditures

The impact of the 1993 Constitutional decentralization reform on states' development can be gauged through two important indicators: one concerns the effectiveness of the 1993 reform on states' development expenditures and the other concerns the effectiveness of the functioning of the third-tier local government, which has a bearing on rural development. With respect to the first indicator, we have used revenue expenditure (or broadly, current expenditures) of the state governments for analysis as they make up about 77 percent of total expenditures today. Within revenue expenditures, "development expenditures" amount to 80 percent of the spending. "Development expenditures" refers to expenditures on various socioeconomic development programs in the social sectors and economic sectors. With respect to the second indicator, we have used the ratio (RPU) of the per capita expenditure of the *Panchayati Raj* institutions to the per capita expenditure of the urban local bodies in each state as a proxy for the state government intention to support rural development relative to urban development.

The development expenditures of the state governments are grouped into two broad categories: social services and economic services. The social services include health and education. The economic services include development programs in different sectors of the economy, particularly in operation and maintenance of infrastructure. For example, revenue expenditures on programs relating to agriculture, roads, electricity, and industries are grouped under "economic services," and these are not capital expenditures.

Data were obtained from the *Handbook of Statistics on State Government Finances* (RBI 2008) and previous publications on state finances by the Reserve Bank of India (RBI). The state-level population estimates are obtained by interpolating decadal census estimates to obtain per capita expenditures for the states. The values in current prices are deflated by the wholesale price index to obtain expenditures and gross state domestic product (GSDP) in real or constant prices.

The coefficient of variation in government development expenditures is shown in Table 7.5, which shows that at the aggregate level there was an increase in the inter-state disparity in state development expenditures over the years before

Table 7.4 Finance Commission, Planning Commission, and non-statutory transfer of resources from the center to the states

A. Vertical transfer

Period	*Transfers from center to states as percentage of gross revenue receipts of the center*						*Total transfer (4+7) (%)*
	Finance Commission transfers			*Other transfers*			
	Share in central taxes (%)	*Share in grants (%)*	*Total transfers through Finance Commission (2+3) (%)*	*Grants through Planning Commission (%)*	*Non-plan grants (Non-statutory) (%)*	*Total other transfers (5+6) (%)*	
1	2	3	4	5	6	7	8
VII FC (1979–84)	22.39	1.96	24.35	12.11	1.66	13.77	38.11
VIII FC (1984–89)	20.25	2.52	22.77	13.56	1.54	15.10	37.86
IX FC (1989–95)	21.37	3.42	24.79	14.48	1.06	15.54	40.33
X FC (1995–2000)	21.40	2.34	23.75	10.57	0.63	11.19	35.79
XI FC (2000–05) (first two years)	20.93	5.20	26.13	10.39	0.82	11.21	37.20

(Continued)

Table 7.4 (Continued)

B. Horizontal transfer

Formula of 12th Finance Commission (2005–2010)

Criteria	*Weight (%)*
Population	25.0
Income	50.0
Area	10.0
Tax effort	7.5
Fiscal discipline	7.5

Gadgil-Mukherjee Formula used in X Plan (2002–07)

Criteria	*Weight (%)*
Population	60.0
Per capita income	25.0
Tax efforts	7.5
Fiscal management	7.5

Source: Authors' compilation from various Planning Commission plan reports and Finance Commission reports

Table 7.5 Trends in disparity in state government development expenditures: coefficient of variation in per capita real expenditures[a]

Year	*Development expenditure*		
	Economic services	*Social services*	*Total*
1980–81	0.101	0.059	0.067
1985–86	0.101	0.073	0.071
1999–2000	0.117	0.072	0.081
2006–07	0.124	0.071	0.081

Note: [a] The figures in the table are coefficients of variation (CV) and are weighted CV using state population as weights (Kalirajan and Akita 2002). The weighted coefficient of variation is calculated as follows: $cv = \frac{1}{Y^*}\sqrt{\sum_i^n (Y_i - Y^*)^2 \frac{P_i}{P}}$, where P_i refers to population of the ith state; P refers to population of the country; Y_i refers to per capita GSDP; Y* refers to per capita national income; and n refers to number of states.

the 1993 Constitutional reform. Nevertheless, it begins to somewhat decline after the reform. On decomposing the development expenditures, it is worth noting that social services expenditure has shown a declining trend in disparity across states after the 1993 reform, while the economic services expenditure has shown an increasing trend. These trends in development expenditure are further examined in a regression model in the framework of the "convergence analysis." Although the underlying theoretical arguments are quite different, the methodology of income convergence analysis of Barro and Sala-i-Martin (1995) provides a useful tool to examine whether the disparity across states in state government expenditures has been increasing following the 1993 Constitutional reform. The analysis is done using data from the periods before and after the reform.

The conditional convergence regression model we used is:

$$\left\{\frac{1}{t-t_0}\right\}\ln\left(\frac{PCRE_t}{PCRE_{t_0}}\right) = \alpha_0 + \alpha_1\left\{\frac{1}{t-t_0}\right\}\ln PCRE_{t_0} + \alpha_2 \ln PCY_{t_0} + \alpha_3 DCI + u \quad (1)$$

Where

$PCRE$ = per capita real state government development expenditures
PCY = per capita real GSDP (average of three years ending in year t from t_0 in all cases; the averages are taken to remove abnormal data points)
t_0 = beginning year of the time period
t = ending year of the time period
DCI = fiscal decentralization index, which is the share of a state's total revenue to a state's total expenditures

We are not particularly interested in the steady state levels of expenditure, but merely wish to examine whether the expenditures across states are likely to be "converging" or "diverging" over time due to decentralization. Convergence would imply that the disparity is likely to be declining and divergence would imply the opposite. In the above equation, if the coefficient α_1 is positive, the per capita expenditures of the different states would be moving at different rates, with the "higher expenditure states" increasing expenditure faster than the "lower expenditure states." Therefore, there would be no convergence of per capita expenditure across states and the disparity would increase over time. If the coefficient is negative, then the per capita expenditure would be converging or disparity would decrease over time. If the coefficient is zero, then disparity would be neither rising nor declining. The role of per capita real GSDP in the equation is to control for overall "initial conditions" of the state economy. If the average income (per capita GSDP) is larger in one state as compared to the other, the expenditures may also be higher because of the availability of larger resources (through own taxes) to that state. Once we control for this variable, the pattern that remains should reflect the influence of other factors, including the impact of the devolution of resources from the central government to the states, on the tendencies of the states to spend. In order to gauge this latter aspect of central government transfer and also the capacity of the state to collect revenue after the 1993 Constitutional reform, we defined a decentralization index (DCI) as the ratio of the state's total revenue to the state's total expenditures. Thus, the DCI has been used as the policy variable in the analysis.

Given our interest in welfare indicators, we have extended the analysis to cover four types of development expenditure of state governments: (1) expenditure on economic services within development expenditures; (2) expenditure on social services within development expenditures; (3) expenditure on medical and public health services within social expenditures; and (4) expenditure on education services within expenditures on social services.

We have examined the pattern of expenditure for two periods:

Pre-reform periods

1980–81 to 1982–83, and
1983–84 to 1985–86

Post-reform periods

2000–01 to 2002–03, and
2003–04 to 2005–06

The results obtained from applying the ordinary least squares method of estimation to equation (1) with different dependent variables (economic and social services), with concerned independent variables explained above, are summarized in Table 7.6. Given our interest to find out the impact of the 1993 reform on the convergence or divergence in per capita real state government expenditure on economic and social services across states, in Table 7.6 we have only reported the signs of α_s and only some magnitudes of them that are significant The expenditures on social services show a statistically significant convergence pattern more consistently than the expenditures on economic services after the 1993

Table 7.6 Estimated coefficients showing the speed of convergence/divergence (α_1), the influence of the initial conditions (α_2), and the impact of decentralization on the growth of development expenditure (α_3) before and after the 1993 Constitutional reform[a]

Development expenditure category	*1980–81 to 1982–83 (Pre-reform)*	*1983–84 to 1985–86 (Pre-reform)*	*2000–01 to 2002–03 (Post-reform)*	*2003–04 to 2005–06 (Post-reform)*
Economic services				
α_1	+0.2853	+	+0.2915	+0.3006
α_2	+	+	+	+
α_3	+	+	+0.0146	+
Social services				
α_1	+	–0.2012	–0.2185	–0.2209
α_2	+	+	+	+0.0012
α_3	–0.0215	+	+0.1652	+0.1774
Med and public health				
α_1	–	–0.2852	–0.2996	–0.3121
α_2	+0.0286	+	+0.1212	+0.1432
α_3	+	+0.1187	+0.1243	+0.1252
Education				
α_1	–	–0.2490	–0.2642	–0.2763
α_2	+	+	+	+0.0085
α_3	–	+	+	+0.0435

Note: [a] The numbers in the table above are the estimated coefficients, which are shown when significant at least at the 5 percent level of probability. In non-significant cases, we reported here only the signs of estimated coefficients.

reform. In fact, the expenditures on economic services show no convergence for any sub-periods considered, while social expenditures show convergence in three of the four sub-periods. Further, the speed of convergence is larger in the post-reform periods for the social expenditures across states, which indicates the positive influence of decentralization.

Within the social services, expenditures on both health and education services show statistically significant convergence in the post-reform periods, indicating that the reform mechanisms driving these expenditures are based more uniformly on the needs of the population across all regions of the country. In other words, decentralization has contributed towards reducing inequality. Further, the coefficients of the DCI are positive and significant at the 5 per cent level for social services, medical and public health, and education expenditures. However, these coefficients are not significant for the economic services expenditures. The initial condition of average per capita GSDP does not influence the dynamics of expenditures.

The above results indicate that decentralization appears to be an important instrument facilitating the convergence and equalization of basic social services expenditures across states. However, what is more important is to examine whether decentralization has contributed to rural development within the third tier of governance, because 70 percent of India's population still live in rural areas.

Therefore, next, we examine the impact of decentralization on rural development within the third tier of governance, which has bearings on the effective functioning of decentralization. Table 7.7 shows states' per capita expenditure through urban local bodies and *Panchayati Raj* institutions in India during the period 2002–03.

The average figure for urban local bodies all states' per capita expenditure was Rs 463, while the average sum for *Panchayati Raj* all states' per capita expenditure was Rs 316. Though the average figures do not differ very much, the figures across states vary widely. In many states, per capita expenditure through

Table 7.7 Per capita expenditure through urban local bodies and *Panchayati Raj* institutions in India, in Indian rupees, 2002–03

State	*Per capita expenditure through urban local bodies*	*Per capita expenditure through Panchayati Raj institutions*
Himachal Pradesh	854	59
Madhya Pradesh	762	110
Tamil Nadu	727	153
Manipur	720	37
Kerala	693	742
Andhra Pradesh	657	898
Gujarat	653	783
Punjab	639	108
Chattisgarh	614	355
Rajasthan	523	382
Maharashtra	489	821
Goa	443	419
West Bengal	426	30
Uttranchal	398	46
Karnataka	329	1147
Uttar Pradesh	315	44
Orissa	395	57
Tripura	287	253
Jarhgand	192	0
Jammu and Kashmir	192	851
Assam	174	3
Bihar	162	40
Haryana	143	24
Mehalaya	124	25
Mizoram	33	34
All States average	463	316

Source: (basic data) Twelfth Finance Commission (2005)

Panchayati Raj institutions was much below the all states average. Thus, the state-wise figures do provide an indication about whether *Panchayati Raj* insitutions are functioning effectively or not. Karnataka State has been in the front in terms of effective functioning of *Panchayati Raj* institutions. Therefore, we use the ratio of per capita expenditure of *Panchayati Raj* (rural) institutions to per capita expenditure of urban local bodies as a proxy measure for the political intention to promote rural development in the context of decentralization. The following regression model was formulated:

$$RPU = \alpha_0 + \alpha_1 LIT + \alpha_2 \ln PCY_{t_0} + \alpha_3 DCI + \alpha_4 WL + u$$

where RPU is the ratio of per capita expenditure of rural institutions to per capita expenditure of urban local bodies. LIT refers to the literacy rate of the state and it is argued that higher rural development will be achieved with a higher literacy rate. WL refers to the ratio of women administrators in rural governance to women administrators in urban governance and it is argued that rural development will be achieved with a larger ratio. The rest of the variables are as defined above. The above equation was estimated using state-wide data from the post-reform period of 2000–01 to 2005–06. The fixed effects model estimates of the equation are as follows:

$$\underset{(0.0522)}{RPU = 0.1482} + \underset{(0.0231)}{0.0463LIT} + \underset{(0.1725)}{0.4051\ln PCY_{t_0}} + \underset{(0.0328)}{0.0712DCI} + \underset{(0.0031)}{0.0076WL}$$

where the numbers in parentheses are *t*-statistics. All the estimated coefficients are positive and significant, suggesting that higher literacy, per capita income, the extent of fiscal decentralization, and women's presence in local administrations all contribute to rural development. For the purpose of this study, the most important finding is that decentralization has contributed positively to rural development by facilitating an increase in per capita expenditure of *Panchayati Raj* relative to urban areas. However, the magnitude of increase is not impressive, even though it is statistically significant at the 5 percent level. The implication is that decentralization needs to be more effective in promoting the activities of *Panchayati Raj* institutions through increasing the provision of resource allocation in the majority of states. Thus, the demand for effective institutional reforms such as decentralization to the third-tier level need not be overemphasized here.

6 Conclusions

The economic and Constitutional reforms of the 1990s in India have given more space to the markets in the allocation of resources as compared to the state relative to the pre-reform days. This shift can be regarded as part of institutional changes for state building. The question is what implication this institutional change has for the spatial equity in development. If the market-oriented policies lead to inequitable development, social and ethnic conflicts may arise, which may jeopardize the reform itself.

In this conclusion, it is important to recognize that the state continues to be responsible for the supply of public goods, including basic human capital and infrastructural development services, across the country. Analyses presented in this study suggest that the mechanisms by which state governments provide for resources for social services, such as public health and education, significantly contribute to higher inter-state equity. If this pattern is a result of equitable sharing of central resources by the states or the effective functioning of decentralization, this element of state behavior is important in keeping the inter-state disparities from widening. This indicates that decentralization has been an important contributor towards political and economic stability by reducing inequality. More specifically, the results point out that the expenditures on basic services such as health and education are spatially pro-equitable to the economic services.

Overall, the results in this study indicate that the government of India within a federal framework has mechanisms that foster development equitably across its states, particularly through health and education expenditures aimed at improving human capital development. In all likelihood, if the reforms, including fiscal decentralization, had led to inequitable development, social, political, and economic stability would have been weakened, which would have resulted in a slower growth rate of the whole economy.

However, the slowly rising disparities in economic services across states warrant the attention of the central and state governments. Further, as the contribution of decentralization to rural development is not impressive, the structural aspect of decentralization needs to be re-examined. Therefore, drawing on Hayami (2001) and Rao *et al.* (2008), it is conjectured that such tendencies arise mainly due to a lack of appropriate and efficient institutions and human capital at the state and central government levels in India, which indicates the need for further institutional reforms. In this context, it is worth noting the following statement that appears in the Planning Commission's Eleventh Five Year Plan: "Much higher levels of human development can be achieved even with the given structure of the economy, if only the delivery system is improved" (Planning Commission 2008: 2).

Notes

* Comments and suggestions by Chikako Yamauchi are acknowledged with thanks. This paper draws on Kalirajan and Otsuka (2012).

1 A pioneering comprehensive study that has analysed the different responses of the states to the reforms initiated by the central government of India is by Howes *et al.* (2003).

2 Fiscal decentralization or autonomy of a state is given by the extent to which it is able to finance its public expenditure from the revenue sources assigned to it. Thus, one measure of decentralization will be the share of a state's own revenue in its expenditures. However, as the statutory transfers are mandated in the Constitution and given on the basis of recommendation by the Finance Commission, an independent Constitutional body, the revenue from shared taxes and statutory grants can be considered on a par

with that of the states' own revenues. Therefore, an alternative measure is given by the share of state revenue including statutory transfers to denote fiscal decentralization.

3 Jha (2007) has provided a concise discussion on the issues concerning the principal constituents of the resources transfer formula between the first and second layers of governments in developing countries. He has argued that the relative weights on these constituents will often be determined by country-specific circumstances.

4 In the Indian case, decentralization has come about more from the center than the states. Many states did not find the need to decentralize below their administrative level until the Constitution was amended in 1993. Decentralization was initiated to provide easy access to public goods locally. There were 247,033 rural bodies known as *Panchayats* and 3,682 urban bodies in 2005. Nevertheless, the Constitution grants strong powers to the central government, including the control of the central executive over state legislation, and the right to take over state administration in a state of emergency (Rao 2005).

5 The Gadgil formula was evolved in 1969 by D.R. Gadgil, who was the first critic of the Indian planning, for determining the allocation of central assistance for state plans in India. The Gadgil formula was adopted for distribution of plan assistance during Fourth and Fifth Five Year Plans, and was later modified to be known as Gadgil-Mukherjee formula.

References

Barro, R. and Sala-i-Martin, X. (1995) *Economic Growth*, New York: McGraw-Hill.

Brown, C.C. and Oates, W.E. (1987) "Assistance to the poor in a federal system," *Journal of Public Economics*, 32: 307–30.

Dreze, J. and Sen, A.K. (1996) *India: Economic Development and Social Opportunity*, Delhi: Oxford University Press.

Hayami, Y. (2001) *Development Economics: From the Poverty to the Wealth of Nations*, 2nd edition, Oxford: Oxford University Press.

Howes, S., Lahiri, A., and Stern, N. (eds.) (2003) *State Level Reforms in India*, New Delhi: Macmillan.

Jha, R. (2007) "Fiscal policy in developing countries: a synoptic view," ASARC Working Paper 2007/01, Australia South Asia Research Centre, Australian National University, Canberra.

Kalirajan, K.P. and Akita, T. (2002) "Institutions and interregional inequalities in India: finding a link using Hayami's thesis and convergence hypothesis," *Indian Economic Journal*, 50 (2): 47–59.

Kalirajan, K. and Otsuka, K. (2012) "Fiscal decentralization and development outcomes in India: an exploratory analysis," *World Development*, 40 (8): 1511–21.

Ladd, H. and Doolittle, F.C. (1982) "Which level of government should assist the poor?," *National Tax Journal*, 35: 323–36.

Oates, W.E. (1972) *Fiscal Federalism*, New York: Harcourt Brace Jovanovich.

Ostrom, E., Schroeder, L., and Wynne, S. (1993) *Institutional Incentives and Sustainable Development: Infrastructure Policies in Perspective*, Oxford: Westview Press.

Pauly, M.V. (1973) "Income redistribution as a local public good," *Journal of Public Economics*, 2 (1): 35–58.

Planning Commission (2008) *Eleventh Five Year Plan 2007–2012, Volume 1 – Inclusive Growth*, New Delhi: Oxford University Press.

Prudhomme, R. (1995) "The dangers of decentralization," *World Bank Research Observer*, 10 (2): 201–20.

Rao, C.H.H. (2005) *Essays on Development, Regional Disparities and Centre-State Financial Relations in India*, New Delhi: Academic Foundation.

Rao, M.G. and Chelliah, R.J. (1995) *A Survey of Research in Fiscal Federalism in India*, New Delhi: Indian Council of Social Science Research.

Rao, M.G., and Singh, N. (2003) "How to think about local government reform in India," in K.P. Kalirajan and U. Sankar (eds) *Economic Reform and the Liberalisation of the Indian Economy: Essays in Honour of Richard T. Shand*, Cheltenham: Edward Elgar.

Rao, M.G., Shand, R.T., and Kalirajan, K.P. (1998) "State electricity boards: a performance evaluation," *Indian Economic Journal*, 46 (2): 51–66.

Rao, M.G., Sen, T.K., and Jena, P.R. (2008) "Issues before the thirteenth finance commission," *Economic and Political Weekly*, 43 (36): 41–53.

RBI (Reserve Bank of India) (2008) *Handbook of State Government Finances*, Mumbia: RBI.

Rodden, J. (2002) "The dilemma of fiscal federalism: grants and fiscal performance around the world," *American Journal of Political Science*, 46 (3): 670–87.

Twelfth Finance Commission (2005) *Report of the XII Finance Commission 2005–2010*, New Delhi: Chatrapati Shivaji Bhawan.

World Bank (2000) *Overview of rural decentralization in India, Volume I*, unpublished report, Washington, DC: World Bank.

8 An inquiry into corruption norms and development

Tetsushi Sonobe

1 Introduction

Corruption hampers state building and economic development. Corrupt officials and politicians embezzle funds intended for the provision of basic public services and the construction of infrastructure (e.g., Olken 2007; Reinikka and Svensson 2005; Shleifer and Vishny 1993). Corruption makes the political legitimacy of the state more dubious and undermines democracy (e.g., Rose-Ackerman 1999). Bribes discourage firms' investments, including foreign direct investments, like taxes (e.g., Mauro 1995; Wei 2000), but bribes damage firm growth more severely than taxes (Fisman and Svensson 2007), probably because the secrecy and uncertainty accompanied by bribery increase transaction costs (Shleifer and Vishny 1993). Cross-country studies find that corruption hinders the economic growth of developing countries significantly (e.g., Mauro 1995).

An approach to combating corruption is to impose severe penalties and increase the probability of detection and punishment. Becker and Stigler (1974) argue that the level of deterrence expenditure is optimal when the marginal cost of deterrence equals the marginal benefit. Compelling evidence for this view was unavailable because of the difficulty in measuring corruption directly. Recently, however, excellent studies by Olken (2007), Fisman and Miguel (2007), Reinikka and Svensson (2011), and Ferraz and Finan (2011) among others have used natural experiments and randomized controlled trials to show that strict audits, media campaigns, and other carrot-and-stick approaches serve as effective deterrents to corruption. For example, one media campaign that provided schools and parents with information to monitor local officials' handling of school subsidies reduced the local capture of the subsidies drastically (Reinikka and Svensson 2011).

These empirical results are encouraging but do not assure success in corruption eradication. As Rose-Ackerman (1999), Fisman and Miguel (2007), and many others argue cogently, citizens, government officials, and politicians in corrupt societies tend to be more accepting of corrupt behaviors than those in clean societies. Such a social norm dampens the enthusiasm for efforts to reduce corruption, stifles the effect of the efforts in the long run, and perpetuates corruption. Finding out how to deal with corruption norms is a challenge for state building and economic development.

This study attempts to address two issues about corruption norms.[1] There is no consensus about the definition of corruption norms. This study refers to them as social attitudes of approval or disapproval toward corrupt behaviors. Recently, an important contribution to the literature was made by Truex (2011). His point is that because corruption comprises various types, corruption norms should be gauged not only by the general extent of corruption acceptance but also by the pattern of attitudes toward different types of corruption. Indeed, he shows that citizens in Kathmandu, Nepal, have varying attitudes toward different types of corrupt behaviors. Since Nepal is a corrupt country according to corruption rankings such as Transparency International's Corruption Perception Index (CPI), he argues that such a variation is a feature of corruption norms in corrupt societies. This part of his argument, however, could be more persuasive if Nepalese society were compared with a less corrupt society. The first issue of the present study is to provide such a comparison group.

For this purpose, a survey of the alumni members of the National Graduate Institute for Policy Studies (GRIPS) was administered through the internet by using a questionnaire that contains the same questions used by Truex (2011). GRIPS is the leading graduate school of policy studies in Japan. The vast majority of its student body consists of mid-career government officials, and two-thirds of them are from outside Japan. In all, 315 graduates from 58 countries responded to this survey, thereby providing a comparison group consisting of highly educated officials in a number of countries with varying CPI rankings and income levels. Our data indicate that in high-income countries, corruption is almost always unacceptable for most respondents regardless of the type of corrupt behaviors, while in low-income countries, such behaviors may or may not be acceptable depending on the person and the details of situation or the context. We also find that government officials in low-income countries and ordinary citizens in Nepal in particular have significantly different attitudes to some types of corruption, and that their differences lack a clear pattern. Such corruption norms in low-income countries would be a source of uncertainty and unpredictability and, hence, high transaction costs.

From these observations, a question arises as to whether developing countries can detach themselves from traditional corruption norms and adopt a new social norm that encourages individuals to maintain strict attitudes toward corruption. Rose-Ackerman (1999: 110) argues that corruption norms are "dynamic and constantly changing." Sah (2007) has developed a theoretical model explaining the dynamics of corruption norms. In this model, public and private actors individually choose whether or not to be corrupt, based on their current perceptions of gains, costs (legal, economic, and social sanctions), and detection probability, which are formed and revised over time based on their personal experiences, acquaintances' experiences, education, media, and all other information, and their choices in turn influence their own and others' future perceptions. Thus, individuals' attitudes toward corruption change with the times, together with their perceptions of the functioning of institutions that affect the gains, costs, and detection probability of corruption.

Although testing or estimating Sah's dynamic general equilibrium model is too much to hope for, our second issue is to examine whether our data of GRIPS alumni are consistent or inconsistent with some of the predictions of the Sah model. Our descriptive analysis finds that the corruption norms of a country are correlated with the perceived quality of the audit system and the media of the country, and with the perceived attitude of the compatriots toward corruption, which is consistent with the model's prediction. We also use a regression approach, looking at the association between government officials' self-rated discipline and socioeconomic characteristics, and find that older cohorts and those living in rural areas tend to be more accepting of corruption, which is also consistent with the model.

The rest of this chapter is organized as follows. Section 2 explains Truex's (2011) well thought-out questions eliciting survey respondents' opinions of different types of corrupt behaviors. The GRIPS Alumni Survey included exactly the same set of questions. Section 3 is devoted to descriptive analyses with a view to reinforcing the results of Truex's study. We then attempt to test the predictions of the Sah model of the dynamics of corruption norms by using descriptive analysis in Section 4 and regression analysis in Section 5. Section 6 contains the concluding remarks.

2 The design of the survey

Corruption is multidimensional. One may accept one type of corruption but not another type. Moreover, opinions may be divided as to which types are acceptable even if people share the same overall level of corruption acceptance. To substantiate this point, Truex (2011) conducted a survey in Kathmandu by using the 13 well thought-out questions that are shown in Table 8.1. Each question describes a problematic behavior, which the respondents rate on a scale of 1 to 5, where 5 means that the behavior is very unacceptable and 1 means that the behavior is very acceptable. The questions are well designed so that a pair of slightly different questions isolates differences in attitudes along a given dimension. For example, Q4 and Q5 are intended to capture different attitudes toward a politician's nepotism and a businessman's nepotism. Similarly, Q1 and Q2 differ in the scale of corruption, while Q2 and Q3 are about the distinction between a gift bribe and a cash bribe. Note that no public actor appears in Q5 and Q8 while the other questions involve one. With a sample of 853 pedestrians in Kathmandu who were willing to participate in the survey, Truex (2011) finds interesting patterns of respondents' attitudes toward different types of corruption, as will be described in the next section.

The present study asks GRIPS alumni members the same set of questions to see how government officials differ from ordinary citizens and how high-income countries differ from low-income countries in the level and pattern of corruption acceptance. In the GRIPS Alumni Survey, hundreds of graduates from GRIPS received an email message requesting that they fill out and return the questionnaire through the internet. This chapter is written based on the 315 questionnaires

Table 8.1 13 problematic behaviors from Truex's (2011) survey

Question: How do you rate each behavior on a scale from 1 to 5?	*Question name*
Q1. A businessman offers a senior official a large amount of money in order to import goods without paying taxes	Grand cash
Q2. A shopkeeper offers a tax collector a small amount of money in order to avoid paying taxes	Petty cash
Q3. A shopkeeper offers a tax collector a small gift in order to avoid paying taxes	Petty gift
Q4. A politician gives a job to a family member even though other applicants are more qualified	Politician job
Q5. A businessman gives a job to a family member even though other applicants are more qualified	Private job
Q6. A government employee gives a job to a family member even though other applicants are more qualified	Bureaucrat job
Q7. A construction contractor gives a government employee a large gift in hopes of receiving a government construction contract	Public contract
Q8. A construction contractor gives a businessman a large gift in hopes of receiving a private construction contract	Private contract
Q9. A government employee awards a government construction contract to a friend's business because he is a friend	Favoritism contact
Q10. Because of a delay, a schoolteacher gives a government employee a small gift in order to make sure that his passport gets processed	Deserved giver
Q11. A schoolteacher gives a government employee a small gift in order to obtain a passport without proper documentation	Illicit giver
Q12. A government employee asks a schoolteacher for a small gift in exchange for giving him a passport without proper documentation	Illicit receiver
Q13. A police officer does not give a taxi-driver a traffic ticket because he is a friend	Favoritism ticket

returned within one month from the end of June 2012. The survey questionnaire includes the 13 original questions and questions eliciting the respondent's opinions of the level of corruption, the functioning of the audit system, the credibility of media, and the citizens' attitudes toward corruption in his or her country. The questionnaire also includes questions about the respondent's socioeconomic characteristics and preferences, such as risk attitudes, patience, and procrastination. Although some respondents left some questions unanswered, the data of 300 respondents from 58 countries are usable.

Table 8.2 lists the 58 countries, their gross national income (GNI) per capita and Transparency International's CPI score, the number of respondents by country, and the country-level averages of the following five variables. PUBSCORE is an average score for the eleven behaviors involving public actors. The country-level average of this variable is our measure of corruption norms. LEVEL indicates the

Table 8.2 Summary statistics by country

Country name	*(1)*	*(2)*	*(3)*	*(4)*	*(5)*	*(6)*	*(7)*	*(8)*
	GNI per capita in 2010	*CPI score*	*Number of respondents*	*PUBSCORE*	*LEVEL*	*AUDIT*	*MEDIA*	*ATTITUDE*
Afghanistan	910	1.5	2	4.45	1.50	2.00	4.00	3.50
Australia	36,910	8.8	6	4.97	4.33	4.17	3.83	4.50
Bangladesh	1,810	2.7	15	4.36	2.33	2.67	3.53	3.20
Bhutan	4,970	5.7	5	4.73	2.80	3.40	3.00	2.80
Brunei	NA	5.2	1	–	–	–	–	–
Bulgaria	13,510	3.3	2	4.23	2.50	4.00	3.50	4.00
Cambodia	2,070	2.1	11	3.68	2.27	2.82	3.55	2.64
China	7,600	3.6	9	4.16	2.00	2.89	2.78	3.33
Colombia	9,020	3.4	2	4.59	2.50	4.00	3.50	3.50
Cuba	NA	4.2	1	–	–	–	–	–
Egypt	6,030	2.9	1	–	–	–	–	–
El Salvador	6,460	3.4	2	4.95	2.50	1.50	2.00	2.50
Ethiopia	1,030	2.7	8	3.93	2.00	2.75	2.00	2.25
Fiji	4,460	NA	1	–	–	–	–	–
Georgia	4,950	4.1	1	–	–	–	–	–
Germany	38,100	8.0	1	–	–	–	–	–
Ghana	1,610	3.9	6	4.86	2.50	3.50	4.00	3.00
Hungary	19,550	4.6	3	4.79	3.33	2.33	3.33	2.67
India	3,340	3.1	8	4.91	2.38	3.75	3.88	2.75
Indonesia	4,190	3.0	43	4.65	2.49	3.09	3.23	2.86
Iran	NA	2.7	1	–	–	–	–	–

(Continued)

Table 8.2 (Continued)

Country name	*(1)*	*(2)*	*(3)*	*(4)*	*(5)*	*(6)*	*(7)*	*(8)*
	GNI per capita in 2010	*CPI score*	*Number of respondents*	*PUBSCORE*	*LEVEL*	*AUDIT*	*MEDIA*	*ATTITUDE*
Japan	34,780	8.0	10	4.68	3.60	3.60	3.40	4.00
Jordan	5,810	4.5	1	–	–	–	–	–
Kazakhstan	10,620	2.7	6	4.50	2.50	3.80	2.33	3.50
Kenya	1,640	2.2	10	4.46	3.00	3.30	3.70	3.40
Korea, Rep	28,830	5.4	2	5.00	4.00	4.00	3.00	4.00
Kyrgyz Rep	2,070	2.1	1	–	–	–	–	–
Lao PDR	2,400	2.2	3	3.42	2.67	3.33	4.00	3.00
Lithuania	18,010	4.8	1	–	–	–	–	–
Madagascar	950	3.0	2	4.68	1.00	1.00	2.00	2.50
Malaysia	14,160	4.3	12	4.86	3.33	3.50	3.25	3.42
Maldives	7,840	2.5	1	–	–	–	–	–
Moldova	3,370	2.9	1	–	–	–	–	–
Mongolia	3,660	2.7	2	4.68	2.50	2.50	3.50	3.50
Mozambique	900	2.7	1	–	–	–	–	–
Myanmar	NA	1.5	3	4.76	2.67	3.67	3.67	3.00
Nepal	1,210	2.2	12	3.86	2.33	3.17	3.17	2.75
Nicaragua	2,660	2.5	1	–	–	–	–	–
Nigeria	2,140	2.4	1	–	–	–	–	–
Pakistan	2,780	2.5	18	4.12	2.00	2.67	3.35	1.94
Paraguay	5,050	2.2	1	–	–	–	–	–
Peru	9,320	3.4	1	–	–	–	–	–
Philippines	3,960	2.6	24	4.76	2.58	2.88	3.50	2.67
Poland	19,180	5.5	1	–	–	–	–	–

Romania	14,300	3.6	4	4.82	2.25	3.00	2.75	2.25
Sierra Leone	820	2.5	1	–	–	–	–	–
Singapore	56,890	9.2	1	–	–	–	–	–
Slovakia	21,870	4.0	1	–	–	–	–	–
Sri Lanka	5,040	3.3	6	4.47	3.33	3.83	3.40	2.67
Tanzania	1,430	3.0	8	4.55	2.43	3.50	3.38	2.88
Thailand	8,150	3.4	15	4.47	2.53	2.93	3.00	2.07
Turkey	15,460	4.2	2	3.91	2.50	2.50	2.00	2.50
Uganda	1,250	2.4	4	4.68	2.25	3.00	3.00	3.00
Ukraine	6,590	2.3	1	–	–	–	–	–
Uzbekistan	3,150	1.6	5	4.40	1.60	2.60	2.20	3.00
Vietnam	3,060	2.9	11	3.90	1.70	2.27	2.82	2.64
Zambia	1,370	3.2	4	4.89	1.50	3.75	3.50	2.25
Zimbabwe	NA	2.2	2	4.36	2.50	3.00	3.00	2.50

Sources: *GNI per capita* in column (1) is taken from the GNI per capita, PPP (current international $) compiled by the World Bank, http://data.worldbank.org/indicator/NY.GNP.PCAP.PP.CD. *CPI score* in column (2) is The 2011 Corruption Perceptions Index (Transparency International) http://cpi.transparency.org/cpi2011/. Data shown in columns (3) to (8) are taken from our survey

1 GNI per capita is "based on purchasing power parity (PPP). PPP GNI is gross national income (GNI) converted to international dollars using purchasing power parity rates. An international dollar has the same purchasing power over GNI as a US dollar has in the United States. GNI is the sum of value added by all resident producers plus any product taxes (less subsidies) not included in the valuation of output plus net receipts of primary income (compensation of employees and property income) from abroad. Data are in current international dollars."

2 The CPI score of a country indicates "the perceived level of public sector corruption there on a scale of 0–10, where 0 means that a country is perceived as highly corrupt and 10 means that a country is perceived as very clean" (http://cpi.transparency.org/cpi2011/in_detail).

4 PUBSCORE is the respondent's average score for the eleven questions about CAS behaviors involving public actors, that is, the questions shown in Table 8.1 other than Q5 and Q8.

5 LEVEL is the respondent's perception of the level of corruption in his or her country rated on a scale of 1 to 5, where 5 means "very few are involved" and 1 means "almost everyone is involved."

6 AUDIT is the respondent's perception of the performance of the audit system in his or her country rated on a scale of 1 to 5, where 5 means "very satisfactory" and 1 means "very poor."

7 MEDIA is the respondent's perception of the credibility of the domestic media in his or her country rated on a scale of 1 to 5, where 5 means "very credible" and 1 means "not at all credible."

8 ATTITUDE is the respondent's perception of the ordinary citizens' attitudes to corruption in his or her country rated on a scale of 1 to 5, where 5 means "very harsh" and 1 means "very lenient."

respondent's subjective evaluation of the level of corruption in his or her country, where 1 means that the country is highly corrupt and 5 means that it is very clean. AUDIT and MEDIA are the subjective evaluations of the performance of the audit system and the credibility of the domestic media of the country, respectively. Similarly, ATTITUDE is the anticorruption attitude of the citizens of the country subjectively rated by the respondent, where 1 means that the citizens are accepting of public corruption and 5 means that they have very strict attitudes toward public corruption. Columns (4) to (8) of Table 8.2 report the country-level averages of these variables except for those countries which have only one respondent. These data are kept secret in order to protect personal information because it may be easy to identify the respondents from such countries.

Our survey data are subject to four biases. The first is the bias in occupation. Most GRIPS students are government officials. The second is the bias toward higher education. All respondents are masters degree holders. These biases are needed to provide a comparison group for Truex's sample of ordinary citizens and are also useful for the purpose of our analysis because those who have similar socioeconomic characteristics may have quite different perceptions according to the Sah model. To be more precise, however, our respondents' occupations are not completely homogeneous because some respondents have left their government posts for the private sector. About 75 percent of the respondents are government officials, and the vast majority of them work at their central governments. About 10 percent work at national universities, and about 15 percent at private or quasi-governmental organizations. As to education, one third of the respondents have another masters degree, and 10 percent have a doctoral degree.

The third bias is the so called social desirability bias (SDB), which refers to the bias arising from a tendency of respondents to give more socially acceptable or respectable answers than their true answers (Arnold and Feldman 1981). SDB would understate corruption norms. Although our questionnaire requested respondents to answer the questions as honestly as they could, this might not be enough to prevent SDB. We hope that SDB is less serious in internet surveys than in surveys in which respondents have face-to-face contact with the enumerator. In this regard, however, we should note that some countries have only a small number of graduates from GRIPS. If the respondents from such countries thought that they could be identified easily, their answers may be affected by SDB. Thus, if there is any systematic difference between the data from these countries and those from the other countries, the former should be excluded from the analysis or their influences should be controlled for.

As Truex (2011) argues, SDB is essentially an omitted variable bias. Thus, in our regression analysis below, we use a number of variables as controls, including the variables representing the respondent's preference for risk aversion, patience, and preference for relative evaluation (as opposed to absolute evaluation) of one's performance, and proclivity for procrastination (i.e. delaying doing something that should be done). Since procrastination carries a disapproving tone, those who admit to this proclivity candidly may be more immune from SDB. Thus, we hope that this variable effectively mitigates the confounding due to SDB.

Finally, our survey data must suffer from selection bias: those who were unwilling to respond did not respond to the survey. In this study, we have no countermeasure to this perennial concern other than taking great care when we interpret the results of the analysis. One way to see the extent of selection bias may be to compare the number of respondents by country and the number of GRIPS alumni by country. Those countries with a large number of alumni would have a greater number of respondents, but the relationship between these numbers may be affected by the extent of corruption if those alumni in more corrupt countries are less willing to answer the questionnaire about corruption. Table 8.3 presents the results of simple regressions intended to examine this relationship. In the first column, the dependent variable is the number of respondents, and the estimated coefficients indicate that an increase in the number of alumni in a country by 10 persons increases the number of respondents from that country by 1.37 persons, and that GNI per capita has a negative and marginally significant coefficient, which suggests that alumni in high-income countries have high opportunity costs of answering the questionnaire. The second column is similar except that CPI is included on the right-hand side of regression as a control even though its coefficient is insignificant.

One may think that the number of respondents in a country would increase in proportion to the number of alumni in that country rather than increasing by 1.37 persons regardless of the size of alumni. If this is the case, it is better to use

Table 8.3 Regressions of the number of respondents by country

	(1)	*(2)*	*(3)*	*(4)*
	Respondents	*Respondents*	*ln (respondents + 1)*	*ln (respondents + 1)*
Alumni	0.137***	0.137***		
	(18.180)	(18.055)		
ln (alumni)			0.518***	0.521***
			(16.593)	(16.239)
ln (GNI per capita)	–0.454* (–1.693)	–0.697* (–1.842)		–0.118* (–1.826)
CPI		0.240		
		(0.910)		
ln (CPI)			0.112	0.296
			(0.881)	(1.592)
Intercept	4.382*	5.643**	–0.141	0.674
	(1.839)	(2.046)	(–0.792)	(1.495)
Observations	86	85	91	85
R-squared	0.806	0.808	0.763	0.779

Notes: Numbers in parentheses are t-statistics. *, **, and *** indicate the 10, 5, and 1 percent levels of significance, respectively. GNI per capita is based on purchasing power parity (PPP) as described in the note to Table 8.2.

the log-log specification. Since alumni in many countries did not respond to the survey, however, we have to avoid the problem of being unable to take the logarithm of zero by using the logarithm of the number of respondents plus one as the dependent variable.[2] In other words, the dependent variable is equal to ln (1) for the countries where no alumni responded to the survey, ln (2) for the countries with only one respondent, and so forth. This ad hoc solution is often used and makes the interpretation of estimation results difficult in some cases, but it does not seem to cause any major problem in our case. Columns (3) and (4) of Table 8.3 indicate that an increase in the number of alumni in a country by 10 percent increases the number of respondents from that country by 5.2 percent, that alumni in higher income countries tend to be unwilling to answer the questionnaire, and that the estimated impact of CPI on the willingness to answer falls short of the 10 percent level of statistical significance.

3 Comparative approach to corruption norms

Table 8.4 shows the scores for the 13 problematic behaviors and PUBSCORE for the residents in Kathmandu in column (1) and the GRIPS alumni in columns (2) to (4). In this table, the 58 countries are classified into three categories according to GNI per capita, and these categories are referred to as low-, middle-, and high-income countries. The naming of the three categories is just for convenience and does not follow the definition given by the World Bank or other organizations. The low-income category has 138 respondents from 24 countries, the middle-income category has 138 respondents from 22 countries, and the high-income category has 33 respondents from 12 countries. Since Nepal is one of the low-income countries in our classification, Truex's sample occupies a column next to that for the low-income countries to facilitate comparison. As one would expect, GNI per capita and CPI score are highly correlated. Their correlation coefficient in the sample of the 58 countries is as high as 0.90. Thus, the above classification of countries is nearly equivalent to the classification into corrupt, less corrupt, and relatively clean countries.

The citizens in Nepal and the GRIPS graduates in low-income countries share almost the same PUBSCOREs, the average scores for the 11 questions about behaviors that involve a public actor. Thus, ordinary citizens and highly educated government officials in low-income countries do not differ in their overall level of corruption acceptance. However, their attitudes toward some behaviors are very different. First, GRIPS graduates from low-income countries are more accepting of a bureaucrat's nepotism (Q6, bureaucrat job) than a businessman's grand cash-giving (Q1, grand cash), while these behaviors are equally unacceptable for the citizens in Nepal. Second, they are more disapproving of petty bribery-giving associated with tax evasion by private actors, such as Q2 (petty cash), Q3 (petty gift), and Q10 (deserved giver). Third, they are more accepting of petty favoritism given by a government employee to a friend (Q13, favoritism ticket). Fourth, however, they are harsh to favoritism if a government employee gives a contract to a friend (Q9, favoritism contract).

Table 8.4 Corruptive behavior acceptance, citizens in Kathmandu vs. GRIPS graduates

Question name	*Kathmandu, (Truex 2011)*	*GRIPS survey respondents from*		
		Low-income countries	*Middle-income countries*	*High-income countries*
	(1)	*(2)*	*(3)*	*(4)*
Q1. Grand cash	4.48	4.49 (0.085)	4.76 (0.066)	4.97 (0.031)
Q2. Petty cash	4.15	4.39 (0.093)	4.78 (0.054)	4.81 (0.083)
Q3. Petty gift	4.10	4.30 (0.098)	4.79 (0.047)	4.75 (0.090)
Q4. Politician job	4.38	4.10 (0.113)	4.49 (0.082)	4.81 (0.095)
Q5. Private job	3.94	3.36 (0.113)	3.35 (0.114)	3.41 (0.219)
Q6. Bureaucrat job	4.44	4.26 (0.086)	4.68 (0.065)	4.88 (0.087)
Q7. Public contract	4.28	4.26 (0.103)	4.65 (0.075)	4.91 (0.052)
Q8. Private contract	3.99	4.21 (0.092)	4.19 (0.098)	4.44 (0.179)
Q9. Favoritism contract	3.83	4.23 (0.093)	4.59 (0.073)	4.88 (0.087)
Q10. Deserved giver	3.86	4.11 (0.088)	4.30 (0.082)	4.31 (0.165)
Q11. Illicit giver	4.45	4.54 (0.075)	4.84 (0.046)	4.81 (0.095)
Q12. Illicit receiver	4.48	4.68 (0.060)	4.88 (0.048)	4.91 (0.069)
Q13. Favoritism ticket	4.35	4.00 (0.101)	4.37 (0.082)	4.66 (0.106)
PUBSCORE (average for the 11 public behaviors)	4.25	4.30 (0.070)	4.65 (0.049)	4.78 (0.065)
Number of observations	853	138	138	33

Notes: Numbers in parentheses are standard errors of the means (but not standard deviations of the scores).

As to Q5 (private job) and Q8 (private contract), which are not included in PUBSCORE because they do not involve a public actor, the Kathmandu sample and our sample from low-income countries show a stark contrast. The GRIPS alumni, regardless of income levels of their countries, have very low scores for the nepotism of a private actor (Q5), compared with the Nepalese counterpart as well as scores for the other questions, on the one hand. On the other hand, the GRIPS alumni do not think that bribery between private actors (Q8) is more acceptable than bribery between public and private actors (Q7) when the stake is a contract.

Is there any clear pattern in those differences between the Kathmandu sample and our sample? Our sample may have a tendency of self-indulgence in the sense that GRIPS alumni appear to be more disapproving of private actors' cheating than public actors' corrupt behaviors. Are there any other differences in pattern? From the comparison between Q9 (favoritism contract) and Q13 (favoritism ticket) or between Q5 (private job) and Q8 (private contract), one may think that the GRIPS alumni pay attention to "contract" or the amount of money involved in the corruption. Note, however, that the GRIPS alumni from low-income countries gave a slightly lower score for Q7 (a company offers a bribe to receive a contract) than for Q3 (a shopkeeper offers a small amount of money to avoid taxes) and Q4 (a shopkeeper offers a small gift to avoid taxes). There does not seem to be a principle or a clear pattern.

We now look at columns (3) and (4) as well. The scores in these columns are mostly near 5 in the high-income countries. The differences in the scores between the middle- and high-income countries are significant at the 1 percent level for Q1, Q4, and Q7, and at the 5 percent level for Q9, and Q13 as well as the aggregate indicator, PUBSCORE. The differences in the scores between the middle- and low-income countries are significant at the 1 percent level for most questions. The exceptions are Q5 (private job), Q8 (private contract), and Q10 (deserved giver) only. While the middle- and high-income countries differ in the overall level of corruption acceptance (i.e., PUBSCORE), they share the same patterns of scores for different questions. Compared with them, the low-income countries are different in attitudes to Q4 (political job) and Q13 (favoritism ticket). But this difference in pattern of attitudes between government officials in the low- and middle-income countries is small, compared with the difference in pattern of attitudes between ordinary citizens and government officials in low-income countries.

Truex's (2011) contribution to the literature on corruption is that he shows that attitudes toward different types of corruption are different. Our addition to his finding is that ordinary citizens and government officials in low-income countries have different attitudes toward different types of corruption and that the difference between them does not have a clear pattern. Although Truex does not emphasize this, he also finds that the corruption acceptance, measured by the scores, varies from person to person and that the extent of variation measured by standard errors varies with the types of corruption. Moreover, standard errors may or may not be greater in the low-income countries than in the middle- and high-income countries, depending on the type of corrupt behaviors.

In relation to the variation just mentioned, we should pay attention to what the respondents think when they give a rating of 4 instead of 5 to a question. Probably, they would be sure that the corrupt behavior described in a question was unacceptable when they rated the behavior a 5. When they rate it a 4 (or less than 5), some of them would mean that they were less acceptable. But some other respondents would think that they were less sure, or that whether the behavior was acceptable or unacceptable would depend on the details of the situation. To the extent that this way of thinking prevailed, the interpretation of the standard error of the score should be carefully considered. Suppose that everyone gives a 4 to a behavior. Although the standard error is zero in this case, the respondents may not really be sure. Some approve of the behavior but others disapprove of it, depending on their mood and the details of the corruption. In short, the variability can be larger than the standard errors suggest.

Thus, although the term "cultural norm" may give an impression that it specifies what is acceptable or unacceptable, cultural norms in corrupt societies are less specific and more elusive. A major message of Table 8.4 is that ordinary citizens and government officials in corrupt society distinguish acceptable and unacceptable behaviors in different ways, but that their differences are elusive. Another major message is that even among government officials in countries with similar income levels, the distinction between acceptable and unacceptable behaviors varies from one person to another and from one situation to another.

These findings offer a new piece of evidence to Shleifer and Vishny's (1993) assertion that corruption increases transaction costs more than taxes. "Corruption is often thought of as like a tax or a fee. Bribes, like taxes, create a wedge between the actual and privately appropriated marginal product of capital" (Svensson 2005: 20). Shleifer and Vishny (1993) point out that corruption is necessarily accompanied by secrecy and uncertainty and argue that secrecy and uncertainty create additional transaction costs. While secrecy is obvious, evidence for uncertainty has been scarce. Table 8.4 can be regarded as a piece of such evidence. The approach pioneered by Truex (2011) will help us supply abundant evidence in future.

4 Correlates of corruption norms

In the dynamic model developed by Sah (2007), individuals' attitudes toward corruption change with the times, together with their perceptions of the functioning of institutions that affect the gains, costs, and detection probability of corruption. Suppose that today's developed countries have actually had such an evolution of perceptions while developing countries have not. It is expected that government officials will be more disciplined in countries where anti-corruption institutions, such as audit systems and the media, are perceived to work well and citizens are perceived to be strongly disapproving of corruption. Or, to put it another way, our respondents' attitude toward corruption (PUBSCORE) is correlated with the perceived performance of the audit system (AUDIT), the perceived credibility of the domestic media (MEDIA), and the perceived attitude of the ordinary citizens toward corruption (ATTITUDE) at the country level.

As a preliminary analysis, we plotted PUBSCORE and AUDIT both at the country level and at the individual level and found that there are outliers whose PUBSCORE is high but AUDIT is low. These outliers are suspected to be subject to SDB. As mentioned in Section 2, the respondents in such countries that had only a small number of GRIPS alumni might think that they could be more easily identified than their counterparts in countries with a larger number of GRIPS alumni, such as Indonesia, the Philippines, and Pakistan. Assuming that the number of respondents is roughly proportional to the number of alumni, we suspected that the respondents from the countries with a small number of respondents would be more likely to be subject to SDB and to have unduly high values of PUBSCORE.

It turned out that 22 respondents from countries with only one respondent, and that their mean PUBSCORE was 4.80, while that for the other respondents was 4.48. The difference was statistically significant at the 1 percent level. Moreover, 61 respondents from countries with four respondents or less, and their mean PUBSCORE was 4.67, which is higher than the other respondents' mean of 4.46 at the 1 percent level of significance. These significant differences deepen the suspicion of SDB inflating the PUBSCORE of some of the respondents from the countries with small numbers of alumni.

Based on these observations and considerations, Table 8.5 juxtaposes three matrices showing the coefficients of correlation among the six variables (PUBSCORE, LEVEL, AUDIT, MEDIA, ATTITUDE, and CPI score) in the full sample of countries, the sub-sample of countries with three or more respondents, and that of countries with five or more respondents, respectively. In Panel A, where all the sample countries are included,[3] the correlation between PUBSCORE and the other variables is generally low and that between PUBSCORE and AUDIT is particularly low. To mitigate SDB, the countries with fewer than three respondents are excluded from the sample. Such exclusion will also help to reduce the impacts of outliers. The result is shown in Panel B, where the correlation coefficient for PUBSCORE and AUDIT is much higher than in Panel A, but the coefficients for PUBSCORE and the other variables are not different from Panel A. To mitigate SDB further, Panel C focuses on the countries with five or more respondents. Here, PUBSCORE is correlated more closely with each of the other variables, and the correlation among the other variables is generally high. Given the nature of subjective ratings, correlation coefficients of 0.4 to 0.7 can be regarded as indicating close correlation. These results are consistent with the Sah (2007) model.

5 Factors associated with attitude toward corruption

In this section, we try to test the following hypotheses derived from the Sah (2007) model: (i) government officials in a less corrupt country tend to take a stronger position against corruption; (ii) older cohorts of officials tend to be more accepting of corruption than younger cohorts within the same country; (iii) those officials living or working in rural areas tend to be more accepting of corruption than those in urban areas; and (iv) government officials with similar socio-economic characteristics may have quite different attitudes toward corruption. As we mentioned earlier, Transparency International's CPI is very closely correlated with GNI per capita. Thus if Hypothesis (i) above is substantiated, it is a piece of circumstantial evidence that economic development reduces corruption.

Table 8.5 Correlation of country averages

Panel A: All countries (N = 57)

	PUBSCORE	*LEVEL*	*AUDIT*	*MEDIA*	*ATTITUDE*
PUBSCORE	1				
LEVEL	0.390	1			
AUDIT	0.031	0.563	1		
MEDIA	0.224	0.390	0.425	1	
ATTITUDE	0.195	0.523	0.426	0.267	1
CPI score	0.381	0.680	0.391	0.327	0.302

Panel B: Countries with three or more respondents (N = 27)

	PUBSCORE	*LEVEL*	*AUDIT*	*MEDIA*	*ATTITUDE*
PUBSCORE	1				
LEVEL	0.375	1			
AUDIT	0.406	0.497	1		
MEDIA	0.181	0.427	0.407	1	
ATTITUDE	0.238	0.641	0.480	0.220	1
CPI score	0.432	0.709	0.390	0.179	0.571

Panel C: Countries with five or more respondents (N = 21)

	PUBSCORE	*LEVEL*	*AUDIT*	*MEDIA*	*ATTITUDE*
PUBSCORE	1				
LEVEL	0.590	1			
AUDIT	0.656	0.788	1		
MEDIA	0.432	0.499	0.408	1	
ATTITUDE	0.466	0.666	0.578	0.231	1
CPI score	0.502	0.784	0.580	0.290	0.667

If Hypothesis (iii) is substantiated, it suggests that corruption is reduced as the center of gravity in economic activities shifts from rural to urban areas. In this section, the unit of analysis and hence the unit of observation is an individual, not a country.

For this purpose, we estimate a regression equation as follows:

$$\text{PUBSCORE}_i = X_i\beta + Z_i\gamma + \varepsilon_i \quad (1)$$

where the dependent variable, PUBSCOREi, is an indicator of discipline for respondent i, X_i is a vector of socioeconomic characteristics, Z_i is a vector of preference variables, and ε_i is an error term. Vector X_i includes the country of residence, age, sex, religion, place of birth, place of residence, occupation, and the logarithm of annual income in US dollars. Education could be included in X_i, because some of our respondents have a Ph.D. or two masters degrees but not just one masters degree, and because Truex (2011) finds a strong effect of education on PUBSCORE in the sample of ordinary citizens in Kathmandu. In our sample, however, education variables do not have any significant coefficients and the inclusion of them does not alter any qualitative results of the analysis. The country of residence is represented by a set of country dummy variables, each corresponding to a particular country. An alternative specification is to replace the set of country dummies by the CPI score of the country of residence. This specification allows us to see whether PUBSCORE is higher (that is, government officials are more disciplined) in less corrupt countries than more corrupt countries. The inclusion of Z_i in equation (1) is intended to mitigate SDB and omitted variable biases. This vector consists of the measures of attitudes toward risk-taking, patience, preference for relative evaluation over absolute evaluation, and the proclivity for procrastination, each of which is the individual's subjective rating on a scale of 1 to 5.

The estimated coefficients of interest are reported in Table 8.6 on pages 174–5, which has 12 columns. The specification with the CPI score is used in the first three columns and columns (7) to (9). In the other columns, the country dummies are included instead. While the first three columns use all the observations that have the complete set of data necessary for this specification, columns (4) to (6) use a sub-sample from those countries that have two or more respondents, and columns (7) to (12) use a sub-sample from those countries with at least five respondents, in order to mitigate SDB. Columns (1), (4), (7), and (10) cover both developed and developing countries, while columns (2), (5), (8), and (11) cover only the developing countries (that is, the low- and middle-income countries), and columns (3), (6), (9), and (12) focus on the low-income countries.

The coefficients on the CPI score are positive in all cases and significant at the 1 percent level for the full sample (see columns (1) and (7)) and the sub-sample of developing countries (see columns (2) and (8)). Thus, government officials in less corrupt countries tend to be less accepting of corrupt behaviors. The relative magnitude of the coefficients as well as the significance levels indicates that this tendency is particularly strong among middle-income countries. These results, together with the differences in PUBSCORE among the three country categories shown in Table 8.4, are consistent with Hypothesis (i).

The age of the individual has a negative coefficient, which is generally insignificant when the CPI score is included in the regression but highly significant when the country dummies are used. The latter specification accounts for country fixed effects, that is, the effects of both observable and unobserved factors common to the country of residence, including the CPI score, on PUBSCORE. Thus, for the purpose of estimating the association between the individual's characteristics and PUBSCORE, the latter specification must be superior. Either the estimated coefficients on age or their significance levels are slightly higher when SDB is mitigated by restricting the sample countries to those with five or more respondents, that is, in columns (10) to (12). These results are consistent with Hypothesis (ii). Note, however, that Hypothesis (ii) can be obtained from two different dynamic processes. The Sah model predicts that when a society becomes less corrupt, every person tends to become increasingly disciplined with age, and a younger cohort starts from a higher level of discipline than an older cohort. Alternatively, Hypothesis (ii) will hold truc in the case in which every cohort starts from the same level and becomes less and less corrupt with age. Thus, while our results are consistent with the hypothesis, they do not necessarily lend strong support to the Sah model.

There is no gender gap in PUBSCORE if the effects of other characteristics and traits are controlled for. In column (8), the coefficient on the female dummy is positive and its statistical significance is only slightly short of the 10 percent level, suggesting that female officials are more disciplined. The coefficient, however, is not at all significant if the country fixed effects are taken into account. Religion is not associated with PUBSCORE, either. As mentioned earlier, a small number of respondents are employees of private or quasi-governmental organizations. The variable named "Private sector" is equal to 1 if the respondent falls in this category, and it is zero otherwise. The coefficient on this variable is insignificant in all columns.

The information on the place of birth and the place of current residence is presented with two variables. One is "Birth in rural," a dummy variable which is equal to 1 if the respondent was born in a rural area and zero otherwise. The other is "Residence in rural," a dummy variable which is 1 if the respondent is living in a rural area and zero otherwise. These two dummy variables divide the sample into four groups: (A) about 40 percent of the respondents were born and are living in urban areas; (B) about 40 percent were born in rural areas but are living in urban areas; (C) a small percentage of the respondents were born and are living in rural areas; and (D) about 17 percent of the sample were born in urban areas but are living in rural areas. In column (1), the coefficients on these two dummy variables indicate that compared with group A, group B scored 0.164 points higher, group C scored 0.164–0.270 points higher (although group C scored actually lower because the difference is statistically insignificant but negative), and group D scored 0.270 points lower. Qualitatively similar results are found in columns (2), (5), (7), (8), and (9), and group C scored significantly lower than group A in columns (4), (10), and (11) as well. The values (in absolute terms) of the estimated coefficients on these variables are larger in columns (2), (5), (8), and (11) than in columns (1), (4), (7), and (10), which suggests that rural residents are more accepting of corruption than urban residents, especially in middle-income countries. In columns (3), (6), (9), and (12), these coefficients are insignificant, indicating that rural residents in low-income countries are not more accepting of corruption than urban residents. This is probably because in low-income countries, even urban residents are considerably accepting of corruption. These results are consistent with Hypothesis (iii).

The coefficient on annual income is positive and significant in every column. Note that the majority of the respondents are government officials, and that the variation in the average income level of the country is absorbed by the country fixed effects or to a lesser extent by the CPI score. The variation in income level that matters here comes from the difference in ranks within a government.

Table 8.6 Regressions of PUBSCORE

	(1)	*(2)*	*(3)*	*(4)*	*(5)*
	All countries	*Developing countries*	*Low-income countries*	*Countries with two or more obs*	*Developing countries with 2+ obs*
CPI score	0.103***	0.235***	0.195	–	–
	(3.986)	(3.528)	(1.299)		
Country dummies	–	–	–	Yes	Yes
Age	–0.010	–0.016*	–0.016	–0.023**	–0.027***
	(–1.232)	(–1.856)	(–1.398)	(–2.632)	(–3.263)
Female	0.129	0.142	–0.089	0.009	0.043
	(1.311)	(1.302)	(–0.323)	(0.084)	(0.371)
Christian	0.173	0.196	0.096	–0.055	0.011
	(1.538)	(1.551)	(0.516)	(–0.487)	(0.088)
Muslim	0.233	0.276*	0.077	–0.024	0.082
	(1.490)	(1.810)	(0.356)	(–0.164)	(0.535)
Birth in rural	0.164**	0.204**	0.236	0.070	0.127*
	(2.285)	(2.643)	(1.706)	(0.943)	(1.779)
Residence in rural	–0.270**	–0.280**	–0.132	–0.317**	–0.374**
	(–2.508)	(–2.060)	(–0.687)	(–2.151)	(–2.213)
Private sector	0.006	–0.006	0.179	0.020	0.012
	(0.046)	(–0.037)	(0.865)	(0.108)	(0.060)
ln (annual income)	0.100***	0.114***	0.145***	0.079**	0.082**
	(3.242)	(3.543)	(2.866)	(2.135)	(2.253)
Risk-taker	0.071	0.072	0.108	0.038	0.051
	(1.448)	(1.446)	(1.210)	(0.632)	(0.879)
Patience	–0.040	–0.027	–0.018	0.008	0.026
	(–0.854)	(–0.509)	(–0.211)	(0.139)	(0.413)
Preference for	0.030	–0.000	0.062	0.011	0.009
relative evaluation	(0.436)	(–0.006)	(0.526)	(0.113)	(0.084)
Procrastination	–0.075	–0.109*	–0.091	–0.076	–0.116*
	(–1.518)	(–1.954)	(–1.222)	(–1.427)	(–2.010)
Constant	3.404***	3.138***	2.633**	4.586***	4.476***
	(5.131)	(4.589)	(2.544)	(6.922)	(6.724)
Observations	275	245	123	256	232
R-squared	0.161	0.180	0.164	0.329	0.330

Notes: Numbers in parentheses are robust t-statistics, clustered at the country level to account for correlation among respondents in the same country. *, **, and *** indicate the 10, 5, and 1 percent levels of significance, respectively. The sample consists of the countries with two or more observations in columns (4) to (5), those with three or more observations in columns (6) to (12).

(6)	*(7)*	*(8)*	*(9)*	*(10)*	*(11)*	*(12)*
Low-income countries	*Countries with 5 or more obs*	*Developing countries*	*Low-income countries*	*Countries with 5 or more obs*	*Developing countries*	*Low-income countries*
–	0.108***	0.258***	0.202	–	–	–
	(3.474)	(3.532)	(1.212)			
Yes	–	–	–	Yes	Yes	Yes
−0.023**	−0.012	−0.017*	−0.021	−0.025***	−0.028***	−0.028**
(−2.208)	(−1.333)	(−1.906)	(−1.742)	(−2.883)	(−3.467)	(−2.668)
−0.245	0.167	0.189	−0.031	0.043	0.071	−0.218
(−0.846)	(1.535)	(1.634)	(−0.108)	(0.399)	(0.624)	(−0.749)
−0.469	0.171	0.202	0.050	−0.049	−0.013	−0.492
(−1.165)	(1.316)	(1.422)	(0.256)	(−0.408)	(−0.096)	(−1.190)
0.021	0.265	0.268	0.066	0.050	0.085	0.036
(0.059)	(1.572)	(1.628)	(0.291)	(0.363)	(0.525)	(0.101)
0.147	0.175**	0.201**	0.260*	0.069	0.105	0.123
(1.002)	(2.172)	(2.301)	(1.784)	(0.965)	(1.462)	(0.830)
−0.159	−0.280**	−0.288*	−0.132	−0.320**	−0.370**	−0.136
(−0.602)	(−2.315)	(−1.922)	(−0.608)	(−2.121)	(−2.100)	(−0.479)
0.211	0.012	−0.017	0.225	0.067	0.050	0.280
(0.863)	(0.085)	(−0.104)	(1.063)	(0.365)	(0.244)	(1.187)
0.111*	0.113***	0.123***	0.173***	0.085**	0.087**	0.126**
(1.988)	(3.555)	(3.763)	(4.200)	(2.360)	(2.421)	(2.352)
0.097	0.059	0.071	0.088	0.034	0.049	0.091
(0.977)	(1.094)	(1.315)	(0.969)	(0.554)	(0.809)	(0.942)
0.021	−0.031	−0.001	0.012	0.017	0.028	0.036
(0.205)	(−0.564)	(−0.024)	(0.130)	(0.290)	(0.423)	(0.342)
0.039	0.033	0.006	0.093	0.018	0.011	0.039
(0.254)	(0.411)	(0.065)	(0.768)	(0.174)	(0.095)	(0.252)
−0.085	−0.092*	−0.113*	−0.106	−0.087	−0.118*	−0.095
(−0.985)	(−1.736)	(−1.911)	(−1.374)	(−1.638)	(−2.039)	(−1.150)
3.706***	3.354***	2.934***	2.487**	4.729***	4.916***	4.598***
(3.125)	(4.533)	(3.798)	(2.306)	(7.314)	(7.095)	(4.031)
117	239	219	112	239	219	112
0.280	0.171	0.189	0.177	0.331	0.331	0.286

The positive coefficient on this variable is likely to indicate that government officials in higher positions tend to be less accepting of corruption. A few explanations for this result come to mind immediately. First, higher positions and higher salaries would induce respondents to express more strongly negative attitudes toward corruption because if they were involved in a corruption scandal, their losses would be larger than those with lower positions and lower salaries. Second, those officials who are less frank or alter answers so as to sound more socially desirable may be more likely to get promoted. That is, candidness is a third factor affecting both annual income and PUBSCORE. Third, those officials who are more disciplined are more likely to get promoted. That is, there is a reverse causation. It is possible that all these causations coexist behind the positive coefficient on annual income.

The coefficients on the preference variables are generally insignificant. Exceptions are the positive and significant estimates of the coefficient on procrastination in columns (2), (5), (7), (8), and (11). A possible interpretation of the positive coefficient is that persons prone to procrastination have trouble disciplining themselves. Another possible interpretation is that officials who candidly admit that they are prone to procrastination are also candid when they answer the questions about the problematic behaviors and, hence, they have lower PUBSCOREs. That is, SDB may be captured by the negative coefficient on the procrastination variable.

The whole result of the regression analysis shown in Table 8.6 indicates that only a very small part of the variation in PUBSCORE can be explained by the country fixed effects, socioeconomic characteristics, and preference or mentality variables. A possible explanation is that the variance of PUBSCORE is inflated by measurement errors. However, it is difficult to imagine that the respondents committed errors frequently when they gave their opinions of the problematic behaviors. To the extent that measurement errors are not serious, one can say that persons with similar characteristics can have quite different attitudes toward corruption, and that the low explanatory power of equation (1) is consistent with Hypothesis (iv).

6 Concluding remarks

This study has attempted to deepen our understanding of corruption norms by extending the pioneering work of Truex (2011). Our sample of GRIPS alumni, together with Truex's sample, has allowed us to find that ordinary citizens and government officials in low-income countries make different distinctions between acceptable and unacceptable behaviors. We have also found that corrupt behaviors are almost always unacceptable for the majority of GRIPS alumni in high-income countries but less likely to be unacceptable for the majority of their counterparts in low-income countries. Thus, the legitimacy of state will improve with economic development not only because development is the target of state building but also because development accompanies reduction in corruption. Moreover, both the descriptive and regression analyses show that even among government officials with similar socioeconomic backgrounds, the distinction of acceptable and unacceptable behaviors varies substantially from one person to another.

These findings recast our image of corruption norms. Like other social norms, corruption norms are standards of behaviors that are accepted within a society, but they are neither very specific nor precisely known to everyone in the society. Corruption norms leave room for the free discretion of individuals and for various interpretations, especially in low-income countries. Thus, corruption norms in such countries would be a source of uncertainty and unpredictability, and, hence, higher transaction costs.

This study has also presented the new piece of evidence that corruption norms are not fixed standards but keep changing. We have found that our data are consistent with some predictions derived from Sah's (2007) model of the dynamics of corruption norms and perceptions related to corruption, such as perceived levels of corruption prevalence, quality of anti-corruption institutions, such as the audit system and media, and compatriots' attitudes toward corruption. The model suggests that sustained efforts to reduce corruption will have lasting effects and to break traditional corruption norms.

A way to increase the speed of changing corruption norms and reduce transaction costs arising from corruption would be to improve citizens' access to information about corruption. Improved access to information may be classified into three types. First, as mentioned earlier, Reinikka and Svensson (2011) report an exemplary case in which the disclosure of information improves the ability of citizens to monitor local government officials, leading to a remarkable reduction in corruption. Second, the results of our study about Sah's model suggest that the increased publicity about the probability of detection and punishment and the legal sanctions levied would also be helpful. The information that the probability is increasing or penalties are becoming more severe will increase the pace of change in corruption norms in a positive direction. Of course, when the probability is decreasing and penalties are becoming less severe, the increased publicity may worsen corruption norms, but it will put pressure on the government to make efforts to prevent such a setback.

The third type of improved access to corruption information involves gathering and disseminating information about the attitudes of other citizens, government officials, and politicians toward various types of corruption. According to the results of our study, this will reduce uncertainty and hence transaction costs. The evaluation of the pros and cons of such a policy is an issue for future study. Another avenue for research is to extend the present study so that the sample includes a greater number of graduates from not only GRIPS but other public policy schools in other countries. Such extended studies will offer more insights into corruption norms and anti-corruption measures.

Notes

* The author wishes to thank GRIPS alumni for responding to the GRIPS Alumni Survey on National Institutional System, thereby providing the data used in this study. He is

also grateful to Karin Hillen for administering the survey, Ayumi Arai and Ryoko Susukida for providing research assistance, and Paul Kandasamy for editing the manuscript.

1 This study focuses on demographically widespread corruption undertaken by a large proportion of government officials. The other kind of corruption includes monopolistic corruption in monarchies, oligarchies, and autocracies. See Shleifer and Vishny (1993) for details.

2 GRIPS has its alumni from 93 countries, but the respondents to our survey are only from 58 countries.

3 In the calculation of the correlation coefficients shown in Table 8.5, Fiji is not included because Fiji does not have a CPI score. Thus, the number of observations is 57, not 58.

References

Arnold, H.J. and Feldman, D.C. (1981) "Social desirability response bias in self-report choice situation," *Academy of Management Journal*, 24 (2): 377–85.

Becker, G.S. and Stigler, G.J. (1974) "Law enforcement, malfeasance, and compensation of enforces," *Journal of Legal Studies* 3: 1–18.

Ferraz, C. and Finan, F. (2011) "Electoral accountability and corruption: evidence from the audits of local governments," *American Economic Review*, 101 (3): 1274–311.

Fisman, R. and Miguel, E. (2007) "Corruption, norms, and legal enforcement: evidence from diplomatic parking tickets," *Journal of Political Economy*, 115 (6): 1020–48.

Fisman, R. and Svensson, J. (2007) "Are corruption and taxation really harmful to growth? Firm level evidence," *Journal of Development Economics*, 83 (1): 63–75.

Mauro, P. (1995) "Corruption and growth," *Quarterly Journal of Economics*, 110 (3): 681–712.

Olken, B.A. (2007) "Monitoring corruption: evidence from a field experiment in Indonesia," *Journal of Political of Economy*, 115 (21): 200–49.

Reinikka, R. and Svensson, J. (2005) "Fighting corruption to improve schooling: evidence from a newpaper campaign in Uganda, *Journal of European Economic Association*, 3: 259–67.

Reinikka, R. and Svensson, J. (2011) "The power of information in public services: evidence from education in Uganda," *Journal of Public Economics*, 95 (78): 956–66.

Rose-Ackerman, S. (1999) *Corruption and Government: Causes, Consequences, and Reform*, New York: Cambridge University Press.

Sah, R. (2007) "Corruption across countries and regions: some consequences of local osmosis," *Journal of Economic Dynamics and Control*, 31 (8): 2573–98.

Shleifer, A. and Vishny, R.W. (1993) "Corruption," *Quarterly Journal of Economics*, 108 (3): 599–617.

Svensson, J. (2005) "Eight questions about corruption," *Journal of Economic Perspectives*, 19 (3): 19–42.

Truex, R. (2011) "Corruption, attitudes, and education: Survey evidence from Nepal," *World Development*, 39 (7): 1133–42.

Wei, S.J. (2000) "How taxing is corruption on international investors?" *Review of Economics and Statistics,* 82 (1): 1–11.

9 Failure and success of development policies for industrial clusters

Keijiro Otsuka and Tetsushi Sonobe

1 Introduction

The last four decades have witnessed a large number of successful cases of industrial development in Asia, but possibly an equally large number of failures in other developing countries, particularly in Sub-Saharan Africa (SSA). While the governments of developing countries are strongly interested in implementing effective industrial policy, development economists have failed to design widely-accepted effective strategies to develop industries.[1] Probably this is due partly to the failure of import substitution policies and partly to the commonly accepted neoclassical presumption that "industrial policies" do not work, and thus governments have to do little to promote industrial development beyond the provision of infrastructure such as roads, electricity, and communication systems.

Such a presumption, however, fails to recognize the variety of market failures that take place in the process of industrial development. We contend that an appropriate industrial development policy that corrects market failures is an integral part of successful state building for development.[2] One major market failure arises from the high transaction costs between manufacturing firms (e.g., assemblers and parts-suppliers) and between manufacturers and traders, which are attributed to asymmetric information and imperfect contract enforcement (e.g., Akerlof 1970; Hart and Moore 1990; Williamson 1985). An obvious institution counteracting this problem is industrial clusters, in which the transacting parties are located near each other to reduce transaction costs (Becker and Murphy 1992). In other words, an industrial cluster can be regarded as an institution that makes markets work by reducing transaction costs. Thus, the government ought to support the development of industrial clusters (Sonobe and Otsuka 2006, 2011).

Industrial clusters are not a panacea, however, because there are other market failures. First of all, the inadequacy of managerial human resources of firms in developing countries has been increasingly recognized in recent literature (e.g., Bruhn *et al.* 2010; Syverson 2011). The case studies of industrial development in Asia and Africa by Sonobe and Otsuka (2006, 2011) reveal that entrepreneurs' managerial human capital plays a critical role in industrial development, as it affects innovation or improvements in production and management efficiency.

More recent waves of randomized experiments demonstrate that the majority of entrepreneurs in developing countries have inadequate knowledge about standard management practices (e.g., Bloom and Van Reenen 2007, 2010; Bloom *et al.* 2010, 2011). As with ordinary human capital, investment in managerial human capital is likely to be socially sub-optimal due importantly to inaccessibility to finance. We argue that the government should facilitate the formation of managerial human capital.

Secondly, industrial clusters thwart incentives to innovate because the geographical proximity of firms within the cluster to each other tends to reduce the cost of imitation, thereby suppressing the private benefits of innovation compared with the social benefits. In order to provide proper incentives to innovate, either the collective action of clustered enterprises or government support policies are needed, as is argued by Nadvi (1999) and Schmitz (1999).

Thirdly, there is much evidence, based on randomized controlled and natural experiments (e.g., Banerjee and Duflo 2005; De Mel *et al.* 2008), that small and medium firms in low-income countries are faced with severe credit constraints. Although industrial clusters may mitigate the effect of credit constraints by stimulating the division and specialization of labor among enterprises, thereby reducing the requirement of initial capital investment (Ruan and Zhang 2009), the cluster does not solve the imperfection of credit markets. It does not follow, however, that a policy toward industrial development should begin with correcting this market failure problem. We argue that the provision of low-interest loans to credit-constrained enterprises is more effective if they are provided to promising entrepreneurs, who may be identified after the provision of technical and managerial training to them.

Fourthly, successful industrial clusters are congested because agglomeration economies attract the entry of new firms until their advantages are wiped out (Glaeser and Gottlieb 2009). The construction of industrial zones and parks is needed to reduce congestion and to promote the expansion of productive enterprises.

The purpose of this chapter is to formulate an effective cluster-based industrial development policy for low-income countries. We believe that the engine of such development is technological progress, including both innovation accompanied by the process of creative destruction and less drastic but practically important improvements in production and management (e.g., Grossman and Helpman 1991; Romer 1986; Schumpeter 1934; Solow 1956). We agree with Gerschenkron (1962) and Deming (1994), among many others, that the major source of innovations is the application of new technological and managerial knowledge imported from developed countries.[3] Because of the information spillovers, investments in the acquisition of such knowledge will fall short of the social optimum. Thus, markets fail, and there is substantial room for the government to play an important role in promoting industrial development. In this chapter, we examine not only how to develop industries by reducing market failures but also how to reduce government failures based on the successful experience of cluster-based development in Japan and China.

The structure of the chapter is as follows. We review typical development paths of industrial clusters in Section 2, while we discuss the advantages of the industrial cluster and its limitations in Section 3. In Section 4, we examine how to promote the initiation of new appropriate industries, which is followed by a discussion of how to sustain the industrial development by stimulating innovations. Section 5 attempt to learn lessons from the experience of Japan and China, and Section 6 concludes the chapter by recapitulating the proposed industrial development policy in the wider context of East Asian development.

2 A review of cluster-based industrial development

More often than not, labor-intensive manufacturing industries, such as the garment, leather shoe, weaving, metal processing, and furniture industries, are clustered in developing countries. Huang and Bocchi (2008), Long and Zhang (2011), Schmitz and Nadvi (1999), and Sonobe and Otsuka (2006), as well as many other studies, report that there are a large number of industrial clusters in East and South Asia and Latin America. Clusters in SSA are studied by McCormick (1999) and Sonobe and Otsuka (2011). These observations indicate that the industrial cluster provides strong advantages for enterprises over non-clustered areas. There are, however, both dynamically growing and stagnant industrial clusters. Also common patterns of the development processes are observed among the successful cases of cluster-based development in Asia and Africa (Sonobe and Otsuka 2006, 2011). Based on our own studies, we present the typical development paths of industrial clusters in this section.

In most cases, the pioneers of new industries imitate the production of imported products. If the production is easy but marketing is difficult, like the garment business, former traders are often the pioneers. On the other hand, if the production is technically complicated, like machinery production, engineers tend to be the pioneers.[4] Those who have worked for large enterprises and foreign firms are often the leading pioneers (see Chapter 10). Thus, marketing and technological knowledge and work experience are critical factors affecting entrepreneurship in the early stage of cluster development.

To initiate a new business, the pioneer must exert great efforts to establish new production methods, find new sources of materials, and cultivate new marketing channels. Once the new business is established, the pioneer receives sizable entrepreneurial profits, despite the low quality of his or her products, because of the large demand for inexpensive products from poor domestic consumers. This profit attracts swarm of imitators to the industry. Many of them are spin-offs, i.e., the former employees of the pioneer, and produce the same low-quality products by using the same low-quality inputs and sell their products on the same local markets as the pioneer. In this way, an industrial cluster is formed, as illustrated in Figure 9.1.[5]

Since the profits are reasonably high, for the time being, entrepreneurs are not particularly interested in introducing new ideas and knowledge. Hence, productivity and product quality hardly improves, but the cluster expands in terms

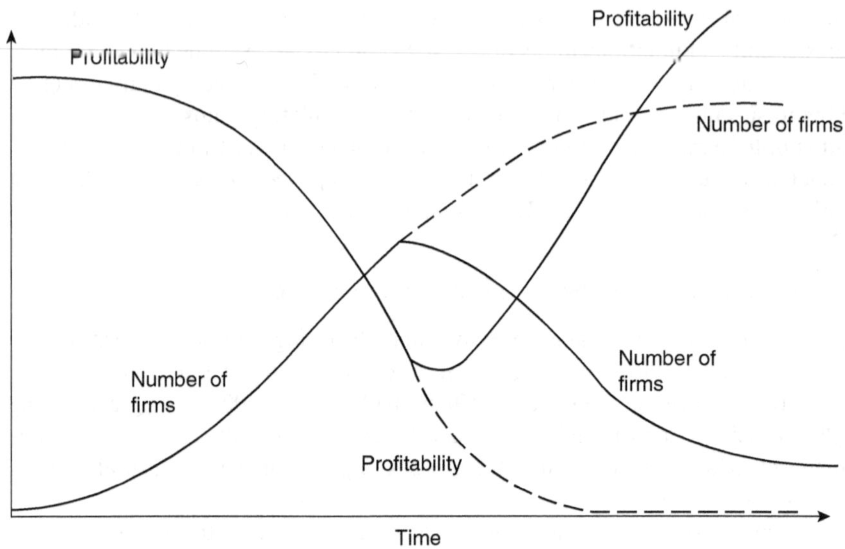

Figure 9.1 An illustration of development patterns of industrial clusters in terms of changing profitability and the number of firms

of the number of firms and the total output. This phase of industrial development may be termed the "quantity expansion" phase.

As a cluster expands, an increasing number of traders buying products and supplying materials come to the cluster, which makes production and transactions in the cluster more convenient. Moreover, some firms specialize in the production of parts. In other words, the division of labor between assemblers and part-suppliers and between manufacturers and traders increases with the market size (Ruan and Zhang 2009; Stigler 1951). In the transaction of final products and parts, transaction costs may arise from asymmetric information about the quality of goods and from imperfect contract enforcement. At this stage of development, however, the problem of asymmetric information regarding the quality is not serious because all the products and parts produced and transacted are standard and of uniformly low quality. The problem of imperfect contract enforcement is reduced by the community mechanism supported by the environment of the cluster in which people know each other and in which information regarding unscrupulous behavior can spread quickly, as in rural communities.[6]

As the entry of new firms unaccompanied by any improvement in product quality and productivity continues, the increased supply of their products will eventually lower the product prices, increase the input prices, and, hence, reduce the profitability. This process, illustrated by Figure 9.1, takes place in the later period of the quantity expansion phase of industrial development. The declining profitability will induce entrepreneurs and managers to seek more profitable products (Aghion *et al.* 2005), which should be of higher quality and differentiated from the inferior products of other firms.

Such an endeavor, however, does not necessarily bear fruit. While a firm may successfully improve product quality by using high-quality materials and employing skilled workers, consumers may not immediately perceive the improved quality and, hence, the new product may fail to command a high price in the market. This firm incurs losses as the cost of production is much higher than before. Akerlof (1970) points out that branding and quality guarantees are effective countermeasures to this problem. However, entrepreneurs in industrial clusters in the quantity expansion phase may not be familiar with such countermeasures. Moreover, since brands may be stolen, branding may have to be supplemented with the use of exclusive sales agencies and own distribution methods (Sonobe *et al.* 2004). Since the improved products use differentiated parts and components and since such intermediate goods embody new ideas, it is also important to establish trust-based, long-term subcontracting relationships with parts suppliers. In addition, to enter the high-quality segment of the market, product quality must be strictly controlled. If these changes are successfully implemented, production can be expanded profitably. As the firm size is enlarged accordingly, the management of cash flows, inventory, and labor will assume greater importance. Good management is not an easy task for entrepreneurs in the cluster, as they have operated only small organizations and may be unaware of how to improve management. In this sense, they are far from efficient managers. They now need to study management or hire competent managers or, probably, both.

The restoration of high profitability involves these multifaceted improvements in production and management (IPM). Although a set of such improvements may not be a genuine innovation, it can be regarded as an innovation in the sense that it is difficult to achieve. Moreover, it is imitated by followers. According to our case studies, the entrepreneurs who achieved the first successful innovation in their clusters and those who imitated it quickly tended to be highly educated. This observation is consistent with Schultz's (1975) hypothesis that the ability to deal with changing profit opportunities can be enhanced by schooling.[7]

The case studies by Sonobe and Otsuka (2006, 2011) also find that these innovative entrepreneurs took advantage of the availability of a variety of human resources in the cluster, such as traders, engineers, designers, and accountants, who gathered in the clusters in the quantity expansion phase. Thus, it is fair to say that the IPM under study is a product of a new "combination" of existing resources, to use the expression of Schumpeter (1934) to refer to innovation.

If entrepreneurs' attempts to improve production and management fail, this will lead the cluster to a long-run equilibrium with low profitability, in which firms struggle for survival (see the dotted curves in Figure 9.1). While such "survival clusters" abound in SSA, many industrial clusters in Asia have succeeded in innovating and have followed a path leading to the dynamic development of the industry with a smaller number of much larger firms, as illustrated by the solid curves in Figure 9.1. The dynamic development phase that usually begins with successful IPM may be termed the "quality improvement" phase.

An increasing number of firms attempt to imitate the first innovation in the cluster, and some of them further improve production and management practices. Those firms undertaking continual IPM will grow steadily, whereas firms that fail to keep pace with growing firms will be forced to exit the industry or will be merged with growing firms. While the number of firms in the cluster will decrease as a result of exits and mergers, the total production value and employment of the cluster will continue to grow, and the products will be sold in larger markets, including export markets. Continual IPM is often achieved by learning from outside of the cluster, especially from abroad. More concretely, innovative entrepreneurs acquire new knowledge of technology and management by visiting foreign countries frequently to participate in trade fairs and training programs, sending workers abroad for training, and inviting foreign experts. They may also be able to learn from foreign firms operating within their countries, as in the case of the pharmaceutical industry in Bangladesh to be analyzed in Chapter 10.

3 Advantages and limitations of industrial clusters

According to Marshall (1920), the advantages of industrial clusters or agglomeration economies are: (1) information spillovers or imitation; (2) the division and specialization of labor among firms producing parts, components, and final products; and (3) the development of skilled labor markets. While we do not have any objections to these advantages associated with industrial clusters, we would like to point out that they are intimately related to each other. For example, information spillovers increase with spin-offs, the poaching of human resources, and with transactions between firms. The three advantages envisaged by Marshall arise commonly from the low transaction costs. These benefits of industrial clusters explain why indigenously developed industries in developing countries are so often clustered.[8]

The fact that the industrial cluster expands through the massive entry of imitators implies that imitation is easy and rampant in the industrial cluster. Although imitation is often blamed for discouraging innovation, it is socially desirable if the probability of further innovation is sufficiently small because new knowledge should be disseminated as widely as possible in such a case (Arrow 1962). But in general, imitation reduces the profit accrued to the innovator, thereby reducing the incentives to innovate. This is a major limitation of the industrial cluster in the development of industries.

A related limitation is the lack of institutions to introduce useful technologies and management know-how from outside, particularly from more advanced regions and countries. In Marshallian agglomeration economies, innovation is missing even though imitation is considered. If the main new ideas come from outside and if it is useful for many, if not all, of the enterprises within a cluster, either collectively supported indigenous institutions or public-sector institutions to facilitate learning new knowledge are needed for the improvement of the collective welfare.

In the quality improvement phase, the problem of inferior quality products tends to arise. A good example is a fake product, which looks similar to improved products but is inferior. The production of such a product may be intentional or reflect a lack of understanding of the improved technology. Selling such a product reduces the reputation of the industrial cluster and, hence, all the enterprises in the cluster may suffer from such a product. Here too, either collective action or government support for quality assurance is needed.

Industrial clusters, particularly if they successfully grow, become congested, as the entry of new firms continues so far as the positive profit lures the entry. Thus, in equilibrium the positive externality arising from the agglomeration economies may be offset by the negative externality arising from the congestion (Glaeser and Gottlieb 2009). In order to avoid the congestion and promote the agglomeration economies, the construction of industrial zones with well-developed infrastructure may be one possible solution. This is important because Eifert *et al.* (2008) indicate that firms in SSA suffer from the poor quality of basic infrastructure, such as roads, electricity, and communication networks. Thus, basic infrastructure should be provided by the government to the industrial zones or areas designated for industries in or near major cities. Also, given the imperfect credit markets, the provision of cheap credit by the government will be needed to relocate promising enterprises to new factories in the industrial zone.

4 Role of the government in cluster development

In order to develop industrial clusters, there are several potentially important roles to be played by the government, which include the provision of knowledge useful for innovation, quality assurance, the prevention of congestion, and financial support. In what follows, we would like to consider more specifically what the government should do in the initiation, quantity expansion, and quality improvement phases of cluster development.

In order to pursue a dynamic development path, competitive market environments must be created and maintained by the government so that the scarcity of resources and the social value of goods are signaled by market prices. This is not enough, however, to initiate the industrialization; the initiation of a new industry is an innovative activity and, as Schumpeter (1934) clearly points out, innovation is likely to be imitated by followers, which tends to depress the incentives to initiate new business. One possible solution is to rely on the leadership of the government in the selection and promotion of appropriate industries. Recently Lin (2009, 2010) and Lin and Monga (2010, 2011) have proposed that governments in low-income countries should identify and promote industries which have successfully developed and become mature in slightly more advanced countries with similar factor endowments. While we agree with these authors that it is a sound development strategy to imitate slightly more advanced countries, we admit that there is the risk of government failure associated with the choice of industries, as is argued by Pack and Saggi (2006), and the ways in which support is provided.[9] Also, the government must identify not only promising industries but also promising entrepreneurs, appropriate locations, and appropriate technologies, which would exceed the capacity of ordinary government. Furthermore, Lin and Monga do not specify how technology and management know-how can be introduced, except for relying on foreign direct investment (FDI).

It is true that entrepreneurs in developing countries often learn production and management knowledge from foreign firms. But whether low-income countries can attract FDI depends on business environments, which are affected by the quality of governance, business laws and regulations, the availability of auxiliary and supporting services, and infrastructure (Blomström and Kokko 2003). Furthermore, foreign firms may not invest in subsidiaries in low-income countries if they anticipate that their products, production methods, and marketing channels are likely to be copied by the local entrepreneurs and their customers are likely to be stolen. While we do not deny the importance of attracting FDI, we believe that it is risky to rely on FDI alone as a source of new knowledge for initiating new industry.

We propose an "entrepreneur-led and government-assisted" approach to the establishment of new industries based on our own observation that there are a significant number of potentially competent entrepreneurs in low-income countries. A possible way of accomplishing this task is to vitalize technical and vocational education and training programs. While these programs have so far focused on the skill formation of workers, management training programs should also be provided for entrepreneurs and hired managers, both present and prospective. The quality of technical and management training programs and other human resource development activities should be substantially improved by hiring competent foreign experts from newly industrialized countries as well as from developed countries.

It is also important to provide both general and industry-specific training. The provision of various industry-specific courses corresponding to a variety of industries will enlarge the opportunity set from which present and prospective entrepreneurs select profitable businesses to enter. Our approach based on private initiatives is consistent with the theoretical proposition of Rodriguez-Clare (2007) that the best policy entails the promotion of clustering in the sector in which the country has a comparative advantage. The provision of credit to competent pioneering entrepreneurs at this stage is infeasible, as it is not possible to identify them from an unknown pool of potential entrepreneurs.

Once an industrial cluster is formed by private initiatives, one possible role of the government is to promote market transactions. In the 1980s and 1990s, local governments in a large number of cities and townships in China built large commercial premises, wherein a large number of parts suppliers and local traders dealing in particular goods and services had shops. This policy contributed to the formation of industrial clusters (Ding 2007; Ruan and Zhang 2009). These local governments also actively constructed highways and other roads and communication networks, which were another major contribution to the quantity expansion of the Chinese economy.

In our view, efforts to improve production and management by learning from abroad are grossly sub-optimal in many industrial clusters, compared with the socially desirable level, chiefly for two reasons. First, rampant imitation, which is characteristic of industrial clusters, drives a gap between the social and private benefits of IPM and thereby discourages entrepreneurs from achieving the socially optimal level of IPM. Only a limited type of knowledge is protected, particularly in low-income countries. Second, the value of gaining new knowledge, particularly acquiring managerial knowledge, is not recognized by entrepreneurs, which drives another gap between the social and private benefits of IPM.

There may be different approaches to altering the behavior and attitude of entrepreneurs. For example, entrepreneurs may be given pecuniary incentives to gain technical and management knowledge. Entrepreneurs, however, are likely to have no idea where to gain such knowledge. Therefore, it seems better to provide a subsidized training program for entrepreneurs, which reduces the cost of learning, including search costs.[10] Training programs would give rise to much more limited corruption opportunities than infrastructure projects (Shleifer and Vishny 1993). Moreover, the knowledge taught in training programs will spill over from participants to non-participants, so that the dissemination of new knowledge is achieved without much cost and hence is efficient.

Since 2007, we have conducted, in collaboration with the World Bank and the Japan International Cooperation Agency (JICA), some pilot projects in which management training programs are provided for small entrepreneurs free of charge in our study sites in northern Vietnam, Addis Ababa, Kumasi, and Dar es Salaam (Mano *et al.* 2011; Sonobe *et al.* 2011). We found, among other things, that participants had very limited knowledge of standard management practices, and that the majority of them were willing to learn such practices. The estimates indicate clearly that the training programs have strong effects on the adoption of standard management practices and the willingness to pay for the admission to a similar training program in future, and that there are significant information spillovers from the training participants to non-participants. Our experimental data also suggest that the training participants are less likely to exit the industry, even though we need longer-run observations to confirm this further.

These results of the training experiments lend strong support to our arguments about the role that management training programs can play in promoting industrial development.[11] However, we must emphasize that the trial training programs that we have offered are not meant to push firms in the quantity expansion phase to enter the quality improvement phase. The content of the training programs was too rudimentary and the training period was too short to expect such a transition to take place.[12] Moreover, the training programs focused on management and did not include any aspect of technical training. Probably, a series of training programs are needed to impart sufficient management knowledge for successful IPM that allows trained firms to transition to the quality improvement phase. Nonetheless, the encouraging results of our experiments suggest that further research is warranted on the impacts of training, the effective contents and design of training programs, and the way in which management and technology training is institutionalized and can be scaled up from a single cluster level to the country level.

However, once firms get started on a continual IPM trajectory successfully, they will expand production, which will aggravate congestion problems, such as insufficient work space, noise, road congestion, and the short supply of water and electricity in their clusters. In many cases, the oldest firms in a cluster are located in the center or the most congested part of the cluster. Their founders' highly educated children tend to undertake IPM earlier and more successfully than other entrepreneurs. These firms have stronger incentives to relocate their production bases to outside of the cluster, partly because of the severe congestion and partly because of the fear of imitation by rivals. Thus, in order to reduce congestion and to stimulate the expansion of the scale of production by rigorously growing firms, the government should invest in industrial zones with improved infrastructure.

In Japan, Taiwan (China), South Korea, and China, the establishment of industrial zones mitigated the congestion problems in the existing industrial areas successfully and contributed to the rapid and sustained industrial growth in these countries (Levy 1991; Henderson *et al.* 2001; Mano and Otsuka 2000; Otsuka 2007; Sonobe and Otsuka 2006, Chapters 2 and 3). According to the theory of agglomeration economies (e.g., Fujita *et al.* 1999; Henderson 1988), the mitigation of congestion allows the central areas to accommodate more innovative industrial activities, thereby contributing to further industrial growth.

High performing firms in clusters in the quality improvement phase require finances to move from their original industrial clusters to more spacious and better equipped industrial zones. These firms are worthy of being granted low interest loans, in view of financial market failures evidenced by a host of empirical studies (e.g., Beck *et al.* 2009; Karlan and Morduch 2009). The advantage of offering cheap credit to assist the industrial relocation at this stage, over the earlier stage, is that it is relatively easy to distinguish between innovative and, hence, promising firms and non-promising firms. It is desirable to link the management training programs with the provision of credit and space in the industrial zone so that firms with improved managerial and technical capabilities and, hence, higher ability to repay loans, tend to receive loans and relocate their production bases.

5 Examples from Japanese history and contemporary China

In the course of the modern economic development in Japan since the late nineteenth century, not only new modern industries, such as the cotton spinning industry (Otsuka *et al.* 1988), successfully developed but also the modernization of indigenous industries, such as the silk and cotton weaving industries (e.g., Hashino and Otsuka 2013), flourished based on the introduction of new technologies from western countries. The indigenous industries were mostly clustered by small and medium-size enterprises. The Meiji government recognized investments in technical education to be the most effective way towards rapid industrialization based on the technology imports for both modern and indigenous sectors (Uchida 1991). The center of industrial development in Japan before World War II was Osaka, where various kinds of technical and educational organizations and research institutes were established by the Osaka municipal and prefectural governments, in order to support the development of small and medium-sized enterprises (Sawai 1999).

According to Hashino and Kurosawa (2013), a large number of trade associations were formed in indigenous clusters of the silk weaving industry in late nineteenth-century Japan. Such associations performed at least two functions: (1) to protect the name brand of the cluster and (2) to introduce new technologies. The associations established training institutes, inspected the quality of products, sent products to exhibitions, and communicated with overseas consulates about the reputation of their exported products. These are precisely the functions that are needed to realize quality improvement in industrial clusters. According to Hashino (2012), many trade associations in silk weaving clusters in Japan established training institutes in the 1880s in order to prevent the production of inferior quality products due to misunderstandings of western dying technology and to restore the brand of the clusters. They also asked the prefectural governments for subsidies for training. Later, the informal training institutes were transformed into formal technical schools managed by the Ministry of Education. Such development makes sense, as local producers know what kinds of new knowledge, skills, and information are needed to upgrade their products, and local governments are in a good position to respond to such local demand.

China's industrialization in the post-reform period is largely cluster-based (Long and Zhang 2011). One of the major issues for the development of industrial clusters in China was to change the perception of consumers about the quality of products, when the cluster attempted to transform itself from low-quality producers in the quantity expansion phase to high-quality producers in the quality improvement phase (Sonobe, Hu, and Otsuka 2002, 2004). According to Ruan and Zhang (2009), trade associations were spontaneously created in Zhejiang province to control the quality of products in the industrial clusters, particularly by suspending the operation of inferior quality producers. According to Fleisher *et al.* (2010), some local governments in Zhejiang province set up quality inspection centers to randomly check product quality and filter out inferior products and producers. In the case of the formation and development of the potato producing and processing cluster in Gansu province, it was the local government that introduced potatoes for commercial production, assisted the formation of trade associations to facilitate marketing, built wholesale marketplaces, and undertook research and extensions (Zhang and Hu 2013). Thus, as in the historical examples from Japan, trade associations and local governments played critical roles in promoting the industrial clusters in China.

The above examples are by no means exceptional. In Taiwan (China), where industrial development is highly cluster-based (Sonobe and Otsuka 2006; Sonobe *et al.* 2003), the Industrial Technology Research Institute has facilitated the import and dissemination of foreign technologies to clustered enterprises by means of adaptive research and training (Hong and Gee 1993). Nadvi (1999) reports that in the Sialkot surgical instrument cluster, which is one of Pakistan's rare examples of consistent export success, the trade association provided information on markets, technology, and other relevant issues to its members by means of training and inviting foreign buyers, and mobilized the state to adopt supportive programs for the cluster.

6 Concluding remarks

The fact that so many industries are clustered spontaneously in various parts of developing countries without receiving governmental support indicates that the Marshallian agglomeration economies are powerful forces to stimulate the formation of industrial clusters. To the extent that markets are undistorted, the development of such industries is consistent with the comparative advantage of the economy. The formation of industrial clusters, however, is not sufficient for dynamic and sustainable development: it requires further support for innovations, quality assurance, infrastructure, and finance. The inaction of the state is bound to lead to the failure of industrial development. While trade associations may play an important role in introducing new, innovative ideas and controlling the quality of products, there is room for local governments to play critical roles in supporting the development of industrial clusters.

The critical question is what motivates local governments to play facilitating roles in the development of industrial clusters. Although we do not have definitive answers, the roles of competition among local governments and learning from other areas should not be overlooked. Sawai (1999) argues that competition among local governments induced the successful application of local industrial policies in various locations in pre-war Japan. Similarly, Hashino (2012) points out that the success of training institutes in some industrial clusters provided a significant stimulus to the establishment of similar institutes in other industrial clusters in pre-war Japan. Zhang (2012) suggests that many successful industrial policies for cluster development originate from the local level in China, due at least partly to competition among local governments. If producers and workers in a locality realize successful industrial development in other localities, they will complain to the local policymakers. If local policymakers want to keep their offices or want to raise their reputation as reliable leaders, they are likely to respond to the demands of the local people. This seems to be an important mechanism underlying the successful development of industrial clusters in Japan and China. Providing autonomy to local governments, strengthening their capacity to support cluster development, and stimulating competition among local governments may be an integral part of the effective strategy to develop industrial clusters. The establishment of such a decentralized system can be a critical part of state building.

Although local governments have to play a role, the state or the central government is also important in providing business environments and investing in human resources. Discussions analogous to the role of local governments can be made for the adoption of successful development policies at the national level in East

Asian countries. Indeed, entrepreneurs and policymakers in East Asia are keen on learning from the successful experiences of advanced neighboring countries. Although statistical evidence is hard to come by, it is generally understood that Taiwan (China) and South Korea learned technology and management know-how from Japan in the 1970s and 1980s when their economies grew rapidly. Later, Indonesia, Malaysia, and Thailand followed the same strategy. More recently, China has been learning from Taiwan (China), Korea, and Japan. At present, Vietnam, Laos, and Cambodia are learning from China, among other countries. By contrast, the importance of learning from abroad is not clearly generally recognized in SSA.[13] Learning from advanced countries seems to be a critical condition for less developed countries to catch up with more advanced countries, as in the case of less advanced clusters learning from more advanced clusters elsewhere. If the state does not recognize the importance of learning from abroad, it is likely to fail in the promotion of industrial development.

Notes

1 There are, however, attempts to formulate industrial development policies; e.g., Cimoli *et al.* (2009), Lin and Monga (2010, 2011), and Page (2011).

2 As is discussed in Chapter 1, successful state building is also the prerequisite for successful industrial development as it assures a stable long-term investment environment.

3 By now, this view has been widely accepted by development economists and other experts (see Chapter 10 for the case of the pharmaceutical industry in Bangladesh). Indeed, Japanese development since the Meiji era provides a vivid example of successful development based on imported technologies (see Chapter 2).

4 Such a shift of jobs by traders and engineers is consistent with the prediction of Hidalao *et al.* (2007) that industrial compositions evolve only gradually.

5 Almost the same path has been followed by industries in which the initiation of the industry was based on new technology brought by FDI, state owned enterprises, and international organizations such as UNIDO.

6 Hayami (e.g., 2009) argues that the community mechanism is effective not only for the enforcement of contract-based transactions but also for the management of local commons and the provision of local public goods in rural communities. In this chapter, however, we focus on the enforcement of contract-based transactions.

7 Bloom and Van Reenen (2007, 2010) find that the education of entrepreneurs is strongly correlated with management scores in their study on management practices across firms and countries.

8 Here we distinguish between a cluster which has been established by local firms and one led by FDI. We believe that the community mechanism of contract enforcement plays an essential role in the former case, whereas the hierarchical relationships between large foreign firms and small local firms play a critical role in the latter case.

9 A case in point is the failure of the import substitution industrial policy, which provided distorted profit incentives to enterprises (Balassa *et al.* 1982; Bhagwati 1978; Krueger 1978). Lin and Monga (2011) propose a simplified industrialization strategy to avoid such failures.

10 Reviewing various policy options to facilitate industrialization in SSA, Page (2011) concludes that strengthening the managerial capabilities of firms and facilitating clustering are key policy measures.

11 These results are highly consistent with the results of other studies involving management training in developing countries (e.g., Bloom *et al.* 2011; Bruhn *et al.* 2010; Drexler *et al.* 2010; Field *et al.* 2010; Karlan and Valdivia 2010).

12 In general we offered classroom training for three hours per day for a total of 15 days. In addition, we implemented on-site visits of management consultants to participating firms twice in the cases of training programs in Vietnam, Ethiopia, and Tanzania.

13 Some enterprise managers in East African countries, however, are learning from other countries by employing technicians and managerial advisers from Asia and by visiting European countries.

References

Aghion, P., Bloom, N., Blundell, R., Griffith, R., and Howitt, P. (2005) "Competition and innovation: an inverted-U relationship," *Quarterly Journal of Economics*, 120 (2): 701–28.

Akerlof, G.A. (1970) "The market for 'lemons': quality uncertainty and the market mechanism," *Quarterly Journal of Economics*, 84 (3): 488–500.

Arrow, K.J. (1962) "Economic welfare and allocation of resources for inventions," in R. Nelson (ed.) *The Rate and Direction of Inventive Activity*, Princeton, NJ: Princeton University Press.

Balassa, B. *et al.* (1982) *Development Strategy in Semi-Industrial Economies*, Baltimore, MD: Johns Hopkins University Press.

Banerjee, A. and, Duflo E. (2005) "Growth through the lens of development economics," in P. Aghion and S. Durlauf (eds) *Handbook of Economic Growth, Volume* 1, Amsterdam: Elsevier.

Beck, T., Demirgüc-Kunt, A., and Honohan, P. (2009) "Access to financial services: measurement, impact, and policies," *World Bank Research Observer*, 24 (1): 119–45.

Becker, G.S. and Murphy, K.M. (1992) "The division of labor, coordination costs, and knowledge," *Quarterly Journal of Economics*, 107 (4): 1137–60.

Bhagwati, J. (1978) *Anatomy and Consequences of Exchange Control Regimes*, Cambridge, MA: Ballinger.

Blomström, M. and Kokko, A. (2003) "The economics of foreign direct investment incentives," in H. Hermann and R. Lipsey (eds) *Foreign Direct Investment in the Real and Financial Sector of Industrial Countries*, Heidelberg: Springer.

Bloom, N., and Van Reenen, J. (2007) "Measuring and explaining management practices across firms and countries," *Quarterly Journal of Economics*, 122 (4): 1351–409.

Bloom, N. and Van Reenen, J. (2010) "Why do management practices differ across firms and countries?" *Journal of Economic Perspectives*, 24 (1): 203–24.

Bloom, N., Mahajan, A., McKenzie, D., and Roberts, J. (2010) "Why do firms in developing countries have low productivity?" *American Economic Review*, 100 (2): 619–23.

Bloom, N., Eifert, B., Mahajan, A., McKenzie, D., and Roberts, J. (2011) "Does management matter? evidence from India," Policy Research Working Paper No. 5573, World Bank.

Bruhn, M., Karlan, D., and Schoar, A. (2010) "What capital is missing in developing countries?" *American Economic Review*, 100 (2): 629–33.

Cimoli, M., Dosi, G., and Stiglitz, J., (eds) (2009) *Industrial Policy and Development: The Political Economy of Capabilities Accumulation*, Oxford: Oxford university Press.

de Mel, S., McKenzie, D., and Woodruff, C. (2008) "Returns to capital in microenterprises: evidence from a field experiment," *Quarterly Journal of Economics*, 123 (4): 1329–72.

Deming, W.E. (1994) *The New Economics for Industry, Government, and Education*, 2nd edition, Cambridge, MA: MIT Press.

Ding, K. (2007) "Domestic market-based industrial cluster development in modern China," IDE Discussion Paper No.88, Institute of Developing Economies, Japan External Trade Organization.

Drexler, A., Fischer, G. and Schoar, A. (2010) "Financial literacy training and rule of thumbs: evidence from field experiment," CEPR Discussion Papers, No. 7994.

Eifert, B., Gelb, A., and Ramachandran, V. (2008) "The cost of doing business in Africa: evidence from enterprise survey data," *World Development*, 36 (9): 1531–46.

Field, E., Jayachandran, S., and Pande, R. (2010) "Do traditional institutions constrain female entrepreneurship? A field experiment on business training in India," *American Economic Review*, 100 (2): 125–29.

Fleisher, B., Hu, D., McGuire, W., and Zhang, X. (2010) "The evolution of an industrial cluster in China," *China Economic Review*, 21 (3): 456–69.

Fujita, M., Krugman, P., and Venables, A.J. (1999) *The Spatial Economy: Cities, Regions, and International Trade*, Cambridge, MA: MIT Press.

Gerschenkron, A. (1962) *Economic Backwardness in Historical Perspective*, Cambridge, MA: Harvard University Press.

Glaeser, E.L. and Gottlieb, J.D. (2009) "The wealth of cities: agglomeration economies and spatial equilibrium," *Journal of Economic Literature*, 47 (4): 983–1028.

Grossman, G., and Helpman, E. (1991) *Innovation and Growth in the Global Economy*, Cambridge, MA: MIT Press.

Hart, O. and Moore, J. (1990) "Property rights and the nature of the firm," *Journal of Political Economy*, 98 (6): 1119–58.

Hashino, T. (2012) "Institutionalising technical education: the case of weaving districts in Meiji Japan," *Australian Economic History Review*, 52 (1): 25–42.

Hashino, T. and Kurosawa, T. (2013) "Beyond Marshallian agglomeration economies: the roles of the local trade association in a Meiji Japan weaving district, 1868–1912," *Business History Review*, forthcoming.

Hashino, T. and Otsuka, K. (2013) "Hand looms, power looms, and changing production organizations: the case of the Kiryū weaving district in early twentieth-century Japan," *Economic History Review*, 66 (3): 785–804.

Hayami, Y. (2009) "Social capital, human capital, and the community mechanism: towards a conceptual framework for economists," *Journal of Development Studies*, 45 (1): 96–123.

Henderson, J.V. (1988) *Urban Development: Theory, Fact, and Illusion*, Oxford: Oxford University Press.

Henderson, J.V., Lee, T., and Lee, Y-J. (2001) "Scale externalities in a developing country," *Journal of Urban Economics*, 49 (3): 479–504.

Hidalao, C.A., Klinger, B., Barabasi, A.-L., and Hausman, R. (2007) "The product space conditions the development of nations," *Science*, 317: 482–87.

Hong, C.-M. and Gee, S. (1993) "National systems supporting technical advance in industry: the case of Taiwan," in R.R. Nelson (ed.) *National Innovation Systems: A Comparative Analysis*, Oxford: Oxford University Press.

Huang, Y. and Bocchi, A.M., (eds) (2008) *Reshaping Economic Geography in East Asia*, Washington, DC: World Bank.

Karlan, D. and Morduch, J. (2009) "Access to finance," in D. Rodrik and M. Rosenzweig (eds) *Handbook of Development Economics, Volume 5*, Amsterdam: North Holland.

Karlan, D. and Valdivia, M. (2010) "Teaching entrepreneurship: impact of business training on microfinance clients and institutions," *Review of Economics and Statistics*, 93 (2): 510–27.

Krueger, A. (1978) *Liberalization Attempts and Consequences, in Foreign Trade Regimes and Economic Development*, Cambridge, MA: Ballinger.

Levy, B. (1991) "Transaction costs, the size of firms and industrial policy," *Journal of Development Economics*, 34 (1/2): 151–78.

Lin, J.Y. (2009) *Economic Development and Transition: Thought, Strategy, and Viability*, Cambridge: Cambridge University Press.

Lin, J.Y. (2010) "New structural economics: a framework for rethinking development," Policy Research Working Paper No. 5197, Washington, DC: World Bank.

Lin, J.Y. and Monga, C. (2010) "The growth report and new structural economics," Policy Research Working Paper No. 5336, Washington, DC: World Bank.

Lin, J.Y. and Monga, C. (2011) "Growth identification and facilitation: the role of the state in the dynamics of structural change," *Development Policy Review*, 29 (3): 264–90.

Long, C. and Zhang, X. (2011) "Cluster-based industrialization in China: financing and performance," *Journal of International Economics*, 84 (1): 112–23.

Mano, Y. and Otsuka, K. (2000) "Agglomeration economies and changes in industrial concentration: a case study of manufacturing sectors in post-war Japan," *Journal of the Japanese and International Economies*, 14 (3): 189–203.

Mano, Y., Iddrisu, A., Yoshino, Y., and Sonobe, T. (2011) "How can micro and small enterprises in Sub-Saharan Africa become more productive? The impacts of experimental basic managerial training," Policy research working paper 5755, Washington, DC: World Bank.

Marshall, A. (1920) *Principles of Economics*, London: Macmillan.

McCormick, D. (1999) "African firm clusters and industrialization: theory and reality," *World Development*, 27 (9): 1531–51.

Nadvi, K. (1999) "Collective efficiency and collective failure: the response of the Sialkot surgical instrument cluster to global quality pressure," *World Development*, 27 (9): 1605–26.

Otsuka, K. (2007) "Rural industrialization in East Asia: its influences, nature and implications," in S. Haggblade, P. Hazell, and T. Reardon (eds) *Transforming the Rural Nonfarm Economy*, Baltimore, MD: Johns Hopkins University Press.

Otsuka, K., Ranis, G., and Saxonhouse, G. (1988) *Comparative Technology Choice in Development: The Indian and Japanese Cotton Textile Industries*, London: Macmillan.

Pack, H. and Saggi, K. (2006) "Is there a case for industrial policy? a critical survey," *World Bank Research Observer*, 21 (2): 267–97.

Page, J. (2011) "Can Africa industrialize?" Paper presented at the African Economic Research Consortium Semi-Annual Plenary Meeting, Nairobi, Kenya.

Rodriguez-Clare, A. (2007) "Clusters and comparative advantage: implications for industrial policy," *Journal of Development Economics*, 82 (1): 43–57.

Romer, P.M. (1986) "Increasing returns and long-run growth," *Journal of Political Economy*, 94 (5): 1002–37.

Ruan, J. and Zhang, X. (2009) "Finance and cluster based industrial development in China," *Economic Development and Cultural Change*, 58 (1): 143–64.

Sawai, M. (1999) "The role of technical education and public research institutes in the development of small and medium enterprises: the case of Osaka between the wars," in K. Odaka and M. Sawai (eds) *Small Firms, Large Concerns: The Development of Small Business in Comparative Perspective*, Oxford: Oxford University Press.

Schmitz, H. (1999) "Global competition and local cooperation: success and failure in the Sinos Valley, Brazil," *World Development*, 27 (9): 1627–50.

Schmitz, H. and Nadvi, K. (1999) "Clustering and industrialization: introduction," *World Development*, 27 (9): 1503–14.

Schultz, T.W. (1975) "The value of the ability to deal with disequilibria," *Journal of Economic Literature*, 13 (3): 827–46.

Schumpeter, J.A. (1934) *The Theory of Economic Development: An Inquiry into Profits, Capital, Interest, and the Business Cycle*, London: Oxford University Press.

Shleifer, A. and Vishny, R.W. (1993) "Corruption," *Quarterly Journal of Economics*, 108(3): 599–617.

Solow, R.M. (1956) "A contribution to the theory of economic growth," *Quarterly Journal of Economics*, 70(1): 65–94.

Sonobe, T. and Otsuka, K. (2006) *Cluster-Based Industrial Development: An East Asian Model*, Basingstoke: Palgrave Macmillan.

Sonobe, T. and Otsuka, K. (2011) *Cluster-Based Industrial Development: A Comparative Study of Asia and Africa*, Basingstoke: Palgrave Macmillan.

Sonobe, T., Hu, D., and Otsuka, K. (2002) "Process of cluster formation in China: a case study of a garment town," *Journal of Development Studies*, 39(1): 118–39.

Sonobe, T., Kawakami, M., and Otsuka, K. (2003) "Changing roles of innovation and imitation in industrial development: the case of the machine tool industry in Taiwan," *Economic Development and Cultural Change*, 52 (1): 103–8.

Sonobe, T., Hu, D., and Otsuka, K. (2004) "From inferior to superior products: an inquiry into the Wenzhou model of industrial development in China," *Journal of Comparative Economics*, 32 (3): 542–63.

Sonobe, T., Suzuki, A., and Otsuka, K. (2011) *KAIZEN for Managerial Skills Improvement in Small and Medium Firms: An Impact Evaluation Study*, Japan PHRD Trust Fund No. TF096317, Washington, DC: World Bank.

Stigler, G.J. (1951) "The division of labor is limited by the extent of the market," *Journal of Political Economy*, 59 (3): 185–93.

Syverson, C. (2011) "What determines productivity?" *Journal of Economic Literature*, 49 (2): 326–65.

Uchida, H. (1991) "Japanese technical manpower in industry, 1880–1930: a quantitative survey," in H.F. Gospel (ed.) *Industrial Training and Technological Innovation: A Comparative and Historical Study*, London: Routledge.

Williamson, O.E. (1985) *The Economic Institutions of Capitalism: Firms, Markets, Relational Contracting*, New York: Free Press.

Zhang, X. (2012) "Clusters as an instrument for industrial policy: the case of China," Draft, International Food Policy Research Institute.

Zhang, X. and Hu. D. (2013). "Overcoming successive bottlenecks: the evolution of a potato cluster in China," *World Development*, forthcoming.

10 Success of industrial development policy in the pharmaceutical industry in Bangladesh

Md. Nurul Amin and Tetsushi Sonobe

1 Introduction

Promoting industries and creating jobs, if successful, would boost economic development and thereby support state building. While politicians and bureaucrats are aware of how important industrial development is, they are unaware of how to facilitate it. In the international development cooperation community in developed countries and international organizations, the commonly accepted view until recently was that industrial policy would not work because market failures prevent industrial development from occurring and, hence, it would be too difficult for developing countries, especially current low-income countries, to address the failures without causing serious government failures. Thus, policymakers in developing countries could not receive encouragement or useful suggestions for industrial development from this community.

More recently, there has been a sea change. Major publications by international organizations, such as the World Bank's *World Development Report 2013* and the African Development Bank and the OECD Development Centre's *African Economic Outlook 2012*, emphasize the importance of creating jobs and generating incomes through improving productivity in the industrial sector. Also, symposiums and conferences on the same issues abound. This change is encouraging for the people of developing countries longing for industrial development. This, however, is just the beginning of the accumulation of knowledge necessary for providing a scientific foundation for the prescription and implementation of a strategy for industrial development. Considerable further research on industrial policy is clearly warranted.

This chapter reports a case study of a successful industrial policy which was proclaimed and enacted by the government of Bangladesh three decades ago. One reason why we focus on a successful case and not failures is that there are already scores of excellent studies on failed industrial policies, such as Balassa (1971), Bhagwati (1978), and Krueger (1978), just to name a few.[1] These studies have made it clear how government interventions that are intended to protect and promote industries can aggravate the dysfunction of markets, create hotbeds for corruption, and widen the gap between the rich and the poor.

A major message of economics is that government interventions enhance economic development only when they address market failure problems. Of course, market failures do not necessarily call for government intervention as they may be mitigated by grassroots non-market institutions based on the community mechanism or other mechanisms, as Greif (2006), Williamson (1985), Hayami and Godo (2005), and other prominent economists argue. Still, grassroots efforts are likely to solve market failure problems only partially because of the transaction costs, and leave room for government interventions. From studies of failed industrial policies, it is impossible to learn whether government interventions are doomed to fail or whether they can succeed in correcting market failures if designed and implemented appropriately. Studies of successful cases of industrial development are expected to illustrate how market failures are mitigated without causing serious government failures and what the effective division of labor among markets, non-market institutions, and the government is. Successful cases, however, are much fewer. Although Baer (1972) and Chang (2003) among others argue that almost all of today's developed countries used protection and promotion policies to develop their industries when they were in their developing stages, such experiences in the West in the remote past may be difficult to apply to today's developing countries. More useful references would be the more recent experiences in high-performing Asian countries.

This chapter deals with the successful development of the pharmaceutical industry in Bangladesh and the critical roles played by the country's National Drug Policy proclaimed in 1982 in boosting this development. One might wonder why the pharmaceutical industry, which seems to be a capital-intensive, high-tech industry, can be developed in a low-income country like Bangladesh. A short answer is that the pharmaceutical industry in this country specializes in the production and sale of generic drugs, which is neither capital-intensive nor high-tech. This chapter attempts to explain how badly the markets for drugs in developing countries in general fail in providing essential drugs for the poor, what characterizes the National Drug Policy as an industrial policy, how the policy addressed the market failure problem, why the policy did not cause serious government failure problems, and how successful the development of this industry has been since 1982. While government intervention was reduced over time, this industry in Bangladesh has continued to grow in size, improve product quality, and enhance productivity. This chapter offers hypotheses on what features of the private sector has made this sustained growth possible, while deferring the empirical test of the hypothesis to a companion paper, Amin and Sonobe (2013).

2 The successful growth of the industry

Pharmaceutical firms in developed countries undertake research and development (R&D) activities to develop new drugs and test them for approval. These high-tech activities require enormous inputs of capital and the efforts of a number of highly skilled, professional pharmacists, biochemists, and other experts. After the drugs' patent expires, however, other pharmaceutical firms copy the drugs at much lower development costs. Although the regulatory body in each country examines whether the copied drug is identical to the original drug in dose, strength, safety, and efficacy, the period needed for its approval is much shorter. While drugs have both trade names made by producers and generic names that indicate their active ingredients, such copies are usually called by their generic names. Probably this is why they are called generic drugs. The pharmaceutical industry in Bangladesh has focused on the production and sale of such generic drugs.

This industry in Bangladesh, moreover, has relied on the import of the most important material, that is, active pharmaceutical ingredients (API), which are available from the firms that invented the original drugs as well as the producers of generic versions of the active ingredients in developed countries, India, China and a few other countries. With active ingredients being purchased, the remaining production process involves mixing them with other ingredients that make it easy for the human body to absorb the active ingredients and serve some other purposes, followed by pressing the mixed substance into tablets and packaging and shipping them. Such manufacturing is not high-tech. It is only very recently that some of the pharmaceutical firms in Bangladesh have begun producing generic versions of API.

Still it is astounding that Bangladesh, one of the least developed countries in the world, has its own pharmaceutical industry. Just before the National Drug Policy was launched in 1982, Bangladesh had 166 approved drug firms, of which about 80 were in operation. Many of them were microenterprises producing folk medicine, and others were small-scale subcontractors for multinational firms.[2] Although the number of firms in operation was large, the total production of drugs in the country, even including the output of the local subsidiaries of the multinationals, met only 35 percent of the domestic demand for drugs. The situation is different now. There are more than 250 approved domestic firms, of which about 150 are producing drugs. They meet 97 percent of the domestic demand for drugs. The domestic production of drugs has been growing rapidly in recent years, as shown in Figure 10.1. In this figure, the bar chart indicates the sales revenue of this industry in million dollars, and the line chart indicates its annual growth rate from 1981 to 2012. The annual growth rate was over 15 percent per year from 2007 to 2012, a pace at which revenue doubles in five years.

Bangladesh is known for its well-developed export-oriented garment industry. Compared with garment production, generic drug production is scientist-, skilled worker-, and capital-intensive. It is reasonable to ask whether the country has a comparative advantage in this industry. The answer is definitely affirmative because the industry recently began exporting its products to other countries without being subsidized by the government. The export destinations include not just other low-income countries but also middle-income countries in Asia, Latin America, and southern Europe, and more recently developed countries including the United States, where the safety regulation is the most stringent in the world.

One might think that such phenomenal growth of an industry in a low-income country is not possible if it is not led by multinational firms. The reality in

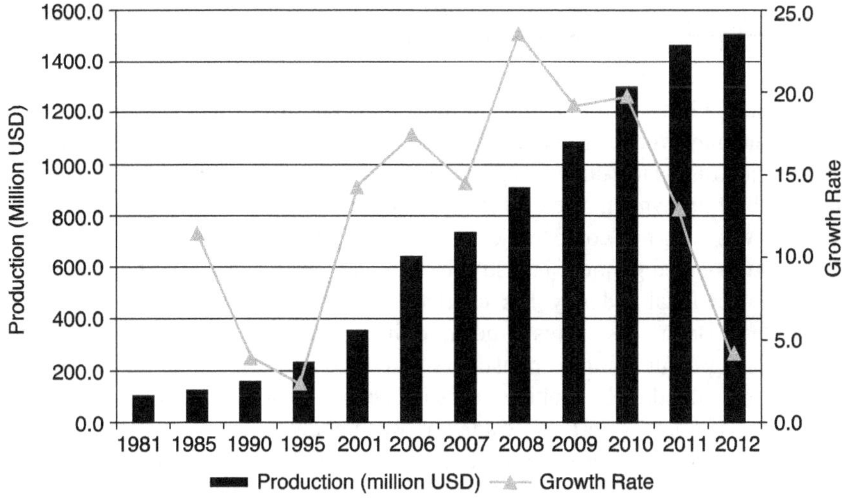

Figure 10.1 Pharmaceutical production in Bangladesh, 1981–2012

Source: (a) Directorate General of Drug Administration (DGDA), Bangladesh for the year 1981, 1985, and 1990; (b) IMS Health, Bangladesh, for the year 1995; (c) our survey in 2011 for the year 2001, and 2006 to 2010; and (b) DGDA for the year 2011 and 2012

Bangladesh is that while multinationals dominated the country's market for drugs earlier, they have been marginalized since the 1980s. Table 10.1 shows the names and ownership types of the 10 largest drug firms in terms of sales on the Bangladesh market in 1985 and 2011. While most of the top 10 firms were subsidiaries of

Table 10.1 Top 10 pharmaceutical firms in Bangladesh in 1985 and 2011

	Top 10 firms in 1985		*Top 10 firms in 2011*	
	Firm's name	*Ownership type*	*Firm's name*	*Ownership type*
1	SQUARE	Local	SQUARE	Local
2	BPI (MAY BAKER)	MNC	INCEPTA	Local
3	GLAXO	MNC	BEXIMCO	Local
4	OPSONIN	Local	OPSONIN	Local
5	PFIZER	MNC	RENATA	Local
6	FISONS	MNC	ESKAYEF	Local
7	GONOSHASTHYA	Local	A.C.I.	Local
8	MSD	MNC	ACME	Local
9	CIBA GEIGY	MNC	ARISTOPHARMA	Local
10	HOECHST	MNC	DRUG INT'L	Local

Source: Author's calculation based on data from IMS Health (2012)

renowned multinationals in 1985, all the top 10 firms are domestic firms owned and operated by Bangladeshi capital and managers in 2011. The multinationals' local production accounts for only 10 percent of the total drug consumption in this country now. Thus, it is not an exaggeration to say that the domestic drug industry in Bangladesh has successfully developed and is rapidly growing.

Still one may wonder whether the rapid growth of this industry has made any contribution to this low-income country if the industry is not very labor-intensive. Indeed, the employment size of this industry is estimated to be less than 100,000 persons, which is not comparable to the employment of 4 million persons by the export-oriented garment industry. Nonetheless, it is likely that the growth of the pharmaceutical industry has exerted considerable impact on the welfare of people in Bangladesh. This is because the increased supply of generic drugs due to the growth of this industry is likely to have reduced the prices of drugs drastically, thereby making drugs accessible for increasing portions of the population. If drugs were freely traded between countries and sold in a perfectly competitive market, the price of each drug would be by and large the same in all countries, and considerable increases in drugs supplied from a small country like Bangladesh to the market would not have any significant impact on the price. In reality, however, drugs are not freely traded but are subject to approval and licenses and other forms of regulations in almost all countries because drug firms, both local firms and multinationals, attempt to differentiate products and to set prices strategically to each national market. It may well be that drug prices vary across countries widely, and that the development of the pharmaceutical industry in a country, especially that of domestic firms, has a substantial impact on the domestic prices of drugs.

To investigate this, we gathered fragmented information on changing drug prices from 1981 to 2012 in Bangladesh and also the current prices in some other countries. The results are shown in Tables 10.2 and 10.3, which deserve a detailed explanation. In Bangladesh, the pharmaceutical industry manufactures more than 500 generic drugs for 6,200 registered brands in over 10,000 different forms of dosages and strengths. In addition to this immense diversity, what makes inter-temporal comparisons of drug prices difficult is that the importance of a drug changes over time because new substitutes are developed and because drug resistance may occur. We decided to focus on the top selling drugs in the years 1985, 2000 and 2011, as well as on representatives from different therapeutic classes, and picked 10 drugs that have been used since the early 1980s or even earlier (which are referred to as "older 10 drugs") and another 10 drugs that were introduced to the Bangladeshi market in the mid-1990s or later ("newer 10 drugs"). Of these 20 drugs, 13 are included in the list of the country's "essential drugs," which is defined by the World Health Organization (WHO) as drugs satisfying the healthcare needs of the majority of the population. Our older 10 drugs include 9 essential drugs and our newer 10 drugs include 4 essential drugs. The older 10 drugs were also included in the 30 important drugs listed in a book authored by Zafrullah Chowdhury (2010), who is a freedom fighter, medical doctor, civil society activist, and one of the masterminds of the National Drug Policy. His book is our source of information on the drug prices as of 1981 and 1991.

Table 10.2 presents the real retail prices of the 10 older drugs in 1981, 1991, 2001, and 2012 and those of newer drugs in 1996, 2001, 2006, and 2012. To calculate the average price of each drug in 1996, 2001 and 2006, we collected the retail prices of all firms producing the particular drug for a particular dosage, mentioned in the first column, from different issues of QIMP (*Quick Index for Medical Preparations*). The numbers in the table are real retail prices in Bangladesh taka deflated by the consumer price index. The data on the retail prices in 2012 were collected through our own survey of 10 pharmacies or drug stores.[3] It should be clear from the table that the retail prices of these life-saving drugs have been drastically lowered. The prices of some of the older drugs, such as atenolol (a drug for hypertension), chloroquine (an antimalarial drug), mebendazole (an antiparastic drugs), and rifampicin (an antibiotic) in 2012 are only one-fourteenth to one-fortieth of their prices in 1981.

The reduction in drug prices is not unique to Bangladesh because new drugs are developed one after another to substitute or replace older drugs. Thus, the question

Table 10.2 Changes in retail prices of 20 important drugs in Bangladesh

Product (generic name)	*Essential drug*	*Real retail price (in taka)*			
(a) Retail prices of older *10 drugs*		*1981*	*1991*	*2001*	*2012*
Amoxycillin cap. 250mg	Yes	5.6	3.2	2.5	1.3
Atenolol tab. 100mg	Yes	19.9	4.2	1.0	0.5
Chloroquine tab. 250mg	Yes	1.3	1.3	0.9	0.4
Diazepam tab. 5mg	Yes	1.0	0.3	0.2	0.1
Mebendazole tab. 100mg	Yes	7.0	0.9	0.6	0.3
Metronidazole tab. 200mg	Yes	2.3	0.8	0.5	0.2
Paracetamol tab. 500mg	Yes	0.8	0.7	0.4	0.2
Ranitidine tab. 150mg	No	10.0	2.6	1.6	0.7
Rifampicin cap. 150mg	Yes	17.2	4.4	3.0	1.2
Vitamin B complex tab.	Yes	2.5	0.5	0.3	0.2
(b) Retail prices of newer *10 drugs*		*1996*	*2001*	*2006*	*2012*
Albendazole tab. 400mg	Yes	3.4	2.8	2.1	1.7
Azithromycin cap./tab. 500mg	No	64.4	30.0	17.4	10.8
Cefixime susp. 50ml	No	n.a	226.3	141.3	70.6
Cetrizine tab. 10mg	No	n.a	1.8	1.4	0.9
Ciprofloxacin eye drop 5ml	Yes	n.a	22.1	16.5	14.5
Diclofenac sodium tab. 50mg	No	1.1	0.7	0.5	0.3
Glibenclamide tab. 5mg	Yes	0.3	0.2	0.2	0.2
Omeprazole cap. 20mg	Yes	12.7	3.7	2.0	1.8
Pantoprazole tab. 20mg	No	n.a	2.3	1.8	1.4
Paracetamol+ caffeine tab.	No	n.a	n.a	0.9	0.7

Source: The real prices in 1981, 1991, and 2001 are the authors' calculation based on Chowdhury (2010: 101) and different issues of QIMP. The prices in 2012 are taken from the IMS Health (2012)

The retail prices are deflated by using the consumer price index.

arises as to whether the price reduction has been more drastic in Bangladesh than in other countries. Table 10.3 compares the current retail prices of drugs in Bangladesh, Sri Lanka, India, the Philippines, Indonesia, and the UK in 2010 to 2011. Sri Lanka and India are selected because they are located in the same region as Bangladesh. Sri Lanka is known for its free provision of public medical services and for its aggressive approach to reducing drug prices, which the country started as early as the 1970s. India is known for its thriving industry manufacturing generic drugs and generic APIs. In the table, Southeast Asia is represented by the Philippines and Indonesia. Both countries are more dependent on drugs produced by multinationals than the three countries in South Asia, but the Philippines was more active in reforming its pharmaceutical sector than Indonesia. As a representative of the developed countries, we select the UK, which is home to some renowned multinational drug firms. We collected data on the prices of 10 drugs selected from the 20 drugs listed in Table 10.2 in Bangladesh, Sri Lanka, and the Philippines through surveys.[4] For India, Indonesia, and the UK, data were taken from the Current Index of Medical Specialities (CIMS), the Indonesian Index of Medical Specialities (MIMS), and the British National Formulary (BNF), respectively.

Table 10.3 Retail price comparison of selected drugs in selected countries (in USD)

Product	*Bangladesh*	*Sri Lanka*	*India*	*Philippines*	*Indonesia*	*UK*
Atenolol tab. 100mg	0.016	0.023	0.065	0.143	0.221	0.182
Azithromycin cap./ tab. 500mg	0.365	0.384	0.514	3.042	2.283	4.500
Cefixime susp. 50ml	2.388	1.943	1.943	5.348	9.805	15.522
Diazepam tab. 5mg	0.003	0.004	0.045	n/a	0.848	0.052
Glibenclamide tab. 5mg	0.006	0.008	0.014	0.018	0.099	0.046
Mebendazole tab. 100mg	0.010	0.012	0.029	0.101	1.566	0.334
Metronidazole tab. 200mg	0.009	0.012	0.015	0.048	0.095	0.376
Omeprazole cap. 20mg	0.061	0.100	0.080	0.295	0.929	0.169
Pantoprazole tab. 20mg	0.047	0.115	0.074	0.475	1.618	0.623
Paracetamol tab. 500mg	0.010	0.012	0.021	0.014	0.065	0.053

Source: For data on Bangladesh, Sri Lanka, Nepal and the Philippines, the IMS Health (2012). For India, Indonesia and United Kingdom, authors' calculation based on data from different issues of MIMS Indonesia, Current Index of Medical Specialities (CIMS), and British National Formulary (BNF), respectively

Pharmaceutical price data from Bangladesh, Sri Lanka, Nepal and the Philippines are for the year 2012. Data from India for 2011, and Indonesia and UK are for the year 2010. Price data on the Philippines include data on generic drugs only; n/a indicates that data are not available.

It is evident that there is no integrated world market for drugs in which the law of one price holds true. Instead there are segmented national markets for drugs. It is also evident from Table 10.3 that almost all of the medicines are sold at the lowest price in Bangladesh, except for cefixime, which is sold at a slightly lower price in the other two South Asian countries. The prices of the other medicines are lower in Bangladesh by 5 percent to 1,500 percent. Thus, the prices of important drugs are exceptionally low in Bangladesh. By contrast, drug prices are much higher in the Philippines, Indonesia, and the UK. The results of the price comparison may lead one to imagine that drug prices are higher in countries which are dependent on multinationals for the supply of drugs and are taking no countermeasures against this. Obviously, it is more difficult for patients in developing countries to pay for drugs than patients in affluent countries.[5] Nonetheless, Table 10.3 indicates that the prices are lower in the UK than in Indonesia for 7 drugs out of the 10. These results present clear evidence of market failures, the issue to which we will turn in the next section.

We conclude this section by mentioning the increasing affordability of life-saving drugs for ordinary people in Bangladesh. In this country, real wages for unskilled workers have increased gradually for the last three decades. The real wage of the lowest-paid unskilled government worker (i.e., grade 20) has increased 2.4 times since 1981.[6] Thus, affordability, measured by the drug prices relative to the unskilled labor wage, has been improved even more drastically than the real prices of drugs have been lowered. Thus, the development of the pharmaceutical industry is not an insignificant matter but a major achievement of the Bangladeshi economy.

3 Market failures and earlier reform attempts

In 1978, the United Nations Children's Fund (UNICEF) and the WHO jointly hosted an international conference in Alma-Ata, USSR and declared "Health Care for All by 2000." The declaration views health as a fundamental human right and asks all governments to formulate national policies, strategies, and action plans. To achieve the goal of healthcare for all, making essential drugs affordable to the poor was considered to be essential.[7] Much to the disappointment of the signatory countries, including Bangladesh, however, the Alma-Ata Declaration was completely ignored by drug firms in the world. Why do firms not respond to demands from the international community? Is it difficult for the government to force firms to lower prices? This section reviews the major reasons why this is so and the countermeasures actually attempted in some countries.

The first reason is that drug firms claim that their pricing is appropriate in view of the need to cover the high cost of developing new drugs. Berndt *et al.* (1995) estimate the cost of launching a new drug to market to be 360 million USD. Patent protection, which creates a monopoly lasting for a few decades artificially, has been the incentive device encouraging drug firms to develop new drugs. Although alternative incentive mechanisms are being proposed, none has so far been implemented on a large scale to reconcile the two conflicting aims of keeping drug prices low and encouraging drug firms to develop new drugs.

Secondly, it is difficult to educate consumers (or patients) and medical doctors to be more price-sensitive buyers of drugs, or to put it in technical terms, to make the demand for drugs more elastic with respect to prices. The less price elastic the demand is, the higher the monopoly price, compared with the unit production cost. The demand for drugs is made less elastic by the fact that "the menu of drugs is so vast and complex that few physicians can inform themselves fully about the available alternatives" (Scherer 1993: 98). The problem is aggravated by the possible moral hazard problem arising from the fact that while it is doctors who choose drugs, they do not pay for the drugs. To inform doctors about the usage and efficacy of drugs, pharmaceutical firms employ a large number of medical representatives and dispatch them to doctors, but it is ambiguous how effective this service is.

Thirdly, drug firms differentiate their products from other products to make the demand for drugs even less elastic, thereby strengthening their price-setting power. An integral part of product differentiation is the creation and proliferation of brand names put on essentially the same products. In the 1970s, the Sri Lankan government decided to reduce the number of imported drugs because the country was faced with a severe foreign currency shortage and because it was heavily dependent on imported drugs. The government could easily reduce the number of imported drugs from 4,000 to 2,100 and then to 600 because many drugs were essentially the same as other drugs (Chowdhury 2010; Reich 1995). Similarly, when the government of Bangladesh started the reform of the pharmaceutical sector in 1982, it banned 1,655 drugs out of the 4,340 registered drugs as either harmful, useless, or therapeutically ineffective. Although the above mentioned medical representatives may help to mitigate the information problem, they are also used to imprint brand names in doctors' minds, strengthen their brand loyalty, and keep the price of each differentiated product high.

A common policy tool to reduce monopolistic prices for the government is to put a price ceiling in place. While this sounds straightforward, its proper implementation requires appropriate information on the costs of production and distribution, which is difficult to obtain due to drug firms' complicated information manipulation (e.g., Laffont and Tirole 1993). In many developing countries, the subsidiaries of multinational firms or their local subcontractor import active ingredients and other materials. Although the custom office should have information on the prices of such intermediate inputs, the reported prices may be much inflated, and such price information may not be used by government bodies (e.g., Lall 1973; Peralta *et al.* 2006). The capacity of the government to set an appropriate level of price ceilings would also depend on how abundantly the country is endowed with human resources with expertise in pharmacy, which could provide sensible advice for the government.

In 1971, the Sri Lankan government mandated that brand names be replaced by their corresponding generic names in the sale and prescription of drugs. The expected effect of this action is to make product differentiation difficult, thereby making drug demand more elastic. The government also mandated that all imports of finished drugs and raw materials be purchased through international tender by the newly established State Pharmaceutical Corporation (SPC). These reforms met with fierce opposition, however. Major multinational firms initially ignored the SPC and continued to sell drugs through their marketing channels. In response, the SPC tried to procure generic drugs from the socialist countries in Europe by amending the country's patent law. This move was blocked chiefly by pressure from the governments of the home countries of the multinationals.

Opposition was also expressed by medical doctors and pharmacists, probably because of their misunderstanding about the safety of generic drugs, their habit of using brand names in prescription, and their loss of direct and indirect benefits that they had received from the importers and multinational firms, such as free samples and promotional materials. Wealthy people and intellectuals who were loyal to well-known brands were dissatisfied with the abolition of their favorite branded drugs. The propaganda campaign conducted by the multinational firms was successful in fueling the confusion and misunderstanding about the safety of generic drugs. The use of generic names was required also in Pakistan in 1971, in India in 1981, in the Philippines in the 1990s and some other countries, but these reform attempts were all short-lived due to protests from multinational firms and physicians (Chowdhury 2010; Reich 1995). The Sri Lankan government went further than these countries and established the SPC, and this step seemed successful because in 1972, the SPC saved about 40 percent of the payment for imported drugs and materials compared with the previous year (Lall and Bibile 1978). Still the policy was so unpopular that it was watered down considerably in subsequent years.

Thus, the market for drugs is associated with a composite of market failures, including indivisibility due to high development costs, asymmetric information, and coordination failure, which are epitomized by the high prices of drugs. Consumer activists in both developed and developing countries have long been criticizing drug multinationals, but they have seldom been successful in changing the behaviors of these firms. Neither mass media nor professionals such as medical doctors and pharmacists are highly motived to fight against the monopolistic power of drug firms, especially multinationals. It seems that the problem cannot be solved without the government's well designed actions.

4 The national drug policy of Bangladesh

Immediate reactions

After gaining independence in 1971, Bangladesh experienced famine, acute poverty, and political turmoil in the 1970s. When Lieutenant General Ershad gained power in a bloodless coup in March 1982, the country was still in the middle of the process of state building. It was this new government that declared the new law called "the Drug (Control) Ordinance, 1982" and the National Drug Policy, a set of policy measures to secure access to essential drugs for all. This benevolent policy could not immediately win the approval of the people of Bangladesh, even though they had suffered from the high prices of important life-saving drugs. Instead the major newspapers regarded the policy a harebrained and populist, improvised by the military government and doomed to be crushed by pressure from abroad. Indeed, the US ambassador came to Ershad immediately and began bringing relentless pressure on the Bangladesh government to reverse the decision, according to Chowdhury (2010). The ambassadors from the UK and Germany soon followed her lead. Their pressure included the threat of stopping assistance from their countries to Bangladesh. Similarly, the multinationals threatened explicitly to stop the supply of medicines to the country completely.

The National Drug Policy was well thought out, however. It was carefully crafted by an expert committee consisting of Professor Nurul Islam of Dhaka University, Zafrullah Chowduhry, and other six professionals, such as military surgeons, with considerable experience and expertise. After being appointed by the government to be committee members, they reviewed the drug situation and the healthcare needs in the country and also the reform experiences of other countries, such as Pakistan, Sri Lanka, and India. Their proposal of the National Drug Policy was swiftly accepted by the government on May 29, 1982. The following description of the events related to this policy and the major contents of the policy are based on our interviews with Zafrullah Chowduhry, Samson H. Chowdhury, the founder of the largest pharmaceutical firm in the country, and other persons who were engaged in this industry and witnessed how events unfolded in those days, as well as Chowdhury (2010).

Less than three months after the coup, Ershad visited the US to meet with President Reagan. Ershad also met with Vice-President Bush, who suggested that Ershad review his drug policy with the help of "independent US scientists" who would visit Bangladesh soon (Chowdhury 2010: 105). Ershad agreed with Bush without knowing that Bush was a shareholder of some pharmaceutical firms based in the US. When a four-member team of "independent US scientists" visited Bangladesh, the health minister, Dr Shamsul Haq, requested the US embassy for their CVs. Although his request made the US ambassador furious, the health minister finally obtained the CVs of the so-called "independent scientists" and found that they were executives and employees of large pharmaceutical firms.

As in Sri Lanka and other countries, the multinational firms succeeded in influencing physicians, pharmacists, and the public through propaganda campaigns. The looming skepticism among the public, together with the threat from the multinationals and the disapproving attitude of the donor countries, made Ershad less willing to move ahead on the drug policy, according to Chowdhury (2010). To encourage Ershad, the members of the expert committee explained the reason why the multinationals would never withdraw from the Bangladesh market. The expert committee designed the new policy, taking into account the reactions of the multinationals and the public. Their policy attempted to extract part of the monopolistic profits that the multinationals had taken away from Bangladesh, but the expert committee was fully aware that the Bangladesh market had to remain attractive for the multinationals. Further, the committee anticipated the propaganda campaign run by the multinationals, the reactions of the donor countries, and the attitude of the public.

Ingredients of the National Drug Policy

Under this policy, the government designated the set of essential drugs, mandated the use of generic names, enhanced public awareness of generic drugs, and had a price cap regulation. The committee, however, was aware that a more drastic measure was needed to achieve the policy goal of ensuring favorable access to essential drugs. As such a measure, Sri Lanka created a state-run monopoly on importing and distributing drugs through international tender. This socialist approach was not acceptable for Ershad, who was looking toward the US.[8] Nor was it effective in fighting against the propaganda by the multinationals because it would not create any supporters, that is, individuals who would directly profit so much from it as to side with the government, as the Sri Lankan experience had indicated. Probably we should also mention, although we do not know whether or not the committee considered this point, that the Sri Lankan approach could have come to a miserable end, if implemented in a corrupt country like Bangladesh.[9]

Instead, the expert committee intended to promote the local production of drugs by local firms owned by Bangladesh capital and operated by Bangladesh managers. Although there were many such firms, they ran tiny businesses. The new policy was intended to promote them and new entrants by using three aggressive measures. The first measure was to prohibit the multinational firms from selling antacids (which prevent acidity in the stomach) and vitamins and ask them to instead concentrate on the development and production of innovative, sophisticated and high-tech products, such as antibiotics. Antacids and vitamins were relatively easy for local firms to produce. The markets for these drugs were fairly large, probably accounting for 16 percent of the whole domestic market for drugs in terms of sales value in those days, according to our interview with Dr Chowdhury on January 15, 2011.

The second measure was to restrict the import of substitutes for the finished drugs and intermediate inputs that were produced by two or more local firms. This measure would be as powerful as the first measure. Take the Ventolin inhaler as an example. This is a drug for respiratory diseases, whose generic name is salbutamol. Before the National Drug Policy, this product was imported by its inventor GlaxoSmithKline (GSK) from outside Bangladesh even though GSK had a production facility for other products in Bangladesh. Ventolin inhaler was one of the top selling drugs in Bangladesh, accounting for 15 percent of GSK's sales revenue in Bangladesh. After the National Drug Policy was implemented, four local firms began producing and marketing copies of this drug. Because of this second measure, their entry resulted in the restriction on GSK's import of the original drug and induced GSK to enter into a toll manufacturing arrangement with one of the four imitators (i.e., GSK asked one of the imitators to produce the drug as a subcontractor for GSK). Once the market knew that the drug was produced by the domestic imitator, the advantage of GSK as the inventor, such as the consumers' perception of superior quality, over local firms disappeared, and the local firms captured large shares of the market for this drug easily.

The third measure for the promotion of the local drug industry was to prohibit those multinational firms without any production facilities in Bangladesh from marketing their products produced by other firms on a toll manufacturing basis. As a result, such multinational firms were forced to establish their own factories in Bangladesh, and local firms working for these multinational firms as subcontractors lost customers. Thus, immediately after the policy was proclaimed, these subcontractors, who were central players in the association of local drug producers, were strongly opposed to the policy. Not long after, however, they learned that a window of lucrative profit opportunity would be opened only if they produced antacids and vitamins and imitated the multinationals' products. Thus, they became staunch supporters of the National Drug Policy even though they would not really welcome the price cap regulation.

It was no wonder that the multinational firms and the governments of their home countries were outraged by these blatantly aggressive measures, which were intended to substitute the products of the multinationals with the products of the local firms.[10] These measures were similar to the measures implemented under the name of the import-substitution industrialization strategy in a number of developing countries in the 1960s and 1970s, which turned into a complete fiasco in most countries. Why did the policy that failed to promote industries in many countries succeed in boosting the development of the local drug industry in Bangladesh?

Why the National Drug Policy succeeded in industrial promotion

To answer this question, we conducted a survey of 148 drug producing firms, together with interviews with persons who played important roles in creating the National Drug Policy and who witnessed the events unfolding in those days. In our firm survey, which was essentially a census of drug firms in operation, we met with the top decision-maker of each firm. As soon as we started these information-gathering activities, we noticed an interesting phenomenon that began immediately after the proclamation of the National Drug Policy. It was the massive shift of managers, engineers, and skilled workers from the multinational firms to local firms. We first recognized that there were a number of top managers who used to work at the local subsidiaries of the multinational firms. Thus, we gathered information on the occupational backgrounds of the top managers and employees and found that 32 out of the 148 top managers had prior experience of working at a pharmaceutical multinational firm, that the percentage is nearly 50 percent if we focus on the relatively advanced 67 firms, and that 14.5 percent of employees of these 67 firms used to work at a multinational firm (Amin and Sonobe 2013).

According to our interviews with elderly respondents, the shift of human resources from the multinationals to the local firms began immediately after the National Drug Policy was proclaimed, thus confirming that the policy played a critically important role in the development of the local drug industry. The shift has continued to date, but the number of persons moving from the multinationals to the local firms has been decreasing over time because the presence of the multinationals in this sector has been declining. The literature on international economics abounds with empirical studies of the impact of foreign direct investment on the development of local industries in the host country (e.g., Aitken and Harrison 1999; Audretsch 1998; Griffith *et al.* 2003; Javorcik 2004; Kokko 1994; Kokko *et al.* 1996; Lipsey and Sjoholm 2005). These studies attempt to substantiate or refute a hypothesis that the operation of multinational firms stimulates the development of local industries because advanced knowledge of production technology, management, and marketing is transferred from multinational firms to local firms. These studies expect that knowledge is transferred when employees who have acquired advanced knowledge while working at multinational firms move to local firms, even though knowledge transfer may also occur through other channels (e.g., Balsvik 2011; Görg and Stroble 2005). The empirical results are mixed, however. Some studies find that foreign direct investments have favorable impacts on the development of local industries and on the productivity of local firms. Many studies, however, find that such impacts are negligible or non-existent.

In the case of the pharmaceutical industry, multinational firms operate in almost every country and have local production facilities in a number of developing countries, including low-income countries. Still, local drug industries were developed only in a small number of developing countries and no country classified as a least developed country, except for Bangladesh. How can the mobility of labor from multinationals to local firms play a critically important role in successful industrial development? Presumably, the answer lies in the remarks of the elderly respondents. According to them, not a few Bangladeshi employees of the multinational drug firms occupied important positions, such as the head of the product development, production, quality control, marketing and senior manager of general management, already in 1982, and, hence, they had hands-on knowledge and experience in pharmaceutical production, marketing, and management. Thus, as soon as they moved to local firms, they could produce the same product as the multinationals produced if the local firms had machinery of the same quality, and they could sell the product at least in the same way as, and possibly in a better way, than they did at the multinationals.

When we asked ourselves why local employees could occupy high positions in the multinationals, the answer was already obvious to us because almost every top manager we met was a graduate of the faculty of pharmacy, the University of Dhaka. Amazingly, Bangladesh began pharmacy education at the university level as early as 1964 with 20 students.[11] We met with two of these first-batch graduates, who were executives at two of the largest local pharmaceutical firms in the country, and learnt that they and their classmates joined multinational drug firms,

Table 10.4 Pharmacy education in Bangladesh, 1964–2011

	1964	*1985*	*2000*	*2011*
Number of universities with pharmacy department	1	2	7	27
Number of approved seats	20	40	450	2,267
Types of universities (public/private)	Public	Public	Public 4 Private 3	Public 6 Private 21

Source: Bangladesh Pharmaceutical Society, http://www.bps-bd.org/university/pharmaeducation.html, accessed October 17, 2011

Dhaka University is the first institute offering pharmacy courses since 1964. 'Number of approved seats' means maximum number of students permitted to be accepted by the respective university.

were promoted to important positions, and moved to local firms at varying times after the National Drug Policy was implemented.[12]

As shown in Table 10.4, the opportunity for pharmacy education has been expanding rapidly in Bangladesh. In 1969, the university started a masters program in pharmacy. In 2003–04, the faculty was expanded and turned into three departments; that is, Department of Pharmaceutical Technology, Department of Clinical Pharmacology, and Department of Pharmaceutical Chemistry, each conferring a masters degree, an M. Phil., and a Ph.D.[13] Currently, there are six public universities and 21 private universities offering undergraduate and graduate courses in pharmacy and having 2,267 approved seats. Needless to say, the operation of pharmaceutical firms requires other expertise, such as biochemistry, microbiology, engineering, and business administration. Bangladesh has offered favorable access to higher education in these subjects and has expanded the opportunity for such education rapidly, compared with other developing countries.

Between 1964 and 1982, a pool of human resources with expertise in production, management, and marketing of drug firms was built up in Bangladesh. Before 1982, such human resources were not working at local drug firms, which were tiny in size and equipped poorly with machinery. They were working at multinational firms, which paid much higher salaries and provided better work environments. By working at the multinational firms, they could acquire a broader range of knowledge and advanced expertise. It is easy to imagine that if there had not been these human resources, the National Drug Policy would have been just one of the numerous failed attempts of import-substitution industrialization.

Of course, human resources were not the only factor needed for the development of the local drug industry. Investment in machinery was definitely needed. According to our investigation, investment in machinery was in many cases financed by banks. Once it became clear to bankers that the National Drug Policy provided enormous profitable opportunities for local drug firms and that human resources with advanced expertise were available, banks were willing to finance fixed capital investments undertaken by local drug firms.

Thus, the existence of the sizable pool of human resources with advanced expertise was critical, as our elderly respondents suggested. Another important reason for the success of the policy to boost the development of this industry dramatically was that the market failures were so rampant that the drug prices were exorbitant. Since the prices were initially very high, the local drug producers, many of whom were at that time subcontractors for the multinationals, found it highly profitable to enter the market for final products, such as antacids and vitamins, by hiring (or poaching) managers and specialists from the multinationals at high salaries, when the policy provided them with the market. The banks accordingly found it profitable to lend money to the local drug producers.

Note that this is just a description of the initial phase of the industrial development. There remains a question of how the industry could sustain its growth after its initial success. Answering this question, however, is beyond the scope of this chapter. Amin and Sonobe (2013) use firm-level data to substantiate the hypothesis that the local drug industry continued to grow in terms of productivity, product quality and diversity, and operation size because it continued to learn advanced technologies and management practices from abroad. Indeed, the results of the econometric analysis indicate clearly that those firms employing highly educated and experienced managers and specialists tended to learn from abroad actively and grow faster, and that such firms tended to be led by highly educated and experienced top managers. In our interviews with managers at various ranks in such firms, they told us that their firms provided them with learning opportunities for more than one month in total per year. Such opportunities take various forms, such as training programs within the firm, short-term training programs held abroad by international organizations, and study at graduate schools abroad. Although employees may quit the firm to move to other firms after receiving training, high-performing firms provide learning opportunities because they otherwise could not recruit talented managers and specialists. Needless to say, we should emphasize again that important roles were played also by university education and multinational firms' training.

It is also noteworthy that rampant rent-seeking and corruption did not topple the National Drug Policy. Although we have no hard evidence for this, we conjecture that two factors helped to prevent rent-seeking and corruption from damaging the policy and the industry. First, the ultimate goal of the policy was not to promote the local industry but to reduce drug prices. The government committed itself to this goal and demonstrated clearly that it could take radical measures to achieve it. If the local firms had pretended that they needed more assistance from the government, the government might have stopped promoting the local industry and instead tried to find sources of drugs elsewhere. Second, due to the multitude of market failure problems in drug markets across the world, drug prices were so high and, hence, the drug business became so profitable in Bangladesh after the reform in 1982, that the local drug firms allocated more resources to the drug business itself than to rent-seeking activities.

5 Conclusions

As soon as we started this study, we could fortunately meet with Dr Zafrullah Chowdhury at his office. In response to our question as to why the expert committee proposed the promotion of the local drug industry, he said that they were sure that without industrial promotion their reform attempt would not be successful, as the Sri Lankan case had suggested. At the time of this interview, we knew little about drug production because we had not visited any factories. We asked him whether it would be difficult for developing countries to produce drugs, and he replied that it was not and that the production of drugs was just an "extension of cooking" if producers are appropriately trained people. From the next day, we spent many days visiting a number of drug factories in Bangladesh and understood what Dr Zafrullah Chowdhury meant by "extension of cooking" and "appropriately trained people." It is now evident to us that developing countries can have a comparative advantage in the production of generic drugs if they have invested in university education in pharmacy, and that this industry can have sustained growth if it continues to learn from abroad.

The accumulation of general and industry-specific human capital, however, is just a necessary condition for this comparative advantage to be materialized. There must be a countermeasure to market failures. If the countermeasure addresses the market failure problems more directly, the industry is more likely to pick up. The case of the pharmaceutical industry in Bangladesh illustrates how strong the impacts of such a countermeasure can be where there are serious market failure problems. As mentioned in the introductory section of this chapter, it is said that even a policy addressing market failure problems falls short of expectations because any policy intervention is prone to rent-seeking and corruption. The case of the pharmaceutical industry in Bangladesh, however, suggests that if the market failure problem is really serious, the benefit from solving the problem is accordingly great, and that the policy intervention can be nicely designed to distribute this great benefit between the private industry and the public so as to discourage rent-seeking and corruption.

This case also suggests that good design of industrial policy must pay attention to the political aspects of the market failure problem. Although market failure is an economic term concerning the efficiency of resource allocation, the correction of market failure affects the distribution of wealth (such as the extraction of monopolistic profit), thereby resulting in distributional conflict, which inevitably has a political consequence, or the political contention of various stakeholders. The continuation of a policy needs political support from both inside and outside the country. Policy planners, like the expert committee that designed the National Drug Policy of Bangladesh, should be able to determine the relationship between particular policy interventions and their political consequences, including the outcome of contentious politics, and design a policy that secures enough support. Thus, we have reached a conclusion appropriate for this book: the development of the pharmaceutical industry in Bangladesh is remarkably consistent with the analytical framework laid out in Figure 1.1 in Chapter 1 on the relationships among state building, economic development, and distributional conflicts.

Notes

1 The excellent analyses of failed cases mentioned above were based on numerous real incidents of the failed applications of the now notorious import-substitution industrialization strategy in a number of developing countries in the 1960s and 1970s. This literature has found, among other things, that protectionist policies make firms very dependent on protection (Soligo and Stern 1965) because these policies never contribute to the productivity gains of firms (Krueger and Tuncer 1982), and are likely to make firms technically less efficient than export-oriented policies (Chen and Tang 1987) and to create environments that discourage productivity gains through learning from abroad (Bruton 1998).

2 In this chapter, a "multinational firm" is defined as a firm whose corporate headquarters is located outside Bangladesh and is in operation in two countries or more.

3 Of these 10 drug stores, 3 are located in Dhaka city, 4 are in its suburb and 3 are in a small town called Lalmohan in the Bhola district. Bhola is the only island district of Bangladesh, located about 150 kilometers south of the capital city, Dhaka.

4 On this occasion, special thanks go to Dr Khondoker Abdul Mottaleb of the International Rice Research Institute (IRRI), Philippines, Mr Chakra Pani Achariya and Mr Thanabalasingam Vinayagathasan of the National Graduate Institute for Policy Studies (GRIPS), Japan, and Mr Aminul Haque, a young pharma-graduate for their great support in collecting pharmaceutical price data from the Philippines, Sri Lanka, and Bangladesh, respectively.

5 According to WHO (2004) and OECD (2005), medicines account for 25 to 70 percent of overall healthcare expenditure in developing countries and only about 18 percent in OECD countries. Morover, patients in developing countries pay 50 to 90 percent of the medicine costs out of their pocket, but patients in developed countries pay much smaller fractions because of health insurance (WHO 2004).

6 This is our calculation based on the relevant National Pay Scales of Bangladesh (BTCL 2010; Ministry of Finance Bangladesh 2009).

7 In 1976, drug consumption was over 50 US dollars per capita in Germany, Belgium, Switzerland, and France, but it was less than 1 dollar in India and Bangladesh (WHO 1988: 12–14).

8 He impressed President Reagan favorably. On October 25, 1983, when they met again, Reagan wrote in his diary: "He's quite a man & is taking that poverty stricken land out of statism & into the world of free enterprise. I like him & his ministers" (Reagan 2007: 191).

9 Bangladesh has been one of the most corrupt countries in the world according to Transparency International's Corruption Perceptions Index and other perceptions-based indices.

10 Probably to keep the Bangladesh market attractive for the multinationals and to help local producers, the price cap regulation was less strict than it could be. The price cap was a certain percentage over the costs of raw materials and packaging materials, transportation costs, and duties and taxes. The mark-up rate was 240 percent for the drugs that are technically the most advanced and the most costly to produce. Four lower mark-up rates were applied to less advanced drugs with the lowest rate being 50 percent. Later on, in 1994, the government made 117 drugs (out of 209 drugs designated as essential drugs) subject to price control. For other drugs, manufacturers were allowed to set their own prices and inform the regulatory body. More recently, most of these 117 drugs have become obsolete (UNCTAD 2011), and accordingly the price control has faded.

11 This is based on our interview with Professor Emeritus Dr Abdul Jabbar, founder of faculty of pharmacy at the University of Dhaka, August 3, 2011.

12 We interviewed Mr Amanullah Chowdhury, Executive Vice President and Director of Rangs Pharma Ltd, on June 4, 2011 and Mr Lutfur Rhaman, Director Manufacturing

of Beximco Pharmaceuticals Ltd, on January 19, 2011. Both were first-batch graduates. Mr Rhaman worked for 15 years in SQUIBB, a US-based MNC, before he joined BEXIMCO. We also met with several early graduates, including Mr Mahbubul Karim, Director Technical Operation of INCEPTA, who had served in two multinational firms (Sanofi and Novartis) for about 25 years in many key positions including head of production before he joined INCEPTA, and M.M. Mosaddek Hossain, Managing Director of UniMed and UniHealth Manufacturers Ltd, who had worked at two multinational firms (FISONS, and ICI) for about 15 years before establishing his own firm.

13 This is based on our interview on December 3, 2011 with Professor A.B.M Faruque, Dean of the Faculty of Pharmacy, University of Dhaka, who was a fifth-batch graduate.

References

Aitken, B.J., and Harrison, A.E. (1999) "Do domestic firms benefit from direct foreign investment? Evidence from Venezuela," *American Economic Review*, 89 (3): 605–18.

Amin, M.N. and Sonobe, T. (2013) "An inquiry into the rapid growth of the pharmaceutical industry in Bangladesh," mimeograph at the National Graduate Institute for Policy Studies, Tokyo, Japan.

Audretsch, D.B. (1998) "Agglomeration and the location of innovative activity," *Oxford Review of Economic Policy*, 14 (2): 18–29.

Baer, W. (1972) "Import substitution and industrialization in Latin Amercia: experiences and interpretations," *Latin American Research Review*, 7 (1): 95–122.

Balassa, B. (1971) *The Structure of Protection in Developing Countries*, Baltimore, MD: Johns Hopkins University Press.

Balsvik, R. (2011) "Is labor mobility a channel for spillovers from multinationals? Evidence from Norwegian manufacturing," *The Review of Economics and Statistics*, 93 (1): 285–97.

Berndt, E.R., Bui, L., Reiley, D.R., and Urban, G.L. (1995) "Information, marketing, and pricing in the U.S. antiulcer drug market," *American Economic Review*, 85 (2): 100–5.

Bhagwati, J. (1978) *Anatomy and Consequences of Exchange Control Regimes*, Cambridge, MA: Ballinger for National Bureau of Economic Research.

Bruton, H.J. (1998) "A reconsideration of import substitution," *Journal of Economic Literature*, 36 (2): 903–36.

BTCL (2010) Bangladesh government national pay scales, retrieved November 2, 2012, from Bangladesh Telecommunications Company Limited, http://www.btcl.gov.bd/home/main/official/National_Pay_Scale.php.

Chang, H.-J. (2003) "Kicking away the ladder: infant industry promotion in historical perspective," *Oxford Development Studies*, 31 (1): 21–32.

Chen, T.-J. and Tang, D.-P. (1987) "Comparing technical efficiency between import-substitution-oriented and export-oriented foreign firms in a developing economy," *Journal of Development Economics*, 26 (2): 277–89.

Chowdhury, Z. (ed.) (2010) *The Politics of Essential Drugs*, Dhaka: Gonoprokashani.

Görg, H., and Strobl, E. (2005) "Spillovers from foreign firms through worker mobility: An empirical investigation," *Scandinavian Journal of Economics*, 107 (4): 693–709.

Greif, A. (2006) *Institutions and the Path to the Modern Economy: Lessons from Medieval Trade*, Cambridge: Cambridge University Press.

Griffith, R., Redding, S., and Reenen, J.V. (2003) "R&D and absorptive capacity: theory and empirical evidence," *Scandinavian Journal of Economics*, 105 (1): 99–118.

Hayami, Y. and Godo, Y. (2005) *Development Economics: From the Poverty to the Wealth of Nations*, 3rd edition, Oxford: Oxford University Press.

IMS Health (2012) 2011 top-line market data, retrieved December 1, 2012, from IMS Health, http://www.imshealth.com/portal/site/ims/menuitem.5ad1c081663fdf9b41d84b903208c22a/?vgnextoid=fbc65890d33ee210VgnVCM10000071812ca2RCRD&vgnextfmt=default.

Javorcik, B.S. (2004) "Does foreign direct investment increase the productivity of domestic firms? In search of spillovers through backward linkages," *American Economic Review*, 94 (3): 605–27.

Kokko, A. (1994) "Technology, market characteristics, and spillovers," *Journal of Development Economics*, 43 (2): 279–93.

Kokko, A., Tansini, R., and Zejan, M.C. (1996) "Local technologies capability and productivity spillovers from FDI in the Uruguayan manufacturing sector," *Journal of Development Studies*, 32 (4): 602–11.

Krueger, A. (1978) *Foreign Trade Regimes and Economic Development: Liberalization Attempts and Consequences*, Cambridge, MA: Ballinger for National Bureau of Economic Research.

Krueger, A.O. and Tuncer, B. (1982) "An empirical test of the infant industry argument," *American Economic Review*, 72 (5): 1142–52.

Laffont, J.-J. and Tirole, J. (1993) *A Theory of Incentives in Procurement and Regulation*, Cambridge, MA: MIT Press.

Lall, S. (1973) "Transfer-pricing by multinational manufacturing firms," *Oxfor Bulletin of Economics and Statistics*, 35 (3): 173–95.

Lall, S. and Bibile, S. (1978) "The political economy of controlling transnationals: the pharmaceutical industry in Sri Lanka (1972–1976)," *International Journal of Health Services*, 8 (2): 299–328.

Lipsey, R.E. and Sjoholm, F. (2005) "The impact of inward FDI on host countries: why such different answers?" in T.H. Moran, E.M. Graham, and M. Blomstrom (eds) *Does Foreign Direct Investment Promote Development?*, Washington, DC: Institute for International Economics.

Ministry of Finance Bangladesh (2009) *National Pay Scales 2009*, Dhaka: Ministry of Finance Bangladesh.

OECD (2005) "Drug spending in OECD countries up by nearly a third since 1998, according to new OECD data," http://www.oecd.org/general/drugspendinginoecdcountriesupbynearlyathirdsince1998accordingtonewoecddata.htm.

Peralta, S., Wauthy, X., and Ypersele, T.V. (2006) "Should countries control international profit shifting?" *Journal of International Economics*, 68 (1): 24–37.

Reagan, R. (2007) *The Reagan Diaries*, New York: Harper Collins.

Reich, M.R. (1995) "The politics of health sector reform in developing countries: three cases of pharmaceutical policy," *Health Policy*, 32: 47–77.

Scherer, F. (1993). "Pricing, profits, and technological progress in the pharmaceutical industry," *Journal of Economic Perspectives*, 7 (3): 97–115.

Soligo, R. and Stern, J.J. (1965) "Tariff protection, import substitution and investment efficiency," *Pakistan Development Review*, V (2): 249–70.

UNCTAD (2011) "Local production of pharmaceuticals and related technology transfer in developing countries," United Nations conference on trade and development, http://unctad.org/en/PublicationsLibrary/diaepcb2011d7_en.pdf.

WHO (1988) *The World Drug Situation*, http://apps.who.int/medicinedocs/documents/s16222e/s16222e.pdf.

WHO (2004) *WHO Policy Perspectives on Medicines – Equitable Access to Essential Medicines: A Framework for Collective Action*, Geneva: WHO.

Williamson, O. (1985) *The Economic Institutions of Capitalism: Firms, Markets, Relational Contracting*, New York: Free Press.

Index

Locators shown in *italics* refer to figures and tables.

For Product Safety Concerns and Information please contact our EU
representative GPSR@taylorandfrancis.com
Taylor & Francis Verlag GmbH, Kaufingerstraße 24, 80331 München, Germany

www.ingramcontent.com/pod-product-compliance
Lightning Source LLC
LaVergne TN
LVHW011126300926
849160LV00008B/525

* 9 7 8 1 1 3 8 9 1 8 1 2 2 *